Grow to Greatness

How to build a world-class franchise system
Faster.

Discover the Five Success Drivers to explosive growth!

STEVE OLSON

2nd Edition

Praise for *Grow to Greatness!*

"I started reading this book with the understanding that it was a comprehensive guide to best practices in franchise development. The wisdom I found in its pages included so much more than I expected. *Grow to Greatness* should be a required read for anyone getting started in franchising or franchise development. It is an excellent reference tool for building and supporting a quality, values-based franchise organization."

Steve Greenbaum, CEO & Founder, PostNet International Franchise Corp.,
and 2008 Chair of the International Franchise Association

"Awesome! Both new and mature systems take heed! Steve Olson has lived and breathed franchise development. His Five Success Drivers are a 'must-do' for explosive system growth. This is the only book I know that addresses the complex world of franchise development. Buy it, read it, take action!"

Nikki Sells, Vice President of Franchise Development, Tasti D-Lite

"This book provides both structural and executional details for start-up franchisors and valuable tips and insights for experienced franchise recruiters. I especially liked the Ready, Set, Grow! chapter summaries that provide checklists for easy review and implementation. I plan to use this book to evaluate our own recruiting efforts."

Scott Haner, Vice President Franchise Development, Yum! Brands Inc.
(A&W All American Food, KFC, Long John Silver's, Pizza Hut, Taco Bell)

"Both new franchisors and established brands going through a re-creation will greatly benefit from reading this book. The willingness to follow a plan is key. The reader should be ready to mark a great idea on every page!"

Lynette McKee, Vice President of Franchising and New Business Development,
Dunkin' Brands (Dunkin' Donuts, Baskin-Robbins)

"Steve Olson has written the definitive book on building a franchise organization that will withstand the test of time. *Grow to Greatness* combines a lifetime of personal experience with case studies from franchise CEOs and lays the path for avoiding the land mines that have tripped up so many systems. This book should be required reading for all franchise professionals."

Keith Gerson, President & Chief Operating Officer, PuroClean

"There's nothing easy about franchising your business. Steve's book offers tremendous guidelines for making the process much easier. I wish this tool existed when we started The Dwyer Group 28 years ago!"

Dina Dwyer-Owens, Chair & CEO, The Dwyer Group Inc.
(Aire Serv, Glass Doctor, Mr. Appliance, Mr. Electric, Mr. Rooter/Drain Doctor in the U.K., Rainbow International), and 2009 Chair of the International Franchise Association

"*Grow to Greatness* is the first comprehensive, practical, and grounded guide to growing a franchise system I have seen. As a young executive tasked with growing a franchise, I was told, 'Learn how to sell franchises.' While I could find skilled individuals to learn from, organized instruction and leadership was nonexistent. The methods described in detail in this book are proven and a must. Thank you for providing such a valuable tool for us—and for every aspiring franchise system. I'm a believer!"

Tom Wood, President & CEO, Floor Coverings International

"Steve clearly outlines how to build a proper franchise recruitment program and how to present a franchisor as a must-buy opportunity for franchise prospects. Written by one of the best in the business, *Grow to Greatness* is the desk reference for franchise development professionals."

Michael Seid, Managing Partner, Michael H. Seid & Associates,
co-author with Wendy's Founder Dave Thomas of Franchising for Dummies

"This is by far the most comprehensive manual on how to build a franchise system I have ever seen, a genuine work of excellence. *Grow to Greatness* is the 'must read' book for successful franchise development. I am so happy you wrote this. It will be extremely helpful to many people."

Linda Burzynski, CEO, VL Service Corp. (former CEO of Liberty Fitness &
Weight Loss and CMIT Solutions and President of Molly Maid)

"Finding the right franchisees effectively and efficiently is as important to a franchisor as its brand and operating system. *Grow to Greatness* provides tools and best practices every franchisor should use. Steve's Five Success Drivers will make a difference for every franchisor who implements them."

Brian Schnell, Partner, Faegre & Benson

Table of Contents

Chapter 4

Chapter 5

Foreword

Revolutionizing the world of small business

Welcome to the extraordinary power of franchising! Generating $2.3 trillion in annual sales, 2,900 franchise organizations in the U.S. economy span a vast, commercial landscape of 75 industries. Currently, franchising contributes more than 10 percent of our nation's Gross Domestic Product, with a new franchise opening every 8 minutes each business day.

Franchising is the champion of small business expansion worldwide. In the United States alone, 41 cents of every retail dollar is spent at a franchise operation. This is quite astounding when you consider that fewer than 5 percent of all small businesses are franchised!

Studies claim that franchised businesses enjoy a success rate up to three times greater than that of independent businesses. Whatever the true number, this is certain: franchising affords significant benefits that provide greater business advantages to owners of franchised businesses. Independent small businesses too often can't deliver the corporate training and support, group purchasing power, advertising clout, and brand strength enjoyed by good franchise systems.

If you can't grow now, you never will!

In this first decade of the 21st century, we are experiencing a franchise renaissance! This rings clear in spite of fluctuations in the general economy. Record numbers of aspiring business owners are reaching out for the American Dream, investing their life's savings and leveraging their homes to do so. They are attracted to the successes of franchised businesses, which combine the best of both worlds: the independence of entrepreneurialism, and the support and proven systems of Corporate America.

Just ask franchise veterans who have been around during the past few decades. Buyers for franchises are more abundant than ever! Stock market uncertainties, job layoffs, and "Enron syndrome" have turned American employees and entrepreneurs away from the once-sacred safeguards of corporate security… and toward the personal empowerment, freedoms, and financial opportunities of owning their own businesses. Franchise concepts have become a safety net for many Americans, reducing their entrepreneurial risks by providing the systems and support that can help ensure their future success.

Extraordinary opportunities await both established and emerging franchisors. But as this book is about to explore with you, how can you optimize best practices to ensure the successful expansion of your franchise organization?

How to profit from this book

"Grow to Greatness" captures the Five Success Drivers for extraordinary franchise growth. It is written to guide you through the "do's and don'ts" for expanding your system, and to avoid the pitfalls that often sidetrack well-meaning development executives. It challenges the thinking of veteran franchisors and will arrest the minds of franchise start-ups. It even provides insights for franchise suppliers, who can gain a better understanding of growth services that can benefit franchise organizations.

This book is the first that focuses on the "business" of building a franchise business. It embraces a monumental subject, encompassing business practices applicable to the 75 categories of business that have been franchised. The book recognizes and offers best practices of hundreds of franchise professionals in retail and service businesses who have achieved successes on both individual and industry levels.

The book can help you in two primary areas: 1) for corporate planning and development, you'll discover a system-wide, strategic approach that can accelerate your franchise growth; and 2) for sales, marketing, and operational implementation, you can immediately adopt "how to's" and step-by-step processes that can improve your performance results in specific development areas.

How to get the most out of this guide

At times, you may take issue with specific development approaches in the book. This certainly is understandable. Even franchisors within the same business require variations in development execution, owing to differences in their ownership, corporate ideologies, franchise program structure, brand strength, expansion goals, and buyer profiles. The detailed processes and tutorials that follow are general guides that can be successfully incorporated in many franchise systems. But keep in mind, they can require modification to be more effective for your franchise growth.

What stands sacred within these pages are the Five Success Drivers for exceptional franchise expansion. They are the foundation for best practices in development and, in one way or another, are part of every professional franchise executive's reason for success. Savvy companies employing these truths have catapulted to glory. *"Grow to Greatness"* is a tribute to these leaders and innovators in the world of franchising.

Growth is the fuel of franchise success

Sometimes there is confusion about what franchising really is. Clarity on this point is key to understanding its business model. "Franchising" is a way of doing business. In its simplest definition, it is a distribution system for products and services that allows a franchisors to expand their brand concept to additional markets without the initial outlay of capital and staffing requirements.

Franchising is an American innovation that is embraced throughout the world. It has contributed to international economies, helping their entrepreneurs profit from the franchise partnership model. Golden arches, sandwiches, postal franchises, and more have created healthy global partnerships, expanding their products to consumers in both industrialized and developing countries.

Growth is the primary reason for franchising a business. It is achieved by partnering with qualified franchisees who, together with the franchisor, can realize business rewards not possible through either one's individual efforts. Without franchise expansion, most franchise systems will not achieve their development goals; without franchise expansion, start-up systems will fail.

Should you franchise your business?

For aspiring franchisors, take a reality check: *"Is franchising really right for you?"* For 28 years, I've seen hundreds of emerging and established franchise companies enjoy great successes. I met Subway founder Fred DeLuca when he had a few hundred franchises. Today he boasts more than 29,000! But I've also witnessed those who needlessly fail in their expansion efforts, not knowing or willing to do what it takes to build a franchise system. Start-up franchisors can be especially vulnerable. Too often, spirited entrepreneurs recklessly launch their successful business concepts into the complex world of franchising, not knowing they lack 50 percent of the core competencies necessary to grow a franchise organization.

Successful franchising is more than slapping together a legal document and hanging a "franchise for sale" shingle on the door. Doing it right requires implementing time-tested strategies, infrastructure, and development practices from the start. You are now entering the business of franchising. The opportunity you offer is not the key to your brand growth and fame—it's whether you have what it takes to succeed as a franchisor. Get your ducks lined up and proceed with caution.

I'll never forget the desperation of a new pet service franchisor who lost $150,000 in four short months, and then called for help. The innocent owners handsomely paid a "packaging firm" to produce boilerplate franchise documents and operations manuals, along with some big and shiny brochures.

"What was your growth plan, marketing strategy, and sales process?" I asked. After a painful pause, the couple confessed: it was to invest $5,000 in local newspapers, which would magically produce at least five dynamic franchises in their first year of operation. This was their recruiting formula for success.

How to safeguard your franchise expansion

This is exactly why I wrote this book. Not to save the world, but as a ready reference that can help start-up and growing franchisors better succeed, without wasting hundreds of thousands of dollars.

To help you further, there certainly are other industry resources for professional guidance. Franchise consultants, seminars, workshops, and conferences are available to companies seeking development expertise. Franchise Update Media Group, the International Franchise Association, *Franchise Times*, *Entrepreneur* magazine, and the *Wall Street Journal* are just a few of several high-quality information providers that can assist you with their franchise publications and conferences.

There also are noteworthy books available on the core mechanics of how to create a franchise, which focus on the legal, operational, and systems development of the business. They are great guides that will provide the tools and foundation to build a better car. This book, *"Grow to Greatness,"* shows you how to kick-start the engine and drive!

My personal motivation

Writing a book at this time is most meaningful for me. You see, I'm not a famous business guru, nor am I a consultant simply observing what it takes to be a winner.

And I'm not yet a "has-been," out of touch with today's best practices. I'm still a player and coach, deeply immersed in business with the scars and stripes to prove it. I've lived the moments: the pain, obstacles, sleepless nights, frustrations, joy, pride, motivation, enthusiasm, exhilaration, and extraordinary achievements of contributing to fast-growth, first-class franchise systems.

I've witnessed "no-name" franchisors surge to fame alongside established national brands. Then again, I've also personally experienced disaster, watching my former franchise system, American Advertising Distributors, dissolve from a healthy 125-franchise network to a pile of vacant printing presses and lawsuits. Franchising is a rewarding journey, but it can never be taken for granted.

I've always appreciated the proverb, *"Teaching is the process of learning twice."* Writing while I'm still in the game certainly is business therapy, and it helps keep me self-motivated in my stubborn quest for excellence. Still in the hunt, I'll sleep very comfortably knowing you'll get your money's worth from this book, whether from a consulting, management, or development executive's standpoint.

How are you going to grow?

Only you know where you aspire to take your business. Whether you are a franchisor, area developer, master franchisee, or franchise supplier, each of us has our own motivations and goals, both professionally and personally. It's up to you to set the direction for your path to achievement.

I hope *"Grow to Greatness"* can make a difference in helping you get there. Let me know if it does… it will make writing this book so very worthwhile.

Advice to Prospective Franchisors

Should you franchise your business?

Franchising is the world's most successful growth strategy for small business expansion. The growth statistics certainly are impressive. Although franchises represent fewer than 5 percent of small businesses in the United States, they account for 41 cents of every retail dollar we spend. Franchising covers most business categories with more than 75 industry categories now franchised, and a new operation opening every 8 minutes each business day.

But behind this franchising dream of becoming the next McDonald's are the realities you must investigate. Is this distribution system for your products and services the best way to grow your business, or is it wrong for you? Let's consider the benefits as well as drawbacks.

Rapid growth at lower cost

What if you could open 5 or more new locations in 90 days, and not pay for any of the start-up or ongoing expenses of running the operation? Although it isn't quite this simple, this picture illustrates how franchising provides opportunities to greatly accelerate your business expansion using other people's money (OPM). The OPM principle has been the gateway for small and large businesses alike to expand into national and international brands through the power of the franchise model.

Staffing growth: not an issue

Franchisees manage their franchise locations, you don't. They handle personnel issues, recruiting, hiring, training, motivating, firing, and replacing employees. Your responsibility is to train and service the franchisees as they invest their talents and energies into building their operations. Traditional business expansion requires more resources and is riddled with the challenges of hiring talented managers, coping with turnover, ongoing expenses, and supporting and overseeing the operation. Franchising certainly streamlines the process for accelerating company growth throughout major markets.

Greater brand recognition

More operations means more customers, visibility, and name awareness. Start-up franchisors quickly gain this bigger-than-before stature when launching initial franchise units within their own markets. Franchising is newsworthy material, which frequently prompts local news coverage and notoriety. This branding recognition only grows with the continuing development of your franchise locations.

Higher unit sales potential

Franchise operations typically outperform company-run locations by 15 to 30 percent, based on historical estimates from established franchise companies that have developed both business models. This makes sense, since franchisees are dedicated, vested operators who are not going to skip work because they had a bad morning. They are "overqualified managers" with business skill sets and personality traits that you have screened for franchise ownership. Unlike employee managers who view their position as a job, the franchisee is an owner with their future on the line.

When sales and operational problems arise, franchise owners are motivated, and forced to find solutions that will protect their hard-earned investment. If they do decide to "quit," they certainly aren't going to abandon the business. Franchisees are highly interested in protecting their investment so they can sell at the highest price. However, a frustrated manager of a company-run location may throw the keys in a FedEx package and skip town in 24 hours.

Group power

Better advertising buys, product purchases, and system networking create operational advantages independent businesses don't realize. The collective business savvy and ingenuity of franchisees is tough to match. It also isn't surprising that many successful franchise products are initially suggested by their owners. Ever heard of the Egg McMuffin? Herb Peterson, inventor of this marvelous breakfast sandwich, was co-owner and operator of six McDonald's restaurants in Santa Barbara and Goleta, California. Peterson, who recently passed away, engraved his indelible mark on the franchise brand. Recognizing his institutional achievement, a substantial press story honoring Peterson in the *Los Angeles Times* read: *"Peterson created the Egg McMuffin as a way to introduce breakfast to McDonald's. He was very partial to eggs Benedict and worked on creating something similar."*

Franchising is a powerful force that fuels greater opportunities for the system and operators through its growth. This partnership of intellectual capital and pooling of talents is at the heart of a healthy franchise organization.

Branding leverage

Franchise unit growth and market penetration create additional sources of revenue and savings. Product manufacturers and service providers view larger franchise systems as a valuable distribution system to bring their products to market, and they will pay for the opportunity to get in front of your customers. These third parties frequently offer cooperative advertising dollars, co-branding programs, sponsorships of your meeting and conference events, and may provide free or at-cost test programs to introduce their goods.

Helping people achieve the American Dream

There is nothing more rewarding than providing the opportunity for individuals to realize their entrepreneurial goals. Franchising is the fabric of small business success. It has changed lives and built fortunes for many who may have never done it otherwise. This is your payoff that can't be measured in dollars and quarters. As a successful franchisor, you'll enjoy close friendships and tremendous personal satisfaction knowing that your business expertise, systems, and support have benefited appreciative franchisees throughout your regional market, the nation, or the world.

What attracts buyers to franchise opportunities?

Nearly 1 million franchise businesses populate the U.S. landscape today. This number grows every year as more individuals seek business ownership offering benefits often not available by starting their own ventures. What motivated me to join a franchise when I left Corporate America? I didn't want to reinvent the wheel, I realized system support would free me to build my business faster, and I knew I'd increase my profits by networking with other successful franchisees. Here are some of the advantages franchise operators in a good franchise program can enjoy:

- best of both worlds—on your own but not alone
- easier entry into the business
- easier to acquire financing
- better site locations
- immediate professional image
- learn the business faster and more effectively
- start with a proven business plan
- save time and money by avoiding costly mistakes

- save money through group purchase power
- profit from experience and knowledge of the franchise network
- gain education, recognition, and social opportunities through conventions
- build more customers through brand awareness
- build more customers through group advertising
- new business opportunities through ongoing research and development
- increased equity and resale value
- higher success rate than independent businesses

Primary considerations in franchising your business

- ***Can your franchisee be successful?*** It's imperative for you to build a sound business model for the franchisees—first. They are the key to your greatness. Plan different scenarios, with low, conservative, and optimistic revenue and expense projections. Your future rides on their successes. Offer a viable, attractive business opportunity and you can succeed as a franchisor. You're asking for trouble if you design your royalties, product overrides, and franchise fees, and then force-fit the franchise model to accommodate your profit objectives.

- ***Can your concept be easily duplicated?*** You may have hit a grand slam with your three local locations, but will your business fly in Des Moines and Boston? If managing and driving the business requires highly specialized talents or characteristics, then you should back off from franchising. You must have a large pool of qualified franchise buyers or there won't be anyone to sell.

- ***You will be in the franchise business.*** You'll enter the world of recruiting, training, educating, motivating, leading, and servicing franchisees; conferences and meetings; franchise technology and communication systems; territory and site analysis; leasing and construction (for retail concepts); product distribution; product research and development; and local, regional, and national marketing. Franchising will become your major business. Your concept is what you are franchising. As a franchisor, your success depends significantly on your leadership abilities to grow and thrive as a franchise organization.

- *Franchisees are business owners.* Franchisees are not employees. They have been granted licensing rights to operate your franchise concept, and legally "independently own and operate" the business. You can't treat them as hired help. They aren't. Realistically, your relationship is a working partnership. Franchisees are outspoken. They will offer their ideas, praise or criticize their franchisors, and push the envelope to maximize their business success. Franchising is both a legal and "partnership" commitment. The strength of your relationship can catapult you to the heights of ultimate glory, or tumble you into a mire of frustration and problems.

- *Financial rewards are long-term.* If your dream is to score a quick killing, kick back, and count the big bucks, then go to Vegas where your odds are much better! You will be investing franchise fees and royalties back into your system from the start, building the necessary infrastructure to ensure healthy growth. Franchising is an ongoing journey of achievements and challenges, and the real monetary and personal rewards will come years down the road.

- *Will franchising help you achieve your goals?* Misconceptions often romance well-meaning entrepreneurs into franchising their successful concepts. I consulted for two business founders in Southern California. One was an Italian family dining and delivery concept, the other a boutique dog boarding and grooming service. The pet operation enjoyed national television and major newspaper coverage for their "muttrimonies" officiated in their doggy chapel, and for limo pickup and deliveries for their high-end clients. The owner was barraged with requests to franchise her unique concept. *"I'll share all my methods to build a great franchise business, train, and help the owners launch their operations. But if they expect me to hold hands and spend time with them, I don't want the hassle. I'm already a babysitter and canines are probably a lot easier."* This entrepreneur realized franchising wouldn't work for her and decided to expand using her own capital and management.

Unfortunately, the second founder, who had started a terrific pizza and pasta restaurant, rushed into franchising, selling to four operators before she discovered this growth strategy was a massive mistake for her. *"My franchisees are draining my resources! They require too much support.*

Can you help me sell my franchised business?" Avoid this entrepreneur's expensive misfire by making sure franchising is the best fit for achieving your objectives. A licensing, dealership program, or other business format may better suit your growth strategy.

Costs of franchising your business

For proper capitalization in today's marketplace, you'll need a minimum $200,000 to create and launch a franchise business. Overly aggressive development specialists or attorneys will tell you that you can franchise your concept for less than $100,000. Technically, they are correct. You can get a "franchise shell" legally packaged for you at that price and hang a franchise shingle on your door. And, if you're a savvy bootstrap entrepreneur with tremendous patience, you can grow your system slowly on a shoestring budget. You will be cash-starved, but with a very conservative expansion plan you can succeed.

The cold, start-up facts that hard-selling packagers don't reveal are: the heavy costs to market your concept; investment in developing a high-performance recruitment program; and the necessary capital for supporting franchisees to help ensure their initial and ongoing success. The greater the satisfaction of your first owners, the greater the growth of your franchise system. That's a guarantee!

Franchise development budget

On a positive note, a big benefit of franchising your concept is that you can enjoy rapid business expansion using other people's money. But to repeat my cautionary note, sometimes prospective franchisors don't realize it requires a serious investment to establish the foundation to successfully build a franchise system. Here's a suggested range of initial development costs required to launch your franchise program. This does not include the cost for initial support services, which is addressed in "Operational costs for supporting your franchisees," below.

Franchise development companies you contact may provide higher or lower figures, but for the most part this will be helpful for benchmarking your research.

Recruitment advertising budget

The advertising dollars you should invest depend upon the aggressiveness of your growth goals; ability to properly support new franchises; estimated acquisition costs for each new franchise owner; and the funds you have available to spend. As a new franchisor, acquisition costs are typically higher because you

Suggested Range of Initial Development

Development Costs	Low	High
Strategic planning and program development[1]	$25,000	$25,000
Franchise documents[2]	15,000	25,000
Operations and training manuals[3]	10,000	25,000
Content and design of core marketing and sales materials[4]	10,000	10,000
Production expenses for print materials[4]	7,500	15,000
Website production[5]	2,500	10,000
Development of sales process and lead generation plan[6]	5,000	10,000
Subtotal	$75,000	$120,000
First-year recruitment advertising[7]	$25,000	$200,000
Total	$100,000	$320,000

Footnotes:

1. Hire an experienced franchise development firm or consultant with a successful resume in launching franchise start-up companies in your business category (e.g., service, retail non-food, retail food).

2. Based on your selection of the franchise attorney you prefer to use.

3. Expert assistance is necessary, even if you initially create your own operations manuals. Do it right the first time, or you will pay much more for it down the road! Outsourced services for experienced franchise manual writers range from $10,000 to $25,000, determined by the scope of the project. This comprehensive library of material is the blueprint for your franchisees' success, detailing every specific aspect of your operations, products and services, management, and sales and marketing procedures and policies. The critical elements of building your business are contained in these confidential documents.

4. Based on the image and quality of the printed portfolio you desire for your promotional materials.

5. Based on the capabilities of and financial arrangement with your current website developer, or if you employ a website developer to produce your franchise site. Note: some franchisors also set up a franchisee intranet in the early stages of their growth, which can cost an additional $10,000 or more.

6. Your franchise development consultant may provide the expertise necessary to launch an effective and successful franchise recruiting program or should refer you to an experienced professional who can help implement one for you.

7. Based on your growth objectives for your first year of franchising. These start-up numbers will differ based on current acquisition costs for your business category and number of franchise buyers generated through your existing customer base.

have no or minimal branding, no proven franchise program, and no pipeline of ongoing prospects. You may get a few referral sales through existing customers, but often not as many as you may expect. Raving fans of your service usually are not qualified, or quickly realize working on the ownership side of the counter is a different world that doesn't appeal to them. Or perhaps you oversell prospective franchisees and scare them away before you learn how to successfully recruit them using a structured process.

We all hear the magical stories of California Closets or Krispy Kreme, and how they grew like wildfire the day they announced they were franchising. But many don't know it took Subway 17 years to reach 200 stores; or that it took Curves several years of re-engineering their concept before the fitness franchise took the country by storm.

The following costs are rough estimates, and assume your concept is within the $50,000 to $400,000 investment range and has a minimum of three successful locations operating.

Growth objectives	First-Year Goal	Marketing Budget
Bootstrap	1 to 3 franchisees	$25,000 to $50,000
Moderate	4 to 10 franchisees	$50,000 to $100,000
Aggressive	11 to 15 franchisees	$100,000 to $200,000

For industry guidelines and research in preparing your recruitment budget, I highly recommend the Annual Franchise Development Report, available for purchase through Franchise Update Media Group (www.franchiseupdate.com/afdr or email sales@franchiseupdatemedia.com).

What do you do after you sell your first franchises?

Once you franchise your business and recruit your first buyers into the system, it's kickoff time for start-up support services. To name a few, you'll provide and monitor pre-training assignments; assist with site location for retail concepts; coordinate office setups, delivery of equipment, supplies, and installation of technology; conduct franchise training school and initial field training at the franchisee locations; and provide customer service by phone, email, mailings, and onsite visits.

How dedicated you are in supporting your initial franchisees will largely influence the success of your franchising efforts. Buyers are attracted to franchises because

"You're on your own, but not alone" and because franchisors share their proprietary formulas and *"blueprint for success."*

This is a tall order. As a young franchisor, you must recognize that your success depends upon your franchisee partners' successes. Savvy start-up franchisors over-support their first franchisees to strengthen their performance and thus ensure good validation when they speak with new prospects. How well they do determines how attractive your concept is to buyers, and can make or break your future franchise growth. You can't just sell sizzle anymore. The reality of your franchise business now makes the difference.

Operational costs for supporting your franchisees

I asked Marvin Storm, founder and managing director of Blackstone Hathaway, to share with you what it takes to develop the infrastructure for a start-up franchise system. He is an industry expert with more than 20 years of experience in franchise development. He was a successful franchisor of a packing and shipping franchise, and he has successfully operated multiple franchises in five different business concepts, managing four different area franchise territories with nearly 100 franchisees. Here's Marvin's advice to prospective franchisors:

Why do many companies that attempt franchising eventually fail, if franchising is such a great business model? The primary reason is that it is harder to operate a successful franchise company than it appears. Although a company may be successful in their core business, this expertise does not necessarily mean a company can successfully execute a franchise model. That is because franchising is an entirely different business with entirely different operational rules.

In a recent discussion with an entrepreneur considering franchising as a strategy for expanding, I asked how he planned to support his new franchisees. The discussion went something like this:

Question: *Have you analyzed how much money it is going to take to adequately train, open, and support your franchisees in the first couple of years?*

Answer: *Not really. We have been doing what we do for 15 years. It will not be hard to train a franchisee to do what we do. We have good people working in the business, and they will be able to provide training, and support. Besides, the initial franchise fee will cover these types of expenses.*

Question: *How did you determine the amount of the initial franchise fee?*

Answer: *I checked what initial franchisee fees were for other franchise companies in our industry.*

During the next hour, I pointed out some of the most common mistakes companies make in franchising their business, some of the issues they needed to consider before venturing into the world of franchising, and the capital required to build a support infrastructure for a new franchise company.

Capitalization

There are two ways to fund the training, opening, and ongoing operational support of new franchisees. One is bootstrapping, and the other is adequately capitalizing the franchise company and investing in infrastructure ahead of the revenue curve.

Bootstrapping model

Many successful franchise companies have successfully bootstrapped their franchising efforts. Bootstrapping generally involves using the initial franchisee fee to underwrite the complete cost of providing training, opening, and first-year support of franchisees. Generally, support infrastructure is added only after franchisees have been recruited. Although highly risky (and why so many franchise companies fail), this model has worked and can work. However, very few companies can successfully deploy this model because their ability to provide support services is contingent upon awarding new franchises.

If franchise sales do not meet projections, there is an enormous temptation to award franchises to individuals who do not meet your original criteria for franchisees. This will allow a franchisor to generate additional franchise fees to cover the franchisee support costs as well as other franchisor-related operational costs. This is generally the first step on the long painful path to failure because recruiting lower-caliber franchisees serves only to increase support costs in the future, as well as to lower per-unit revenues.

Capitalization of a Franchise Support Model: Bootstrapped		
Support Function	Low	High
Franchise Training[1]	$0	$15,000
Franchise Opening[2]	$5,000	$25,000
Franchise Field Support[3]	$60,000	$100,000
Total	$65,000	$140,000

1. In many cases, training takes place in the flagship location, provided by the founder with no direct cost.
2. Franchise openings are done by the founder or by a long-time employee serving as the jack-of-all-trades trainer.
3. The franchise support department is a jack-of-all-trades employee who splits their time between providing franchisee support and their duties in the core business.

Even if a new franchise company succeeds using this bootstrapped model, the number of new franchisees awarded and their rate of growth are generally lower than that of companies using a fully capitalized operational model (FCOM).

The fully capitalized operational model

The FCOM calls for a more aggressive approach by anticipating and planning for a high level of support for franchisees. Properly establishing the initial franchise fee is also a necessary component of the FCOM. The main difference in this strategy is that the financial resources are available to provide high-caliber training, opening, and ample first-year support to franchisees, regardless of the rate of awarding new franchises and the collection of initial fees.

The franchise company is in a much stronger position when it isn't necessary to recruit marginal franchise candidates to generate additional franchisee fees to pay for operational overhead or payroll. The better funded franchisor can focus on recruiting high-quality franchisees who attract other high-quality franchisees. Motivated franchisees are generally competitive and focused on success without a lot of handholding—hence, lower support costs with higher average revenue per unit. Eventually a culture of performance begins to emerge in the franchise system.

Capitalization of a Franchise Support Model: FCOM		
Support Function	Low	High
Franchise Training[1]	$100,000	$150,000
Franchise Opening[2]	$75,000	$150,000
Franchise Field Support[3]	$150,000	$200,000
Total	$325,000	$500,000

1. Training is viewed as a core function of the business. A training director is hired prior to awarding of the first franchise. This individual can assist in providing opening and field support for the first few franchisees.
2. A director of franchise support services is hired very early in the franchising process.
3. As the franchise system grows, a full team of support personnel is systematically recruited with the objective of providing high-caliber support to franchisees.

Validation is another important dynamic created by the FCOM. Validation of your business model is generally better because franchisees can execute at a higher level and are more profitable. When this type of support is present, more franchise candidates want to join the system. This increases the velocity for new franchisee recruitment, excitement within the system, and cash flow for the franchisor.

Finally, the most important dynamic created by using the FCOM strategy is value creation through brand dominance. When highly qualified franchisees are recruited, higher average unit revenues are generated. This eventually builds dominance over the competition and branding in the marketplace because branding yields pricing power. Pricing power enables franchisees to maintain their margins as the market matures and becomes more competitive. Long-term value grows as higher margins enable franchisees *to provide a higher level of customer service than their competition, which creates even greater market dominance.*

Branding and customer service may also be achieved using a bootstrapped model, but the timeline is generally much longer.

How you answer the question of bootstrapping or raising capital in launching a franchise will, to a large extent, determine your eventual success. Companies adopting the fully capitalized operational model have the opportunity to realize greater unit growth, higher unit revenues, more franchisee satisfaction, and creation of more value over a five-year period than those using the bootstrapped model. The following chart illustrates the potential performance differences in multiples, assuming all other factors are equal:

	Bootstrapped	FCOM
Franchisee satisfaction	X	2X
Franchise unit growth	X	3X
Revenue per unit	X	4X
Company valuation	X	5X – 10X

(My thanks to Marvin Storm, founder and managing director of Blackstone Hathaway, for his contribution of the preceding section.)

So, is franchising right for you?

Launching a franchise is a major commitment. With the right leadership, business model, and timing franchising could catapult your business concept to regional, national, or global success. For openers, you should have a profitable business operating a minimum of three years, at least three locations, and a minimum of $200,000 capital to invest to franchise and market your system. If you bootstrap your franchise growth, recognize that it will take longer and present more challenges during the initial development years. To aid your review process, here's a reality checklist to see if you are on the right track:

Seven questions for decision-making

1. Can franchising help you achieve your short- and long-term goals?
2. Do you believe your business can be easily duplicated?
3. Do you have compelling business advantages and benefits that will attract

qualified owners to invest in and be rewarded by your opportunity?

4. Do you believe you can provide the leadership, training, systems, marketing expertise, location assistance, and other tools to help franchisees build their own successful businesses?
5. Can you adapt to the relationship of having franchise owners who in reality are "partners" in your business?
6. Will you be comfortable with the legal responsibilities and obligations of a franchise?
7. Will you commit the necessary capital, time, and resources to develop a successful franchise system?

How to discover for yourself

Do your homework by contacting recognized experts in franchise development to help guide you in making the right decision. Focus on those with track records in launching successful franchise systems. Ask franchise attorneys, Franchise Update Media Group, or the International Franchise Association for referrals.

If you still aren't sure if franchising is the best pathway to your growth, hire a consultant to conduct a feasibility study before you commit to investing your valuable time, capital, and resources into a franchise program. Expect to pay between $5,000 and $12,000 or more, depending on the depth of research, which can include, for starters:

- analysis of the competitive environment and future growth, both of your industry and within the franchise sector;
- potential customer demand for your franchise service;
- key points of differentiation your business can offer;
- development of a viable franchise model that can both attract and reward your franchisee partners and satisfy your franchising goals;
- forecasting of initial and long-term investment and infrastructure requirements;
- structural packaging of your franchise program for direct single-store or multiple-store development, or through an area development, area representation, or master licensing system; and
- budget projections for franchise development, operations and support, recruitment, staffing, and legal services.

If in fact you determine franchising is right for your business, congratulations! Welcome to an exciting journey that can bring professional and personal rewards to you, your franchisees, and employees throughout the U.S. and the world!

Chapter 1

Success Driver I:
Total Management Commitment

Franchise success starts with leadership...

and so does franchise failure.

Success Driver I:
Total Management Commitment

What it takes to succeed

Without any doubt, this first success driver for launching explosive development—total management commitment—requires significant attention. A separate franchise book could embrace this single theme. Time and again, top management can become a critical roadblock, preventing their franchise system from realizing its full potential. Most of the time their heart is in the right place, but sometimes their head is somewhere else!

Franchise success starts with leadership... and so does franchise failure. To achieve greatness requires passion and a relentless commitment to successful growth. *"Whatever it takes"* is the mandate and no excuses are acceptable.

I've had the pleasure of working with some extraordinary chief executives who have achieved the seemingly impossible... leaders with open minds who re-energized their franchise development by checking their egos and biases at the front door.

Building a better franchise

Money Mailer, a national direct mail franchisor, aggressively grew to more than 400 franchises in its first 20 years. But as with nearly every franchise, the company finally hit some pretty rough waters in its life cycle. In a summary that is much too short, in 2000 Money Mailer was reeling from an exodus of senior staff following two turbulent years of significant franchise losses fueled by disgruntled, struggling owners.

President Godfred Otuteye knew a quantum leap was required to turn around, revive, and rebuild his system. All the stops were pulled out as the entire franchise operation was evaluated and re-engineered. Meetings with franchisees were held throughout the country, soliciting their input and participation in returning the company to its glory days. Godfred hired new executive staff and pressed those few remaining managers to make sacrifices for the cause. Consultants were brought in to assist in his "Mission Impossible" campaign. I was one of them.

Ironically, six months prior I had cautioned another consultant on the futility of trying to save the sinking ship at Money Mailer. *"They are too far gone at this point,"* I advised. Fortunately, I was proven wrong. I won't bore you with the details, but I learned in working with a group of "reborn crusaders" that achieving the impossible is possible... if you are willing to take extreme measures.

In the midst of the storm, Godfred convinced his entire organization to help rebuild their brand and contribute to recruiting new franchisees into the system. An aggressive campaign was created to visibly support their vice president of development, Dennis Jenkins. Posters, postcards, and campaign buttons declaring *"I am Dennis"* were distributed to each franchise owner, their employees, corporate secretaries, accountants, field operations personnel, and even building maintenance employees.

Godfred's leadership stabilized a hemorrhaging franchise from negative growth and upheaval to an astounding 600 percent increase in new franchise sales within 18 months (from 6 to 7 annual deals to 42). Dennis, along with Marketing Director Beth Swade and staff, pulled off an amazing victory with total support from franchisees, employees, and customers. I've had the great fortune of being part of other turnaround teams, but never of this magnitude!

This leader's burning desire to build an extraordinary company conquered his not-so-perfect storm and ignited higher levels of greatness for the Money Mailer system. Sometimes it takes a sinking ship to build a much better ship.

20 percent of you will achieve greatness

There are formulas that can produce astonishing results for your system. During different phases of their growth, I have enjoyed working with a handful of savvy franchise executives who have embraced these success principles and catapulted their organizations from attrition and mutiny to extraordinary growth.

Not surprisingly, these executives are among the elite 20 percent of today's franchise leaders, driven by their "whatever it takes" obsession to make it happen... those who commit all the time, financial, and human resources to multiply their growth efforts several times over.

Most franchisors however are not blessed with these trailblazers. This book caters to this 80 percent majority who, with guidance, have the opportunities to achieve significant breakthroughs in their development. I admit a few in this group seeking accelerated growth will fail, not because of lack of desire, but because of insurmountable hurdles now confronting their organization and/or leadership.

But for most of you with the motivation to move forward, there is a process that can launch you to new heights of franchise expansion. Half the battle is recognizing where the land mines to growth are buried. This discovery itself will provide a greater understanding of your franchise operation, help identify the real challenges, and provide better direction on how to more effectively lead your organization to a bigger and better future.

Here are common management traps that can ambush healthy franchise growth. Realizing these potential land mines can help overcome resistance before you activate your growth plan.

No pain, no gain!

Unfortunately, some leaders are unable to navigate the rough waters of transition, an overwhelming project that requires significant change. Senior executives often are uncomfortable dealing with the consequences of disruption. Attachment to their comfort zone can block the aggressive tactics and actions necessary to catapult their organization forward. It certainly isn't a simple task.

Changes create immediate challenges. The dilemmas of disorganization, second-guessing, new and additional roles for personnel, and tossing past practices for new will definitely turn the corporate environment upside-down. We all can talk about and plan for making changes. That's the easier part. Success lives or dies in the execution.

A high-end landscaping company with successful branch offices throughout the U.S. decided to franchise in smaller markets where owner-operators made much better business sense than branch locations. Unfortunately, the franchising model wasn't succeeding as planned, so the founder asked for consulting assistance to help turn the situation around.

Several meetings were cancelled, so nothing was ever accomplished. The founder finally admitted that his president didn't want the hassle of dealing with these "franchise stepchildren." *"He really doesn't care for or have time or energy to deal with them."* The pain wasn't worth the gain, and the founder backed off from battling with the president, who, incidentally, was married to his daughter!

Shatter the walls of resistance

Control and leadership authority will be tested, and in some instances requires direct confrontation to prevent roadblocks. I'll never forget my frustration sitting before the corporate legal counsel of a 350-unit service franchise, trying to convince him to add earnings claims (now called financial performance representations) to their Franchise Disclosure Document (FDD). Their franchisees' profitability was very impressive and certainly would be a key attraction to qualified candidates considering this franchise opportunity.

"Do you enjoy fishing?" was the initial response to my suggestion! I was taken aback, but it became clear this attorney wasn't about to rock the boat with this pain-in-the-butt project since he was retiring next year. It was obvious there was no way he would disrupt his smooth sailing. The franchise would have to develop earnings claims on someone else's watch. The CEO should have stepped in, ripped the fishing rod from his fantasies, and instructed him to get those earnings claims into their documents. But he didn't. The employee rode on a different bus than his peers, at the expense of the organization's development efforts. Was it the attorney's fault for retarding their selling impact? No. It was the failure of leadership to demand he get with their program or pack up and go fishing now.

Technology departments certainly can be land mines that stall the quest for progressive growth. Smokescreens hidden behind the walls of cyberspace and techno-babble too often hold senior management hostage. One frustrated president of a major household franchise brand was told by national headquarters, *"It will take two years before our technology team can produce a franchise recruitment website for you."*

Recently, I asked a C-level executive when final modifications to his company's new website would be completed. He had absolutely no clue: the technology officer was just whisked off to work on a huge new project. At another company, a 300-unit food franchise, the CEO was hostage to his 25-year-old whiz kid. Eighteen months earlier his chief geek had promised a bigger, better website with all the whistles! Still nothing had happened. Who's in control here? Certainly not the executive leadership.

Do-nothing management

Much worse are the companies that never implement changes after spending expensive time, money, and research to discover valuable solutions to ramp up their development efforts.

During the late '90s, I was hired by a multi-concept retail franchise that ignored six months of our market studies and franchisee interviews. Our research revealed one of their concepts should put the brakes on its recruitment efforts. A problematic change had occurred in this concept's market and was hammering their unit economics. Franchisee satisfaction was tanking as technological improvements and price reductions no longer allowed their owners to compete in metropolitan areas. The concept screamed for re-engineering, with desperate pleas to do so from loyal, victimized franchisees. Rather than take corrective action, the executives ignored repairing the structural problem. They continued to waste marketing dollars and attempted to recruit more franchisees doomed for failure. The dying concept was sold several years later to a new owner who re-invented the franchise and began rebuilding the brand.

Through the years, C-level "naysayers" and "indecision-makers" have personally been my biggest frustration. They drag down high-performance growth companies. The market is too competitive, and development issues must be swiftly addressed, reviewed, and resolved. I have consulted and worked with masters of non-commitment. Diffusing issues through inaction jeopardizes opportunities to leap ahead in the quest for expansion. The inability to make hard decisions can cripple companies. Astute leaders realize it's better to make a wrong decision on occasion rather than make no decisions at all!

As a frequent example, why do successful franchisors with compelling stories still hesitate to provide Item 19 earnings claims (now called financial performance representations, FPRs) in their Franchise Disclosure Document (FDD)? It helps their buyers and it helps their growth. The FTC publicly encourages earnings claims in the FDD because of buyer demand for such meaningful business information. Don't we want prospects to make more educated decisions by sharing real financials with them that they can work with? In addressing liability risks, franchise attorneys confirm that lawsuits involving earnings are predominantly with companies that don't provide financial information in Item 19. High-growth franchises know that today's buyers seek earnings claims from franchisors, and that their absence can be a warning signal. Competitors making FPRs certainly play this up. I closed multiple deals where earnings claims noticeably influenced a franchise buyer's decision. And never with repercussions.

I'm also puzzled by leaders of companies boasting high franchisee satisfaction rates who sidestep the practice of providing referral incentives to franchisees who introduce new prospects to their offering. You can do it, just disclose it. With a well-developed campaign, you'll sell more qualified franchisees at a greatly reduced acquisition cost. As a former successful franchisee, I appreciated corporate's "thank you" for prospect referrals, especially considering the multiple hours I contributed promoting the system to countless candidates calling for validation.

Select your best to lead

Through the years I have been known for my impatience with mediocrity, which can lead only to disappointment. Extraordinary goals cannot be achieved through ordinary efforts.

Peter Shea, CEO of Entrepreneur Media, had aggressive plans to ramp up his company during the mid-'90s. From the get-go, he shared his vision and expectations in a company-wide session with his 100 employees. It was probably the most appreciated and well-received communication I have ever witnessed in an organization. His upbeat yet cautionary message went something like this:

"We are entering exciting times that present greater opportunities for all of us at Entrepreneur. *With your hard work and help, many of you can make meaningful contributions and enjoy the rewards along the way. But there will be changes, trying times, and confusion during this transition. Perhaps some of you won't be able to adapt to this time of growth, and I respect that. It certainly doesn't mean you are a poor employee. It just means this isn't working for you, and it's time for you to move on. And that's okay."*

No punches were pulled, and opportunities were available to those ready for the challenge. The CEO's message was clear. Employees were respectfully alerted to trying times ahead. The paths they chose were in their hands. Some who couldn't cope with the changes jumped ship; those incapable of taking on their new responsibilities were let go. The majority stayed the course for what evolved to become a boom period in the organization's growth. From the very start, through old-fashioned straight talk with his employees, Shea inspired his best to embrace his challenge. No smoke and mirrors, just the simple truth. His invitation motivated those with the talent to rise and help lead the charge. He let his people know he needed the right people in the right seats, headed in the right direction on his journey for growth. Those who stepped up were amply rewarded with promotions and raises.

Rally the troops to the cause

Turnaround missions crumble if franchise management doesn't prepare employees for the oncoming changes and disruption. Clear communication and education to the staff and their employees are mandatory. How each employee will benefit from the growth must be individually defined. Otherwise, you will spawn unnecessary resentment and resistance. Change is pain, and for many employees isn't worth it… unless they understand the payoffs for working longer hours, restructuring their roles, learning new skill sets, and maintaining grace under extraordinary pressure.

A former senior development executive with a 350-unit personnel franchise masterfully recognized that "buy-in" from support services was essential to accelerating her department's sales growth. She was experiencing difficulty in getting contracts prepared for approved franchise candidates. As we know, time kills deals: documents must be prepared quickly and delivered for signature by the new franchisee. One day of delay is one step closer to a lost sale, whether it's from buyer's remorse or visiting Uncle Bill the accountant. There always are naysayers lurking around the corner, lusting to squash a franchise deal.

This senior executive sat down with the resistant employee causing the roadblocks. She enthusiastically shared how great it was that the employee was processing more contracts, because more franchise sales meant they would both personally profit from higher company stock values. The employee's hot button zoomed from red to green, and from then on agreements zipped back to the executive's desk.

How "selling CEOs" drive development

In 1983, when Steve Greenbaum was in his early 20s, he went to work for his father selling business opportunities in the pack-and-ship industry. Rising to the challenge, he led the company, Coserco, to explosive growth with the development of more than 450 independent mail and parcel centers before buying his father out in 1990. Taking the reins as president and CEO, he decided to go a different route, wound down the operation in 1992, and founded PostNet International Franchise Corp. with his friend and business partner Brian Spindel. Today PostNet is the largest and fastest-growing privately held company in the postal and business services industry, with more than 900 franchises in 12 countries.

In 2008, this consummate "selling CEO" and repeat winner of several STAR Awards for recruitment performance by *Franchise UPDATE* magazine, also was serving as chair of the International Franchise Association. Steve generously shared his leadership insights for achieving high-performance growth.

Steve, why has it always been important for you to be involved in your recruitment efforts?

SG: Without a successful selling organization you have nothing to support. You don't have an organization to build. Once you have a growing organization, you must commit 100 percent to do whatever it takes to successfully lead and support your franchisees, build a culture, a values-based organization, and buy-in to the future growth of the system."

What attracts buyers to your PostNet franchise?

SG: First, it's the business concept and how it works. But what really brings them in is our commitment to values and who we are. When we ask new franchisees why they came aboard, they talk about the enthusiasm, energy, and momentum of our organization. These are the primary reasons they join us.

What are some of the key factors driving your development?

SG: Responsiveness to franchise inquiries. If someone takes the time to contact you and you don't immediately follow up, what does that say about how you respond to your existing franchisees? For us, image and quality are number one in everything we do. Our website, emails, promotional materials and Discovery Day represent our brand and who we are. Our communications are direct and succinct. We have effective lead management systems and measurement tools for moving candidates through our sales process. As an online recruitment pioneer back in '96, we continually push the envelope seeking new avenues for prospect generation.

How important is your selling process?

SG: With a strong sales process in place you don't need to rely as much on top selling skills to close deals. Don't get me wrong, I certainly want sales talent on our team. However, a powerful systematic approach is by design an effective, self-closing process that doesn't require as much "selling" to get the deals done. The process helps our sales person establish control and manage the candidate's expectations with anticipated outcomes. The candidate agrees to established time frames and works by appointment bookings. The spouse must be involved. Expectations are managed from the start. We use the Franchise Disclosure Document as a selling tool, and my partner Brian or I conduct an executive interview prior to Discovery Day. We leave nothing to chance at our Discovery Days. Candidates come understanding this is "closing day" pending our executive committee approval.

Have you made changes in your franchise development process since your first years of franchising? What impact do the economy, buying habits, and the digital world play in today's recruiting market?

SG: The world has changed the way people shop and buy. Our recruiting approach has expanded from a four-step process to a nine-step process. It's still a four- to six-week time frame, and the fundamentals are the same. But now it provides more interaction, engagement, momentum, and relationship-building than before. It's like moving down a hallway of doors: close one door, open the next. Where our recruitment was more dependent on the sales person previously, now it's more in the sales process. It's managed more efficiently, supported by more technology, and introduces interim steps that maintain and increase our candidates' enthusiasm and engagement. Buyers tell us they love the process. They know where they're going and what to expect. The process itself culminates in the close, and selling is really more informational and instructional and less about closing. If you have to close a prospect at Discovery Day, something's wrong. The process should have closed them along the way.

What development advice would you give to other established franchise systems?

SG: If your organization isn't evolving and responding, you're dead in terms of growth. View everything your prospect touches through the eyes of a prospective buyer: your website, printed materials, the ways you communicate through your sales people. Continually challenge your process. Okay, so it's gotten tougher to recruit good candidates. Stop complaining about the economy, and start adapting to the market needs. Pay close attention to environmental conditions and the things you can't control. Our industry was affected by the UPS takeover of Mail Boxes Etc., followed by the FedEx-Kinko's merger. PostNet had to respond to this, and to newer technologies and customer expectations. But this isn't the first time. Since 1983, we've had to change from a traditional pack-and-ship business to a postal business and communications center, to the digital diversified business center we are today. If we hadn't retooled our organization based on how buyers buy and impending economic challenges, we would have been in big trouble.

Ready, set, grow!

The mission of this book is to offer best practices to help your franchise grow to greatness. The good news is that these practices are not unique. They apply to every concept, including yours… whether service or retail, or food, sales, or automotive! Franchising is a business unto itself. Core organizational, operational, marketing, and sales principles are all the same.

Embrace the Five Success Drivers in this book, and this is what you can expect to accomplish with your franchise development:

✓ **See results in 6 to 12 months**

It takes "total management commitment" to make a difference. Hang in there, plant the seeds, and you'll reap the rewards. Seventy percent of franchise leadership who walk the talk can enjoy development payoffs. What you invest on the front end comes back in measurable results.

✓ **Realize dramatic increases**

Radio Shack soared in the late '90s, transforming shrinking stores to extraordinary unit growth by completely repackaging their franchise program and successfully partnering in small markets with complementary retail concepts. Work smarter, not harder.

✓ **Turn things upside-down**

To achieve superior results, you can't continue operating your business the same way. Minor changes usually produce minor results; major changes can produce newsworthy breakthroughs. Prepare the troops for the shakeup. It's a bumpy road, but those who stay and steer the bus in the right direction can celebrate the success of the journey.

✓ **Nothing and nobody is sacred**

Have you ever fired an incompetent employee too soon? Doesn't happen. Yet a retail soft goods franchise gave their sales executive nine lives to start producing deals. Wow, was that expensive! After months of professional training, coaching, retraining, motivating, and threatening, the results were still the same: unacceptable performance. The CEO admitted he had wasted tens of thousands in marketing dollars and lost prospects. If you can't get rid of a struggling sales person because he's your brother, transfer him to the mail room where he won't mess up your development efforts!

✓ **There are no shortcuts**

Sorry, magic bullets just don't exist in franchise development. Growth is dependent upon not just one, but all five key drivers for successful development. A common misconception is that a better lead generation plan or hiring a top sales gun will solve faltering recruitment efforts. Not so.

✓ **Enjoy new strength and vitality**

Everyone loves to win. New success sparks greater enthusiasm, confidence, loyalty, and passion for growing franchise organizations. It's always a thrill when you can enjoy the victories on the journey to greatness. Problems remain, but are much more manageable when your energized team is rising up with you, not against you. You can see it in their eyes and watch it in their swagger. What a difference a day makes!

Chapter 2

Success Driver II:
Strong Franchisee Satisfaction

Shared vision, values, and purpose…

the fuel that ignites greater franchisee

loyalty and satisfaction.

Success Driver II:
Strong Franchisee Satisfaction

A few years ago an enthusiastic candidate interviewing for the COO position of a retail food franchise asked me, "What do you believe is the key to an outstanding operations and support program for this company?" Leaning across the desk I exclaimed, *"Happy franchisees!"*

Satisfied franchisees are everything

Happy, well-treated owners are the life support system of every healthy franchise system. Certainly, achieving this is not a simple or easy task, and it requires tremendous, energy, resources, and time. But the payoffs are enormous! Your system cannot help but flourish when your franchise partners know you care about their well-being, communicate with them openly, respond to their needs, and provide them with the opportunities, support, and training to help them realize their personal and financial goals.

I'll always remember the boardroom of Franchise Concepts Inc. (FCI), a multi-concept franchisor in Houston. Emblazoned on their wall lived the mission statement they practiced every day: *"Our franchisees are our top priority."* Steve Lowrey, their president at the time, was walking the walk and had helped build Deck the Walls, The Great Frame Up, and Framing & Art Centre into the largest framing franchise company in the world.

The company's commitment to its operators hit home when I interviewed their new group of Great Frame Up franchisees, acquired by FCI during the late '90s. Contrary to some mergers, this union was a huge hit with the transitioning owners.

For the first time ever, I witnessed a lovefest of "reborn" business owners. They were ecstatic about FCI's greater support, product inventory, and purchasing power. Responsiveness and expanded services helped revitalize their attitudes and business growth. New management's sensitivity and interest in their success sparked their enthusiasm for the new parent company. Wake up, naysaying franchise owners who believe franchise buyouts can only hurt their business!

Franchisee validation drives system growth

What is the relationship between franchisee satisfaction and the growth rate of new franchisees entering franchise organizations? Franchise sales execs know there's a direct connection, but is there any documentation to prove this? To answer this question, I asked Eric Stites, president of Franchise Business Review (FBR), to conduct research to find out. FBR is a franchise marketing company specializing in independent franchisee satisfaction reports and ratings.

The study, based on data from 130 franchise companies, revealed that companies with high levels of franchisee satisfaction grew at an annual rate six times greater than that of companies with low satisfaction levels. Small franchisors (especially start-ups) were excluded from this survey since they would skew the results because of much higher year-over-year growth as a percentage, and because they had less of a track record for measuring franchisee satisfaction.

The 130 companies in the study had a minimum of 50 franchise units at the end of 2003. Systems ranged in size from 50 to 3,915 units, with a median size of 165 units. Median annual growth for these companies over a three-year period was 12.5 percent. The sample was split into four quartiles based on franchisee satisfaction, as measured by FBR in this franchisee satisfaction survey. The average rate of survey participation by franchisees was 58 percent. The research clearly documents that higher satisfaction produces greater franchise growth.

The study also helps answer the frequent question, Do the fastest-growing franchise companies experience lower franchisee satisfaction? There's an industry perception that rapid growth often creates disgruntled franchisees because of eroding support and services. In this study, there wasn't any conclusive evidence to support this. In fact, the 50 fastest-growing companies of the 130 surveyed had a median franchisee satisfaction rating slightly higher (3 percent) than the rest. So clearly, there are many companies growing quickly and still maintaining high satisfaction levels with their franchise owners.

Who is your ideal franchise owner?

Unfortunately, many franchise companies don't know! If you have franchised for more than two years, there is no excuse for this. You can achieve greatness only if you discover how to identify and attract top-quality candidates, and avoid the trauma of under-performers who will continue to drag down the growth of your system.

If you are a start-up franchisor, you have a legitimate excuse: you can't really know who your best performers are until you have franchisees with at least two years of experience in your system. At that stage, you begin identifying those owner profiles that do well in your program. Consequently, you can adjust your sights toward buyers with the attributes and qualities possessed by these more successful franchisees.

Building a high-performance franchisee network starts with your selection process. And the key to successful selection is to know exactly who you are looking for. At times, franchisors forget to employ this simple principle. Caught up in the flurry of growth quotas, marketing projects, changes in the franchise program and in sales personnel, companies become vulnerable and have been know to stray from their buyer formula.

Who is your current franchise owner?

If you don't know, you'd better find out fast! Five years ago, when Money Mailer was reeling from system challenges, the franchisor had been recruiting general business people from "all walks of life and backgrounds." Unfortunately, this was fanning the flames of failure and they didn't know it. It had been quite awhile since the company analyzed the career experience, skill sets, and characteristics of their operating owners. Unknowingly, the system was fueling its downward spiral by inviting the wrong people with the wrong capabilities to join their franchise. Money Mailer needed to get back on track quickly before their train derailed.

During the same period, a food franchise also was feeling some "partnership pains," sweeping in 40 new franchisees within 24 months of starting to franchise. Other than sizing up the attributes of the founder, the company didn't have an owner profile for success to build a perfect candidate model. But with several stores open, the franchise chain now could sort out the better store owners from the stumbling operators. Would they actually do this?

Both the 20-year Money Mailer veterans and the younger food concept management team now had the experience base to remedy their misguided recruiting methods and avert potential disaster.

Establish your success profile

The president of the food franchise drilled deep, seeking answers to why certain owners were making it while others were simply missing the boat. It became apparent that in their business model absentee and part-time owners didn't work; that specific personality characteristics were critical that weren't necessary in other food-related businesses; and that a franchisee's career background and training often had a significant impact on their success.

At Money Mailer, close self-examination of their owner base paid off quickly: they were chasing the wrong prospects with the wrong marketing messages. Scoping out and separating the winners from the losers within their franchise was the bullet they needed for targeting the right candidates with the right stuff. Specific selling skills were a key trait of the successful Money Mailer franchisee, something that had not previously been required. As noted above, buyers "from all walks of life" had been recruited. Within 60 days, the company readjusted its lead generation sources, marketing materials, sales process, and profiling tools to speak to their real, qualified candidates!

Identify your best and worst performers

Successful performance is a result of the experience, skill sets, interests, and behaviors that match the requirements of your franchise system.

Identifying your ideal candidate is not difficult, but it does take research and some time. Every franchise system has three groups of franchise owners: the stars at the top, the mainstream middle, and the bottom-beaters who struggle every day.

To strengthen your franchise system's opportunities for success, identify the winning characteristics of the best 20 percent in your system. If these owners are very process-oriented, mechanically inclined with analytical behaviors, don't be wooed by candidates boasting great personalities and sales experience who fall short on organizational and managerial skills. Also identify the behaviors and experience levels of your bottom 20 percent, those owners who "just don't get it" and fail to improve even with continual support and assistance.

Profiling the bottom 20 percent of your franchisees accomplishes two objectives: 1) it alerts you to variations in behavioral styles that are contrary to your success model, and 2) it more clearly distinguishes the desired characteristics unique to your top performers.

Analyze the top and bottom 20 percent of your franchise system if you haven't within the past two years! You will uncover key factors that tune you in to your current franchise performers. Money Mailer certainly benefited from this exercise, adjusting its qualification criteria 90 degrees to successfully align with what really counts in their partnership model.

Profiling tools help you qualify

Many franchisors use behavioral surveys as part of their franchisee selection process. This can be a smart investment, considering the size of the payoff and the risk. Understanding the personality makeup of your top franchise owners can guide you to more intelligent decision-making when awarding your franchises. Knowing more about a candidate's personality makeup, goal-orientation, sociability, analytical and compliance traits leads to better choices, benefiting both parties.

Behavioral surveys can provide effective insights into the natural characteristics of potential franchisees throughout the qualification process. Do they have the drive and dominance factors you are seeking? Are they too independent or too indecisive to operate your franchise? Do they have the social skills you demand to build relationships with repeat customers?

This behavioral information brings you closer to the real person sitting before you at Discovery Day, the approval visit for prospective buyers at franchise company headquarters. It's show time at this event, and both interested parties are interviewing each other. This is the final "date" before the franchise marriage begins, so the more you learn about your prospective partner along the way, the better the decision you can make.

The franchise candidate's behavior may or may not mirror *"who this person really is"* during the group and individual meetings at Discovery Day. You'll witness greater and lesser performances, depending on the adeptness of candidates to sell themselves to the home office staff. How many times have we seen a borderline candidate barely squeak through the approval process, who then turns out to be one of your best and brightest franchisees?

Then again, we have all been surprised by candidates who were masters of the interview, only to pay the consequences as they floundered to keep their head above water as your franchisee. I'll never forget the dashing, charismatic new franchisee that wowed our franchise approval committee at American Advertising Distributors, a marketing franchisor. He had all the right moves, and better yet, was the leader and motivator in his corporate training class. This guy had it all, so much so that he never even opened his franchise, walking away from the business before he started!

We have all been duped on occasion, so it's imperative to minimize these painful experiences, which can be very costly for both you and the franchisee—especially when awarding master or regional development agreements, where the stakes are much higher and a bad choice can damage your franchise expansion in a major market. Personality and behavioral surveys are helpful in discovering who people really are. Knowing the inherent characteristics of interested candidates provides you with another tool for determining whether they may fit your owner profile.

One cautionary note: Behavioral surveys reflect natural behavioral tendencies only, and should be used as indicators, not decision-makers. Profiling firms stress this point as well, since all of us have adaptive "learned behaviors" that can override our natural traits. I am not a naturally social person, yet I have consciously learned social skills that are effortless within others. Some older tennis fans may remember watching Jimmy Connors achieve greater levels of success once he learned to control the temper tantrums of his early career. Bjorn Borg was inherently in total control of his behavior, so much so that he was coined "the Silent Assassin" of professional tennis!

Accord Management Systems, Caliper, Franchise Navigator, and Performance Dynamics are some of the profiling services that specialize in assisting franchisors identify and benchmark their franchisee success profiles.

Franchisor Profiling Study #1

What proof is there that franchisee surveys pay off for both the franchisor and franchise operator? The following performance study of CertaPro Painters shows specific unit revenue improvements that were achieved by developing and implementing the right profiling tools in the recruitment selection process. Here are excerpts from the report produced by Caliper:

CertaPro Painters contracted Caliper to identify the specific personality traits most associated with running a successful franchise. With this information, CertaPro and Caliper could create a job-matching process to precisely identify individuals who would be a good fit for this complex role.

Creating the solution

In late 2003, Caliper had conducted an initial study with a small group of 24 franchisees to establish the validity of the Caliper Profile traits in predicting franchise performance. This study identified six traits—aggressiveness, empathy, risk taking, urgency, accommodation, and thoroughness—that differentiated between high and low levels of performance.

In 2006, when a larger sample size became available, Caliper ran the study again and was able to gather franchise performance data and Caliper Profile results on 75 current franchisees. In addition, Caliper and CertaPro Painters worked together to do a job analysis, setting up informational interviews with the stakeholders and successful, reasonably experienced franchisees from across the CertaPro franchisee network. Based on the data gathered from these interviews, a survey was created that would be given to all prospective franchisees. It provided them with brief but clear guidance regarding their suitability to the franchisee role.

Then, with the data from the job analysis of current CertaPro franchisees, Caliper created a structured interview for the franchisee role.

Profiling performance results

Caliper's follow-up study in 2006 confirmed and extended the results of the 2003 study. During this time frame, CertaPro effectively hired and retained people who were much more in line with the Ideal Profile of a successful franchisee.

The average monthly sales for people who fit the Ideal Profile were substantially higher than for those who did not fit. By selecting the people that Caliper recommended and passing on candidates whose personality characteristics did not fit with the Ideal Profile, CertaPro was able to generate long-term positive results.

As shown below, individuals who received a positive recommendation had, on average, over $100,000 more sales per month than those who were not given a positive recommendation:

Average Monthly Completed Sales for Franchisees with Positive vs. Negative Caliper Profile Recommendations		
Recommendation	Average Monthly Sales	No. of Individuals
Positive	$259,200.84	13
Negative	$151,716.54	11
Difference*	$107,484.30	

*This difference in sales is statistically significant [t (22) = -2.36; p<.05].

As the table indicates, by going against Caliper's advice and providing 11 individuals who were not recommended with the opportunity to open a franchise, CertaPro essentially lost an average of over $1 million per month in sales.

Franchisor Profiling Study #2

Another established franchisor contracted the profiling firm Accord Management Systems to help increase franchise unit performance by implementing assessment tools and personality surveys in their recruitment programs for qualified franchise candidates, as well as for qualified franchisee employees. The program paid off. The franchisor generated additional royalty revenues in excess of $500,000 over a measured time period based on identifying candidates with behaviors and attributes most suitable for the franchise business.

As in the first study, it's clear that candidate selection can make an eye-opening difference in the success of your system. The following chart summarizes the findings of the Accord survey as it relates to royalty generation by the composite behavioral profiles of each group.

Engagement Survey of Leading Franchisor	
Franchise Suitability	Average Annual Franchise Royalties
Optimum Profile	$52,000
Good Profile	$24,000
Average Profile	$11,000
Wrong Profile	$ 6,500

Getting the right people on your bus

Take the step if you haven't. Profiling tools can work whether you develop them in-house or "out-house." They can help drive growth faster and reduce your failure rates. This comes from a convert, yours truly, a tough skeptic who once considered profile surveys just a waste of time and money!

Helping the wrong people off your bus

So what do you do with franchisees that "aren't making it happen?" The ones who don't fit your formula and, realistically, will never turn things around? How do you make the best of a bad situation? The solution is logical.

Be responsive and take the lead. Clean house where necessary by providing exit strategies for unsuccessful operators. Struggling or problem franchisees are simply a drain on themselves and their franchise systems. They are not happy and are often resentful, worried, and have lost their motivation. They face growing financial difficulties, and have stressed-out families who share the burdens of their failing business.

Unfortunately, some franchisors tend to sweep these owners under the rug, hoping they will somehow go away by themselves. The less they hear about these unwanted stepchildren the more they procrastinate in confronting the issues. When calls come in from these operators everyone runs for cover. Defenses spring up on both sides. Documented conversations and formal letters cross paths. The franchisor and franchisee have lost confidence, credibility, and trust in each other. Not a good situation.

Franchisors who proactively address failing locations can minimize strained relationships and ugly conflicts with poor operators. Provide options and exit strategies to assist failing franchisees and help these owners cut their losses and move on as quickly as possible. It's your obligation to make this offer, if they haven't asked already. The why, what, and who is at fault makes no difference at this point and helps maintain respect for one other. Use a straightforward approach, whether your owner is still in compliance or not with your agreement. It certainly could head off painfully slow deaths or lawsuits that might ensue.

Establish a resale referral program so your struggling owners can turn to you for guidance in preparing, positioning, and selling their business. (Make sure you consult with legal counsel on how to advise these franchisees and avoid any potential liabilities.) Franchise owners sincerely appreciate a well-structured exit program. It's a significant franchise benefit you can sell when they are considering entering the business.

Those of you with successful resale programs know the value to both the system and the existing owners. I've used testimonials from former franchisees when recruiting new owners. In fact, I sold a new franchisee referred by a prior owner who struggled in managing her business! Our operations team had spent a lot of time helping her make her business marketable, and then we found her a buyer. She still believed in our program, but recognized the business simply wasn't right for her.

De-branding has become a newer franchisor alternative for resolving problems at certain locations. Simply stated, both franchisor and franchisee sign releases of liability and agree that the undesirable operator may convert the location to an independent business, eliminating all signage, identity, products, and proprietary procedures that are identifiable with the franchise brand.

Partners in profit

First, I do apologize by referring to franchisees as "partners." Franchise attorneys correctly remind us that franchisees are not franchise partners or owners. They are franchisees who are granted licenses to operate a franchise business under the agreements authorized by their franchisors. Yes, this is the legal definition and relationship of a franchisee. (Thanks for the reminder, guys!)

In practice, however, franchisees are business owners and the franchisor's business partners. The franchisor succeeds when the franchisee succeeds. When the register rings, both profit. When the register collects dust, both fail. Mutual dependency is the success model, and both partners must work together to enjoy the rewards.

Living this partnership principle strengthens your franchisee relationships and expansion throughout your franchising life! Unfortunately, during the 1990s I was part of a highly successful business service franchise that lost this cooperative bond. The CEO and major stockholder pushed out key management in an active takeover and destroyed the company within a few years. His unfriendly approach and dictatorial management drove respected franchisees out of the system and triggered numerous lawsuits. The once-thriving 125-unit franchise organization died in shambles and bankruptcy.

Both you and your franchisees pass through predictable life cycles. Understanding this natural evolution will provide valuable insights to better understand, adapt, and lead your organization—and improve your changing relationship with your franchisees. Both you and your franchise partners will profit. Here are some growing experiences every franchise company must address to foster franchisee appreciation and enthusiasm.

Life cycle of the franchisee

Franchising is a marriage that successfully blooms when both parties work together to achieve their individual and mutual aspirations. The journey will certainly encounter bumps along the road, but with willing adjustments both franchisor and franchisee will reach their destinations.

Emerging franchisors: open your eyes wide and prepare for this marriage! Otherwise you'll get blindsided with unexpected turmoil within the first two years. The following identifies the stages of the franchise relationship. The key to a harmonious union is the franchisor's responsibility to anticipate and respond to these life cycles with guidance and leadership.

- *Courtship:* Franchisor and candidate are excited about the opportunities they can offer one another.

- *Honeymoon:* The strong mutual attraction leads to the Discovery Day ceremony at franchise headquarters. Joining hands, the franchise certificate is inked and plans for a rosy future begin. There are times of frustration, exuberance, and fear during the new franchise training and pre-opening stages, but in most instances the union holds and the deal is consummated.

- *Infancy:* The business is born and reality hits as the franchisee realizes the amount of support and nurturing the franchisor must provide to ensure the survival of their business. The humbled franchisee now looks even more to the franchisor for their business wisdom, recognizing their dependency in surviving this trying start-up period.

- **_Teenage rebellion:_** Independence sets in as the franchisee's business begins to blossom. Ideas, changes, and challenges may create tensions with the franchisor, whose policies and procedures now seem a bit "old school" and dated to the budding franchise owner.

- **_Adulthood:_** The franchisor is now viewed with greater maturity as the franchisee regains respect and appreciation for the integrity of the products, services, and brand consistency that have supported their successes. The operator has conquered the formula for building the business and now seeks education, guidance, and opportunities from the franchisor that will take them to a higher level of growth.

- **_Community:_** Advisory councils and advertising committees are a natural outgrowth of the need for healthy communication within the franchise partnership. As a best practice, the franchisor should initiate the formation of these councils and committees. If they don't, I can almost guarantee that the franchisees will, sometimes for misguided reasons and with misdirected objectives.

Stages of franchisee competency

I once ruffled an area developer's feathers by telling him his initial sales expectations were wrong for his new service franchise. Arrogantly I exclaimed, "_Jack, even though your friends say they will become clients, most of them won't. Believe me!_"

Several months later at a conference, Jack sheepishly admitted I was quite right with my earlier comment. He was a little standoffish, and I realized our once-comfortable relationship would never be the same. I'd made a major error: I forgot how to respond to a new franchise owner facing business situations that were second nature to the franchisor. I initially jumped on Jack, who had excitedly shared with me what he believed was a good thing. I had rained on his parade, which embarrassed him. I should have addressed his naivete more diplomatically, and shared with him why he couldn't count on most of his friends. As a new area developer, Jack was still incompetent. His friends had given him only verbal commitments with no contracts signed or money in hand. Jack had assumed they all would sign up with him. It wasn't his fault. He didn't know any better at the time.

There are four stages of competency in how we all learn, whether it's how to raise a child, play a piano, or master our current job. This is no different in the franchise business. You must appreciate that business buyers are attracted to your franchise because they know you can provide them with the competencies they currently lack. Franchisees will grow through these four stages of competency:

- *Unconsciously incompetent:* New owners don't know what they don't know! Expect some frustration or panic once these fledglings start up their businesses and quickly discover they haven't a clue how hard or consuming it really is going to be.

- *Consciously incompetent:* The franchisees realize their naivete and gain greater respect and appreciation for your expertise and assistance. They straighten up and focus on learning your system, what they have to know and do, and how to best use their skill sets to become successful owners.

- *Consciously competent:* With experience and some successes, the franchisees gain expertise and confidence as the business builds. They see the light at the tunnel's end and recognize their abilities and know-how to achieve their goals.

- *Unconsciously competent:* These are your master builders, those franchise partners who do it naturally, and with a grace and assurance that is now inherent in their way of doing your business. They are your star performers and leaders, trainers and board members, and confidants and partners who you and other franchisees can now learn from.

Prepare your staff for the predictable ignorance of new and growing franchise partners, and how they must be patient and encouraging, even when virgin franchisees get fixated on "dumb" or "meaningless" activities or ideas. This will eliminate frustration and misunderstandings for both you and your franchise partners.

As a franchisor, you've built the vehicle and the road. Your franchisees are granted the keys and license that entitle them to drive the business and enjoy the potential rewards. They will swerve, run into jams, and hit a ditch or two. That's okay, because through their well-meaning efforts they don't have all the competencies or experience to run a straight course. That's why they bought your business expertise: to guide them on the right path to success. Let's face it, we've all touched a hot stove a few times!

When I consulted for a California retail franchisor, the corporate staff kept commenting about the "silly" suggestions that new franchisees were convinced would spiral their business to heights of grandeur. The new operators were exuberant about their flashes of marketing brilliance and operational enhancements. *"What's wrong with these franchisees?" exclaimed the upset marketing director. "Why are they fighting the system? They're going to be troublemakers, and we need to shut them down quickly."* I settled the frustrated exec down and explained that these new franchisees are excited and really do mean well, but they are just naive about the business. They were in the unconsciously incompetent stage of development. *"Be patient, acknowledge their good ideas, and let them know other operators have already tested them. Share with them what we hoped would be marketing home runs, but what actually happened, and why they ultimately failed."*

During the second year of a franchisee's business, two field trainers complained, *"What happened to Joe and Ray? They went by the book in starting their operations, but now they keep pushing us to add more specialty drinks and bring in breakfast items. I tell them it absolutely won't work, but they won't let up."* I smiled at one of the trainers, exclaiming, *"Welcome to the teenage rebellion cycle of franchisees! These owners have learned the basics and are now flexing their muscles as they grow. They no longer instantly say 'Yes.' They're testing the parental wisdom of the system. It's a natural progression that they'll seek better mousetraps for their business. Remind these owners that we do welcome their ideas, but that they must be good for the customers, good for the other owners, and good for the brand. In this case, they just didn't pass the test."*

Proper screening is critical to a healthy relationship with incoming franchisees. To qualify for a franchise, interested buyers must agree to follow the policies and procedures of your system and recognize that sometimes they'll have to make compromises for the good of the system. If a franchisee's independence keeps flaring up, you probably didn't screen that individual well enough to reject them during your selection process.

Life cycle of the franchisor

Franchisors also evolve and develop through definite stages. The good news is these stages are predictable and quantifiable, and that with preparation you can act to ensure a smooth transition through each cycle of your growth.

The size of your franchisee organization, based on number of franchisees, is often the driving factor that determines your management infrastructure, staffing needs, support programs, and ongoing development strategies. These unit levels can vary according to your concept, industry, and other mitigating factors, but these are the basic three:

- **0 – 50 franchises:** Launching your franchise program requires strong support functions in franchise sales, real estate, training, marketing, and customer service. Founders often will multi-task, performing most of these roles themselves during the start-up phase. At this stage, the CEO has personal relationships and frequent contact with the franchise owners. As franchisees are brought into the system, additional personnel are hired with competencies in the various functions.

  Franchise advisory councils and advertising committees are implemented when approaching 25 franchise owners, in order to provide a collective communication channel between corporate and the owner network. The first national convention is initiated to foster system unity, share best practices, recognize the top franchisees, and provide networking opportunities.

- **51 – 250 franchises:** The franchisor is no longer a small company and is now feeling the pains of growth. It is more difficult to be responsive to individual franchisees, and the CEO must step back from daily tasks and adopt a strategic planning and leadership role. With the maturing performances of franchisees, the organization now has success profiles for its better-performing operators. Early franchisees who were poor selections are identified and provided assistance with exit strategies.

  The franchise is now becoming a professional, mid-sized organization, with CRM tools, intranet systems, marketing research, and product development.

- **251 – 1,000 or more franchises:** The franchisor is gaining recognition in the marketplace and solidifying itself as a business that is standing the test of time. High-level professional managers are brought in as the organization morphs into a large business. National and regional advertising funds begin to deliver the branding benefits and cost efficiencies inherent in the franchise model. More professional marketing, merchandising, and real estate services are available at the unit level, funded by increasing royalties and other revenue streams enjoyed by the burgeoning brand.

A strong culture breeds greatness

Some visionary franchisors energize their growth by creating a cultural power in their business environment that propels their branding strength to a higher level. More than ever, today's franchise buyers are seeking a community that defines and shares their value systems, business principles, and vision. "Common purpose" is definitely a catalyst for attracting like-minded business owners who can transmit your business principles to their customers, employees, and within your organization. It's the special fuel that ignites greater franchisee loyalty and satisfaction.

I'm always excited to experience a company's unique culture in action. In the rental car business, I believe Enterprise Rent-A-Car has instilled a value system that towers above other companies. They have, on numerous occasions, provided extraordinary service beyond my expectations in a way that I just don't get from the robots behind other car rental pickup counters.

During one of my recent travels, I was again enamored with the magic of Enterprise. Jeff, a stoutly former football player, picked me up, with my wife Jane, and whisked us away to their rental center with the enthusiasm of a sports fan at the Super Bowl.

Curious about the cultural phenomenon I was experiencing, I asked the dynamic lad, *"What's it like working for Enterprise? I hear it's a different kind of place."* Sporting a big grin Jeff exclaimed, *"Great company. The founder's in his 80s and going strong as ever! Did you know that Enterprise has more employees earning over $100,000 than any other large business in the U.S.? Plus, you 'gotta' be a college grad, and very few survive our tough training or the grueling 60-plus-hour work weeks. For the right person like myself, it's a great place to work and make good money. You see, each one of us is trained to operate this business as our own business, and we're recognized for our performance. I'm accountable, and the better I do the more I'm rewarded."*

I was blown away. Jeff was passionate and appreciative that he was part of the Enterprise Rent-A-Car organization. Jane and I got excited just listening to him, but then came the grand finale, that special moment few consumers ever experience. The energy was brimming over as we entered the retail office, populated by other Jeff-like employees dashing to and fro assisting customers at the counter and on the phone... all on top of their game amidst the controlled chaos.

Then disaster struck. Jeff escorted us to the only rental they had remaining on such short notice: a 50-foot tricked-out pickup truck you'd more likely see jumping barrels at a "Monster Wheels" auto show. Seeing the terror in our faces, Jeff gracefully slipped back into the office and returned smiling. *"Here, take these keys to my new car. I'll take the pickup for the next few days."* Thank you, Jeff!

A celebrated moment in customer service had just occurred. The power of an outstanding corporate culture has leveraged this organization from good to greatness. It certainly touched Jeff, who had become a recruiting billboard for the Enterprise Rent-A-Car system. It's not surprising *Business Week* magazine has ranked Enterprise as one of the top five "Best Places to Launch a Career."

Core values grow ordinary to extraordinary

Express Employment Professionals (formerly Express Personnel Services) is a best practices company passionate about the success of its franchise partners. And they know it. With humble beginnings as the "Johnny-come-lately" in their highly competitive industry, the Oklahoma company soared to an industry leader in temporary employment services. One only has to hear franchisees speak about their franchise experiences to realize the culture that the company's founder, Robert Funk, has instilled throughout the organization. I never had heard owners repeatedly use words such as *"ethics, credibility, caring, genuine, and sincere"* when describing their corporate team. Even those who struggled recognized the well-meaning efforts the company invests with franchisees to improve and grow their operations.

Discovery Day at this organization is an exceptional experience for franchisee candidates. The hospitality and magnetism the corporate staff extends to their guests provide a memorable and convincing experience that has produced phenomenal closing results for the organization. When consulting with Tom Gunderson, former vice president of development for Express, I was awed by his personal attention to ensure my experience at their Oklahoma City headquarters was outstanding. His team members were the most appreciative and gracious staff I have ever worked with.

Hospitality went above and beyond what could be imagined. After we spent a full eight hours on franchise marketing strategies, Tom escorted me on a memorable tour at the stables of Mr. Funk's famous Clydesdale horses, and then to the auction house for his prize cattle on his magnificent ranch grounds. I was the supplier they were paying, yet they treated me as their most valuable client. This was both alarming and inspiring. And I must say this was an exceptional experience for me.

Tom gave his time way beyond the call of duty with a consultant, not because it was his job but because it was his pleasure. I then knew why franchisees spoke so highly about their staff with potential owners. They truly were interested in the welfare of their franchise partners.

Are you walking the walk?

Most franchisors miss the mark because they don't activate their message throughout their system. Seize this opportunity and you will become one of the exceptional companies that do!

Mission statements, goals, and visions must be more than catchy words on franchise sales materials and employee brochures. They must be demonstrated daily through the actions of the corporate team and franchisees. Savvy franchise buyers see beyond the sizzle. Too often they have been shortchanged by empty promises in their former careers and are still licking old wounds.

I once sold a franchise to a senior executive who was on the rebound. He had just visited a franchise that promoted its "family values," only to discover it wasn't at all true. *"At their Discovery Day, they only cared about getting my money. They weren't interested in what was important to my wife and me in making this life-changing decision."* Too bad he wasn't considering Express Personnel!

Linda Burzynski now owns VL Service Corp., a franchise development firm. Before that, as CEO of Liberty Fitness & Weight Loss, she was a walking brand for her franchise. Throughout her executive career, Linda has earned an outstanding reputation for immersing her soul in the franchise companies she has led. She sees, feels, and breathes the business from the ground up. As president of Molly Maid, she donned a worker uniform and toiled side by side with the maids, scrubbing floors and dusting cobwebs. Her insights into the challenges and motivations of hourly workers generated better employee recognition and recruitment programs for the system. At Liberty, she embraced her own fitness and weight loss program, worked out religiously, lost more than 50 pounds, and today enjoys a healthy lifestyle she'd never experienced before. Realizing the customer benefits for herself helped prompt additional services that have enhanced the franchise concept and opportunity.

Linda makes it her business to really connect with her staff, franchisees, their employees, and their customers. Would you as president do what Linda does for her franchisees at an advisory meeting? At 9 p.m. she's finished the first 12-hour day with her board members. Or has she? At 2 a.m. she's buying gifts at a 24-hour department store. At 3:30 a.m. she's back home writing special appreciation letters to each of the 10 board members. At 8:30 the next morning she's back in the conference room with a twinkling eye, raring to go for day two of the event. Amazed by this experience I asked, *"Linda, what's this all about?"* She looked confused, as if this were no big deal. I inquired further with staff members and franchisees. Countless examples flew expressing respect and admiration for Linda, and for her total commitment to connect with the people she leads and manages. *"This is Linda, what she's all about!"*

Getting it right with your franchisees

Core values are today's "X factor" in franchise development. To succeed in this business, franchisors must effectively position their concept in the marketplace, offering compelling benefits to both customers and potential franchise buyers. By creating a dynamic culture you'll add a powerful dimension to your brand, which can catapult your organization beyond the competition.

Dick Rennick, founder and former CEO of American Leak Detection, was named Entrepreneur of the Year at the 1998 IFA Convention. What was so stunning about this celebration was witnessing the nearly 100 franchisees who had flown in at their own expense to celebrate and validate their leader's compassion, values, and relationships instilled within their system. Dick's inspiring comments focused on his owners and employees, the builders of his successful franchise family. An explosive, standing ovation followed, bathing the general assembly in the infectious warmth of his franchise fans clapping, whistling, and cheering for their leader. This extraordinary ceremony of franchisors and franchisees has never been duplicated at an IFA convention in the past 25 years. We all experienced the power of corporate culture at that momentous event in Dick's business life.

Rennick also received the "Lifetime Achievement Award" in 2006 from the American Association of Franchisees and Dealers (AAFD), recognized for developing fair, franchisee-friendly franchise documents. Dick's humanitarian actions expanded to the consumer population throughout the U.S. He founded and championed the Franchise Emergency Action Team (FEAT) of participating franchise systems that have donated many hours, services, and products to assist U.S. communities during times of disaster. Rennick had the "X factor." He created culture, inspiration, and pride within his franchise organization, and made a difference giving back to the general population when it mattered most.

Recognition and rewards

Show your franchise partners that you care. Most franchise owners want to be recognized and rewarded for their achievements. If they didn't, most franchisors probably wouldn't want them as part of their system. Find ways to thank owners for their contributions. Newsletters, meetings, conventions, phone calls, personal letters, and visits are multiple opportunities to show appreciation for your owners, both one-on-one and among their peers. "Showcase" your top producers. Reward them for their winning spirits and what they have achieved in building successful businesses.

Franchise owners buy into your message that they are joining a family of franchisees who share and exchange ideas and best practices within an active network sharing common goals. They like the fact that franchising is a people business, and is relationship-driven between the franchise owners and the corporate team. Group power and the value of "on your own, but not alone" was certainly an attraction that drew me to join a franchise system in 1980.

About 12 years ago, I visited a former master franchisee of a 3,000-unit cleaning franchise who developed one of the top regions in the country. Because he was a big producer, corporate headquarters frequently recommended franchise candidates visit his operation. The owner would spend hours with these prospective buyers sharing his business successes and promoting the franchise organization. As a result, candidates who bought into the program would occasionally call and thank him for taking the time to visit and answer their questions.

Unfortunately, corporate headquarters never recognized the master franchisee for helping out, which really bothered him. Corporate failed to recognize his support by spending time with these buyers, not once applauding him for promoting their system. *"I wasn't looking for a referral fee, all I wanted was to be recognized for my efforts."* The master eventually sold his region and started his own franchise program. Never lose touch with your franchise owners, no matter how large your system becomes!

How recognition inspires owners

The power of recognition often motivates franchisees to achieve greater accomplishments and give back more to the system. In 1983, during the opening ceremony of our national convention, my mentor and partner Frank Duffy and I were crowned franchisees of the year before a few hundred peers and their families. For the next three days we were rock stars, basking in the limelight of other owners. They wanted to speak with us, asked if we would spend time with them at the event or by phone after the convention. *"What were our secrets to setting new performance records? How did we successfully attract and develop our employees when they couldn't? What advice could we provide to help them with their circumstances?"* I really felt good sharing our successes with our franchisee partners, who could benefit from our contributions and experience. It was a special moment of celebration and personal growth. I realized then how recognition and reward fuels the strength of franchise networking. Years prior to that event, we were the students gleaning information from our business neighbors. Now Frank and I were the professors with the ability to give back to others.

Balancing the differences

Franchisors and franchisees will always face the challenge of living harmoniously in two business worlds that are not quite the same. As local small business owners, franchisees must make compromises for the strength of the national network and brand. Likewise, corporate must also be sensitive to the genuine needs of its franchise partners, and not quickly dismiss business challenges that may be unique to their markets. Swiftly addressing issues and creating solutions is the conduit for building franchisee and franchisor satisfaction.

I was shocked years ago when I overheard some corporate employees name-bashing their franchisees, only to discover that their senior executives were participating in the mutinous behavior. I asked the director of franchising if the CEO knew this was going on. In disgust he fired back, *"He's the one who started it!"* This condescending attitude reared its ugly head a few years later with some costly lawsuits. I wasn't surprised.

Ask owners to rate your performance

Make periodic reality checks to see how you're doing with your partners. Poll your owners annually to find out how your organization scores with your franchisees. If you don't know where you stand with your operators, how can you effectively respond to their needs and interests? Franchise advisory councils, committees, and task forces are invaluable in representing the interests and challenges of your franchisee network. But acting as filters, they don't expose you to the individual voices of your system owners so you can hear exactly what's happening on the franchise streets of San Jose or Brooklyn.

Franchise development surveys are great feedback tools that allow "the masses" to clearly communicate their messages to you. They are easy to develop, administer, and analyze. But beware: Don't ask owners what they think if you aren't going to respond to their input. Surveys can be extensive or limited, depending on what feedback you are seeking from your franchisees.

Rather than automatically using a staff member for your survey, consider hiring an outside firm or qualified individual to conduct the interviews. An outside firm builds credibility with your franchisees and can be more objective in gathering information. Their third-party relationship usually makes owners more comfortable in expressing what they really think about the franchise. Also, the project will be completed much faster, rather than taking a backseat to your staff's more pressing daily activities.

It's all about exceeding expectations

Franchise buyers get excited by franchise organizations that listen to their customers and align their services and values with what's important to their patrons. It's all about the experience, not the transaction. You know you've arrived when customers of It's A Grind Coffee House get excited because your employees know to serve their lattes in a nice ceramic mug rather than a paper cup. Or, when franchisees of We The People see a client's heartfelt appreciation for resolving family business matters by preparing standard legal documents they couldn't possibly afford from an attorney. Inspired franchisees proudly tout their victories to inquiring prospects who want to know why customers are so attracted to their business.

Getting it right with your customers

Another way to know you've arrived is when your *customers* experience and buy into your core values. Every day since he began franchising in 2001, Marty Cox, the founder of It's a Grind Coffee House, focused on identifying, sharing, and communicating the organization's core values. This founder's commitment and attention to customer alignment was a powerful catalyst that helped attract more franchise buyers to It's A Grind than to any other competitor. Patrons repeatedly exclaim, "*I feel so comfortable in your cafes. Your environment is so much more inviting, your employees are upbeat and more friendly, your staff knows me by name and brings my coffee and bagel to my table.*" Their community within four walls turned strangers into daily friends, and at times became the celebration place for birthdays and engagements.

"*Providing exceptional experiences to enhance the lives of the people we meet every day*" was the credo at It's A Grind. And it is the foundation of what spawned the company's success in the fiercely competitive coffee space. Franchisees, as well as corporate staff in operations, real estate, and sales had to buy into this ideology. This passion to serve and create special moments for customers ran up and down the organization. Candidates commented about the franchisees' almost cult-like commitment to the franchise's value system. As Cox stressed, "*If our mission doesn't reflect who you are, our franchise is not a fit for you. You'll become frustrated and struggle in our business.*"

Capture what the customer wants

Distinguish your franchise by knowing what creates steadfast customer loyalty to your brand. Franchisees profit from this consumer connection, which drives repeat business. At American Advertising Distributors I capitalized on our point of differentiation by arming our retail clients with marketing intelligence that was superior to any other service at the time, producing more successful campaigns for their businesses. I bragged to prospective franchisees about our powerful corporate research and development, which was instrumental in our 82 percent customer retention rate. Our retail market craved expertise for building their businesses, and our system delivered the goods beyond their expectations. We had raving customers who championed our brand because we provided them what they wanted.

Does your brand's culture cater to your customers? If it doesn't, your concept, franchise partners, and their employees will suffer. Young franchisors may say they can't afford to hire a mystery shopping service, research firm, or conduct consumer focus groups. If so, then implement this low-cost solution: provide questionnaires in your locations for customer feedback, or have field operations staff conduct random interviews at your franchise locations. Here's a simple survey used by a bootstrap haircutting franchise to gain insights into their customers' wants, needs, and experiences:

- As a customer, what attracted you to this salon?
- Are there any other reasons you go to the salon?
- What characteristics make this salon stand out from other haircutting shops?
- What services do you receive here?
- Would you rate the quality of their service as fair, good, very good, or excellent? Please tell me why.
- How would you rate the quality of your hairstylist, and why?
- What is the atmosphere and environment like?
- In a sentence, how would you describe your experience in this salon?
- Have you been to any other salons that compare with this salon? Please explain:
- What improvements in service or products would you like to see in this salon?
- What two suggestions do you have that can help the owner, who is sincerely interested in knowing how to make their salon even more appealing to you?
- If someone thinking about going to this salon asked you about its service, what would you say to them?

Customer surveys are critical, especially for monitoring whether customers will refer friends or associates to use your business products or services. Not too long ago, I had an aggravating experience with a national franchise car rental agency. (Of course, it wasn't with my heroes, Enterprise Rent-A-Car!) After the rental fiasco, I received their customer satisfaction form from corporate headquarters. I filled it out, wailing about melting in the Florida heat with no airport pickup service for 45 minutes and other frustrations. Venting on the customer satisfaction form cleansed some of my anger. Will they read and respond to my complaint? Will they apologize for their unacceptable service and perhaps pay me off with a free rental day or other gesture of goodwill? Whether I use their Orlando airport location again (or any other facility of theirs) was totally in their hands. Because they chose not to respond, they lost me as a customer and referral forever.

Are your franchisees your biggest fans?

Strong franchisee validation drives greater system growth. Owner satisfaction spells success in franchise recruitment. Choose the right partners, cultivate a strong marriage, and your development efforts will soar. Adversarial relationships, with an "us vs. them" atmosphere, will bring your expansion efforts to a wicked halt. If you don't have your team's support, how can you win the game?

Robin was our franchisee service rep for our Houston franchise at American Advertising Distributors. She was very good at her job, but known for her occasional "attitude" and apathy in assisting owners. She wasn't a team player. That changed quickly on her first visit to our franchise. Two days before she arrived, headquarters screwed up by printing "$15 off" instead of "$5 off" on a shoe repair promotion for one of our multi-location clients. Customers flooded their stores, and their managers, fearful of losing future business, gave up explaining the error. Our client was in a rage, so we said our corporate representative was coming to town and would personally fix the problem to his satisfaction. We told Robin on the way to the client's main store about this massive problem, and that she would be handling it, not us. *"No, you can't make me do this, please!"*

Robin took the bullets from our screaming client that day, and transitioned from cavalier corporate employee to caring team player. For the first time, she stood in the shoes of the franchise owner. She made good on corporate's error and took care of our client, providing $10 credits for each customer redemption he honored at the higher price. She also offered some value-added marketing services for free, which the store owner said wasn't necessary. We became Robin's biggest fan after this experience, which strengthened the connection with our corporate partnership. She was now working together with us.

Ready, set, grow!

Build franchisee satisfaction and you'll build faster system growth at reduced costs, attracting more quality buyers through franchise owner and customer referrals. It's a simple message, but not that easy to execute. Aggressive start-ups that dazzle buyers with smoke and mirrors pay dearly. Selling sizzle without the steak burns right back. Here are key development tips for growth from this chapter's checklist:

✓ Build strong relationships and mutual respect with your franchise partners. Monitor your customer service, training, and operations departments to ensure they are working side by side with owners, not across the table from them. Keep 'em happy, demonstrate you care, and you both win.

✓ Identify and profile your successful owners. You'll grow your organization with better performing franchisees and minimize poor candidate choices. Using more intelligent qualification and selection tools will reap greater payoffs for you and your franchise partners.

✓ Develop an exit program for those unhappy franchisees who continue to struggle in your business. Work with them to help sell their operations, providing guidance to best prepare for the transition. Taking proactive steps increases the opportunities to remedy difficult situations and avoids the inevitable conflicts that result from taking no action at all.

✓ Understand the life cycles a franchisee experiences and teach your staff how to lead effectively in responsive, productive ways that keep your owners in tune with your system's policies and procedures.

✓ Create a brand culture that embraces all levels of the organization, from CEO to employees and customers. It can be the "X factor" that sets you above your competitors.

✓ Recognize and reward your franchisees openly for their contributions and achievements through conventions, meetings, newsletters, and personal correspondence. Special appreciation from the top when you're working hard in the daily trenches counts more than you think.

✓ Ask your franchisees to rate your performance in support services, products, and commitment to help them achieve their professional and personal goals. Periodic surveys and polling will sharpen your franchise programs and improve your connection with your revenue-producing franchise partners.

Chapter 3

Success Driver III:
Compelling Franchise Program

Keep the doors open and think beyond

the walls of tradition.

Success Driver III:
Compelling Franchise Program

Franchisors should continually ask themselves, *"How attractive is my franchise opportunity now? Does it still deliver what it takes? In what ways do I stand out among competitive opportunities?"*

As a reality check, review your franchise program each year to ensure it remains strong and provides the sizzle and power of an attractive, viable business concept. Does it continue to satisfy the goals and interests of your existing owners? Does your concept capture the attention of new buyers? Or is your opportunity growing stale, losing a little steam? And then you must grab your mirror and ask yourself, *"Is yesterday's buyer still the owner I want today?"*

Look at our roller-coaster marketplace. What works today may not work as well tomorrow. Business and consumer environments change, never remaining the same. It's easy to lose sight of new and evolving competition, trends, and other influences that motivate franchise buying decisions today.

The competitive landscape for qualified franchise buyers has increased significantly. Industry growth is at a record pace, with more than 1,000 new franchise concepts springing up in the past four years (through the end of 2008), according to FRANdata. Consequently, franchisors are working with prospects who are considering more opportunities than ever before.

In addition to a healthy new menu of franchise concepts, opportunity seekers can discover almost any franchise company in existence by surfing the web from their office or home. Cyberspace has given small companies the power to compete at a fraction of the cost that traditionally prohibited their national exposure. The playing field has definitely expanded. Established franchises certainly enjoy branding and credibility advantages, but the competitive gap isn't as large as in prior years.

What's your long-term strategy for staying ahead of the curve? Preparation and adaptation are what keep high-performance companies on top of their game. Take the lead and you'll increase your opportunities for stronger system growth over the long haul.

Respond to market demands

"Tired brand," "dated concept," "no legs," and "industry disaster" all are fatal labels for a franchise brand. Unfortunately, we all have watched systems erode to shells of their former glory days. The need to adapt to a changing environment is illustrated in the stories of two franchises, one that famously overcame a PR nightmare that could have wiped out their system; and another that ignored danger signs that toppled their market dominance overnight.

Some of us "seniors" remember the disturbing news decades ago when uninspected meat from Australia slipped into some Jack in the Box burgers. Unbeknownst to the franchisor, the foreign beef had been delivered to a few stores. Although this isolated incident was instantly fixed, it didn't matter. The damage of the national press hammered hard. The franchisor minimized the blow with an ingenious response, replacing its burger menu with an impressive sandwich line that took off. Years later, as consumer memories faded, Jack in the Box quietly reintroduced hamburgers, complementing its now popular sandwich and other product choices. Today, the company's food-quality and safety program has been recognized as the most comprehensive in the industry.

Losing touch invites disaster

The second company, an automotive franchise, unfortunately decided to brush off impending disaster and paid dearly. First to market with a product innovation, the company was the buzz of the service growth sector. Franchise recruitment soared as buyers lined up to secure their piece of the action. The first years were fabulous, with no real competition. Barriers to entry kept others from also cashing in on their concept. But the franchisor wore blinders and ignored the inevitable. Rather than evolving its program beyond any "me too" companies that were springing up, the franchisor did nothing. The fall came hard as competitors developed similar services with more attractive offerings to buyers. The company stubbornly resisted the reality. As their franchise recruiter blindly retorted, *"We created the industry, we're the original deal! These guys are all knockoffs! Why would anyone buy their programs?"*

Household brands reinvent themselves

Let's take a look at another franchise system that also hit rough development waters in the 1990s—except this company was far from start-up status. This time growth challenges had struck the legendary Radio Shack brand.

Leonard Clegg was a longtime operations executive with Radio Shack, a household brand that had faced flat franchise growth for the past several years. The franchise model was becoming tired, with any forward progress offset by backward steps. Len Roberts, the new CEO, was impressed with Leonard's reputation and performance in operations and appointed him to "do what it takes" to turn up the dial and revitalize franchise expansion. Clegg went to work, taking dramatic measures to build a new Radio Shack opportunity that was ideal for smaller markets, where the company was struggling to establish more presence.

He trimmed the store model to 600 square feet, slashing inventory to the top 20 percent of merchandise that was driving 80 percent of store sales. He repackaged his opportunity for a new audience: successful owners of hardware stores, home improvement centers, and other complementary retail environments.

The "Mini-Shack" he created offered a $60,000 start-up program, with a one-year satisfaction guarantee. Should a franchisee for any reason decide to leave the system during their first year of operation, Radio Shack would buy back all of the existing inventory.

Growth exploded for Radio Shack, as the brand's trimmed-down, refocused franchises populated smaller communities. Buyers applauded the chance to bring a powerful, customer-building, national brand into their localities! The potential rewards blew away the low financial risks.

Often franchise leaders are reticent to leave their comfort zone to re-engineer their concepts. Reinventing a franchise concept can be scary, exciting, exasperating, disruptive, expensive, and exhilarating. Hopefully, the examples of visionary management who cured fundamental cracks in their franchise foundations will inspire others facing similar challenges. Nobody ever said this is easy. The higher the stakes, the higher the risks.

When all cylinders aren't firing

Mobile Bankers, a California-based franchise, was at a crossroads threatening its growth in the early '90s. At that time, the check cashing "on wheels" concept was a cottage industry that lacked standardization and was controlled by independent chains.

For those unfamiliar with this hidden industry, here's how this check cashing concept works. Servicing large factories, hotel chains, and other business with minimum-wage workers, armored franchise trucks would arrive on payday and cash employee paychecks for a fee at the work sites. This service was a real benefit to employees, since they were part of the 25 percent of U.S. workers without checking accounts. The fees charged were lower than at check cashing stores, and the service eliminated the transportation hassles, expense, and time needed to go off-site. Most important, employers welcomed the service since it was beneficial to the employee and eliminated problems of workers returning late for their shifts (or sometimes not at all!).

Unfortunately, Mobile Bankers was unexpectedly blindsided by a major problem. Most of its franchisees were not acquiring new company accounts, despite the fact that the service was highly attractive and in demand. Headquarters responded by sending personnel to help build new accounts while visiting with the owners. But after they left the franchisees once again floundered.

Ralph Ross, the founder and a franchise expert, quickly discovered what was wrong. Mobile Bankers had missed the mark in positioning his concept, attracting the wrong owner candidates. The program was packaged as a mom-and-pop, blue-collar opportunity for those seeking a profitable route business servicing hundreds of regular customers. After careful analysis, he realized that his few successful owners had management skill sets and a different vision of the business operation.

These top performers were operating Mobile Bankers as an executive franchise that provided a valuable employee benefit service for blue-collar workers in manufacturing, production, hotel, and other labor-intensive industries. They focused on marketing and selling the program to company presidents, vice presidents, and human resource directors, and then supervised their fleet of check-cashing vehicles servicing the accounts. The key to their business success was acquiring and maintaining strong relationships with large commercial accounts, not driving armored trucks.

Mobile Bankers had now pinpointed their error in developing the concept. They had designed and promoted their franchise program to the wrong franchise buyers! The company successfully reformulated the opportunity and re-launched its new executive franchise tailored for upper-management entrepreneurs seeking a unique business-to-business service. The revamped program immediately attracted the right candidates and the concept was off and running.

Unfortunately, within the next few years, other challenges prevented Mobile Bankers from realizing its vision. But they gave it their very best, always extremely focused on developing a compelling franchise proposition that rewarded both franchisee and franchisor.

How to hit a grand slam

In 1984, I met Fred DeLuca, co-founder of Subway, then a 19-year-old retail chain with approximately 300 stores. Many of us would be happy with such development success. But not Fred. He had envisioned thousands of his Subway stores operating throughout the world. At the company's expansion rate, however, he would never see his dream come to fruition.

Fred was determined to turn his vision to reality and needed to find the formula for explosive growth. Impressed by the success of the Century 21 model, he decided to develop a franchise expansion concept to accelerate his growth. As I recall, he handpicked his best store owners and awarded them development rights within their markets. This move was revolutionary. It contradicted the basic franchising model, which required healthy fees to obtain area development rights. This was unheard-of at the time, and still is today. In return for this opportunity, these "development agents" had to agree to aggressive recruitment quotas.

Fred now had a highly motivated, successful Subway team who were provided with an exciting expansion model to make a lot of money. On the other hand, he could just as easily yank this development opportunity from a development agent who was underperforming, since they paid nothing for the privilege.

Second, he reduced his franchise fees, a brash move revolutionary within industry circles. But he wanted to make his concept extremely attractive for aspiring business owners, who now could join his Subway program and open a store for less than $50,000. So what happened? The lower barrier to entry helped catapult Subway to the top of the food chain with franchise buyers. You couldn't find a more attractively priced start-up package.

Third, Fred demanded simplicity in his program. Ease of operation within a simple box is still the heart of Subway's success. Keep it neatly packaged without extras that can lead to inconsistencies and confusion.

Finally, he devised an ingenious revenue structure to help ensure a "win-win-win" for all parties: franchisor, franchisees, and development agents.

Because new franchisees would receive on-site support, Fred boosted royalty fees to 8 percent. This provided strong financial incentive for his handpicked development agents, who would receive a percentage of the franchise fee for recruiting new owners and one third of ongoing royalties.

Because of the very affordable start-up costs, new franchisees didn't mind paying higher royalties on the back end and rushed to sign up with Subway. Fred created an additional market of business buyers who previously couldn't afford to own a franchised food business like his. The price of admission was right and the opportunity extremely attractive. The development agents were successful Subway store operators who would provide new owners with local real estate assistance, training, and ongoing support to help launch and grow the new franchisees' businesses.

More than 20 years and nearly 30,000 stores later, Subway, its development agents, and its franchise partners certainly have stood the test of time and success!

In essence, Fred revolutionized his sandwich business by introducing two monumental changes to his franchise program: 1) establishing a national sales force of successful franchisees who exponentially expanded his system, and 2) offering his franchise to a broader buyer market that didn't have the skill sets or financing required by most franchise programs.

Fred took a huge gamble, introducing extreme changes in his Subway development model. In his case, the rewards have been monumental. Today, Subway is a global household brand that continues to bring its classic sandwich concept to every nook and cranny of the world. And just when you think the franchise program might be growing stale, along comes greater success with Subway celebrity Jared, followed by a popular expanded menu of bread choices and competitively priced products.

Some critics point to challenges Subway has faced during its meteoric growth. This certainly is expected, whether you're Subway, McDonald's, or Starbucks. Such astounding and sustaining achievements could not be possible without a strong, viable franchise program. Today, in 2008, Subway is the fastest-growing franchise in the world approaching 30,000 restaurants in 87 countries. Great job, Fred.

Area development

Is area development right for you?

To address this question I asked Marc Kiekenapp, managing partner of Kiekenapp & Associates, to share his experiences. Marc is a master sales professional, and a 29-year veteran in leading and launching development programs with both single-unit and area development strategies. He has recruited, managed, and trained area developers (ADs) for many years. His insights into the successes and frustrations of building and operating AD programs are quite revealing.

After all the long months of preparation, attorney's fees, training manuals, and writing and registering your UFOC, you thought you were happy with your current system. Then someone says, "Did you ever think of operating your company as an area developer model"? Now what? Do you change everything you've put together? Is this model right for you? Is it the same as a regional director franchise or a master license?

So how does a franchisor determine if this model can enhance their current program or if it would be detrimental to their franchise system?

Within the franchise industry, several names are used to describe these types of franchise opportunities. For the purpose of this exercise, let's work with the following description for area representation through a business model for area developers: An area developer agreement requires the franchisee to 1) award franchises, 2) assist in the opening of the franchise units, 3) support and assist the ongoing training and services, and 4) in some cases, operate a unit.

An area developer is a unique individual who is, in the simplest terms, a "mini franchisor." This franchisee is an extension of the corporate culture and the protector of the brand in the market granted to them. Great care must be taken in selecting these individuals. Rarely do they have the same profile or financial background as the franchisees in your system today. Granted, I'm sure most of us could identify one or two performers in our current system that would appreciate an opportunity to start such a program.

Now that we are working from an understanding of responsibilities and duties, what benefits and challenges does an AD program present?

Reasons not to implement an area developer program

1. *You don't have a proven, successful concept.*
2. *You view the program primarily as a way to produce significant cash for your franchise.*
3. *You are having problems awarding franchises and believe this could help.*
4. *Your concept is brand new and systems are not in place to support franchisees, yet alone area developers.*
5. *You have built a fully staffed infrastructure directly supporting existing franchisees, and the business model of splitting royalties and duplicating services doesn't make sense.*

Reasons to consider an area developer program

1. *Your product or service is marketed and customized to specific markets where local knowledge and support could be a great benefit.*
2. *Your franchise development plans are to build out the entire United States from day one.*
3. *You can create a larger staff for selling franchises*
4. *You will be able to map potential territories or acquire real estate sites faster*
5. *Fast expansion reduces corporate travel and support issues that could be managed locally through an AD program*
6. *Your franchise concept needs more than national support staff to be successful.*

Maintaining control of your program

As the franchisor, there are five key components of the business for which you must maintain decision-making authority; you have to protect your backside. If an area developer leaves the system, you will inherit the franchisees and all the baggage that could follow. The five areas are: 1) the approval process for new franchisees; 2) initial training; 3) system updates; 4) web hosting; and 5) royalty collections.

A well-designed area development program can be a wonderful and exciting franchising decision. To name a few, companies that have successfully implemented area developer programs include Century 21, Subway, Mail Boxes Etc. (now The UPS Store), Planet Beach, and Max Muscle.

Strategies for recruiting qualified area developers

Experience is an invaluable asset in the franchise business. Recruiting seasoned candidates who have successfully operated other area developer programs is a great place to start. In most cases, if an area developer has managed a system they have already created relationships with construction companies, advertising media, and developed support and training programs. An experienced AD can be a little intimidating to a franchisor, but my rule has always been to "hire up." You should consider a customized offering in your FDD for recruiting experienced area developers.

The next best candidate for the area developer franchise could come from within your system. Always keep in mind that this candidate isn't necessarily the highest unit producer, but in most cases is a solid operator with an excellent support staff. The franchisee may be getting bored and need a new challenge. They are most likely the franchisee that is always there to help, do training, validate with new owners, and most of all is a team player. (Be sensitive, as this could be a slippery slope with a danger of perceived favoritism toward a particular franchisee.)

Since an area developer franchise resembles a "mini franchisor," this certainly is not a franchise that can be run by an individual. It requires a person who can pull together a team of experts to grow the designated territory. Management and recruitment skill sets are critical to the success of an area developer. Typically, an AD excels in one or the other. Require your area developers to hire the talent they will need to ensure strong performance in both sales and operational functions. Otherwise, the model will not succeed. In short, they must hire the skill sets they don't have. Over the years, I have only met a handful of area developers strong in both business management and sales.

Without franchise sales, an area development business plan never comes together. When creating a business plan, it's exciting to forecast projections where you have opened 20, 30, or 40 units. But nothing can happen until the first units are awarded. In my experience, the number-one downfall of the area developer program is the lack of a skilled sales person awarding franchises to the right people.

I've been in franchising for more than 29 years, predominantly involved with recruiting and granting franchises to qualified candidates. This is a skill that takes years to acquire. As the franchisor, don't fool yourself and do what I call area developer math: "If I have 10 ADs and they each sell 10 units we're going to be rich!" *Wrong, nothing is that easy. You will need to develop a training program for them, and/or allow your area developers to work closely with your national sales team to develop effective recruiting skills.*

Financial models and performance quotas

You've determined that your franchise system can benefit from the introduction of an area developer program; you've created an FDD that gives you control of the key components of your business; and you've identified a person with the right attributes for the AD franchise. All that's left is the key question: How do we divide the money in a way that rewards and motivates the area developer to effectively build the brand in the defined markets and maintain a unified franchise system across the country?

Most area developer programs will share in royalty payments, franchise fees, and transfer fees. Some franchise companies also manufacture and/or distribute products in the system. In some cases, the franchisor will share a percentage of the product margin.

Deciding on how to structure your AD program depends on margins, what the AD's contractual responsibilities are, etc. Compensate your ADs for what they provide and do for your system. If the area developer supports and trains the franchisees, share the royalty. Share the franchise fee if the AD is responsible for sales, and do the same with product overrides.

Building an area developer franchise is not a get-rich-quick scheme. The ultimate goal for the AD is to create an annuity flow from the hard work they put forth in the early years of the business. Without franchise sales, the plan will not bear fruit.

Since franchise recruitment is most critical, don't be greedy about sharing initial franchisee fees with your AD. I recommend a minimum of 50 percent and as high as 75 percent, depending on the amount of the franchisee fee. If considering an AD program, you should have a minimum of $30,000 as the franchise fee. Both the franchisor and the AD must put 100 percent effort toward driving sales through training and creative local lead generation programs.

Quotas should be realistic, with a team effort to grow the brand regionally. Do not confuse "sales goals" with quotas. Create an environment for success and growth. Gradually increase the quotas over the term of the agreement. As experience grows, so will sales. Offering assistance from your national sales team is a great way to get your ADs off to a fast start.

Royalties are the lifeblood of your national company and should be what drives most of your business decisions. You must create comprehensive training programs for the

ADs to protect the brand and system. I recommend the AD receive from 40 percent to 60 percent of royalties, depending on the level of support you expect them to perform.

Non-performance is the most talked-about subject when considering an AD program, and what gives most franchisors pause. As you craft your area developer agreement, conflict resolution on the subject of quotas should be thought through very carefully. Realistic quotas along with sensible conflict resolution will be your best avenue to success. One clause that can help is the option for the national office to take over franchise sales and rework the shared commission structure at the franchisor's option. The area developer may have a great support and training system but struggle in the franchise sales arena.

Making area development happen

I have implemented several area developer programs. The correct training, franchise sales assistance, and structure can allow franchisors, their area developers, and their franchisees to enjoy greater market penetration, unit sales, branding, and growth. Max Muscle is a current example of area development success. Within three years, system-wide satisfaction has increased significantly, new stores are opening weekly, and more than 80 percent of the ADs are at or exceeding their quotas for sold and opened units. Max Muscle's driving commitment and dedication to its area development program is a performance model that has rewarded franchisor, area developers, and franchisees alike.

In summary, the most important issues to consider in implementing an area development program are:

1. *Are you creating an AD program for the correct reasons?*
2. *If you decide this structure is a good fit for your system, select the right AD franchisees.*
3. *Support, train, and assist your ADs in building their territories.*
4. *Protect your brand by maintaining control of the key elements of your business.*

Do not take the consideration of an area development program lightly. This is a decision-making process that should involve the management team and key franchisees. Don't pull the trigger unless you thoroughly understand your concept, and how an area development program can assist you in sustaining growth and support for your franchise system in the future.

(My thanks to Marc Kiekenapp, managing partner of Kiekenapp & Associates for his contribution of the preceding section.)

Multi-unit programs

Attracting experienced franchise operators

Many franchisors lust for experienced multi-unit franchisees to buy their concepts. These seasoned business builders manage and operate their own units (not to be confused with area developers, who sell and support franchisees in defined territories). Multi-unit operators have the management expertise, infrastructure, and track record for building successful franchise businesses. The risks, training, and operational support required from corporate are often less costly, and market expansion significantly accelerated. What does it take to capture a growing multi-unit or multi-brand owner successfully operating 15 to 100 franchise locations? When you look around and see that Burger King, Choice Hotels, Dunkin' Donuts, SuperCuts, and Qdoba are doing it, the question is *"Why can't I?"*

Multi-unit franchisees discussing business sound a lot like stock brokers strategizing with clients about their portfolios. These high achievers seek opportunities to keep building and growing for numerous reasons: they have saturated their market with an existing brand; they want to spread their investment risks among several concepts; they seek franchises to generate income on their real estate properties; they are developing multiple franchise locations for future acquisition by investor groups. So how do these "mega" franchisees build their brand portfolios? How do they shop for new brands? What components of a franchise system do they look at? What type of research do they conduct? What turns franchisees off to franchises they are exploring?

Here's what some big guns of franchising say. At a recent Multi-Unit Franchising Conference produced by Franchise Update Media Group, I had the opportunity to interview a focus group of six prominent, multi-concept veterans. Together, they represented more than 25 franchise brands and 1,000 operating franchises in the U.S. These were truly builders of America's franchises, spanning industry sectors from hotels and fast food to tanning salons. These seasoned pros offered the following suggestions for recruiting multi-unit operators:

1. *A "one size fits all" mentality doesn't work.* These are professionals at building franchise operations, devoting serious investments and resources to build out their markets. Make sure you structure agreements recognizing that these are experienced operators. Consider allowances that acknowledge and address this larger business relationship, its short- and long-term benefits and challenges.

2. ***Experienced franchisees read and understand your FDD.*** There's no use trying to dance around items and conditions that have open interpretations. Tell it straight and clarify everything in writing. Mature buyers quickly pick up on restrictions and procedures not typical in other franchise documents. They also applaud the more favorable elements you offer. Study your agreement language so you clearly understand what it all means. Too often franchise CEOs can't tell you, and call legal counsel to unravel the confusion. This may not present you in the best light with these educated prospects.

3. ***Sophisticated buyers scare easily from agreements that heavily favor the franchisor.*** Multi-unit operators seek healthy and balanced relationships. Be prepared. You may get away with non-reciprocal indemnification with franchisee neophytes, but you can hit concrete walls when you deal with these savvy buyers.

4. ***ROI is key to their decision.*** If the business model doesn't fit their requirements or work within their infrastructure, experienced operators will pass. Be prepared to address this so these buyers can build pro formas to properly assess your opportunity. If your franchise can't produce the returns, don't waste time and money in wooing multi-unit pros.

5. ***Decisions are based on logic.*** They are driven by your business model, not by the emotion and romance that often attract single-unit buyers. They want earnings claims from you and your multi-unit franchisees. They'll seek out your top producers who can openly share key metrics and performance factors to help them evaluate your brand. They will dig deep and expect direct answers to satisfy their decision-making process.

6. ***Demonstrate your commitment to multi-unit development.*** Do you consistently market in the publications, shows, and other venues multi-unit owners frequent? Do they read and hear success stories about your multi-unit partners? Is your brand name recognized enough in their world to make their "check you out" list? These mega-owners stress the need for franchisors committed to a multi-unit development strategy that is ready to go, and not just testing it out as a new expansion method. Sticking your toe in the water with this crowd doesn't work, and word spreads fast.

7. ***Multi-unit conferences require a different recruiting approach.*** Relationship-building and networking at these events produce the best results. Unlike public franchise exhibitions, these aren't mom-and-pops stuffing their bags with your literature. Don't expect herds of enthusiastic attendees completing your inquiry forms, or long in-depth conversations. Experienced operators are low-key, analytical, and cautious in expressing interest. Put yourself in their shoes. They know they're recruitment targets and move under the radar screen. Recognize this as you answer their questions and stay away from canned sales pitches.

8. ***"Mega" franchisees rely on referral networks.*** They keep their antennae up, checking with savvy franchisees, franchisors, consultants, and investors who know what's hot and what's not in the franchise community. Get your word on the street through your influential contacts, including any suppliers that service expanding multi-brand operators.

9. ***The multi-unit investigation process is much longer.*** Be patient if you are new to selling this market. The significant investment by both franchisee and franchisor requires a different recruitment process. Timing, competing concepts, business analysis, and negotiations all are factors affecting the closing period. These are not formula sales. Certainly no 90-day deals here. It could take nine months to two years!

10. ***Multi-brand owners may want a "test" location first.*** This initial step makes sense in hammering out large deals with experienced operators. Both franchisee and franchisor want to ensure a successful launch, and they may begin with one unit. If both parties are satisfied with initial performance levels at the beta site, the franchisee then signs up for an agreed-upon commitment to roll out the market expansion.

Should you grow internationally?

The allure of worldwide presence has prompted many franchise brands to investigate the potential profits, greater brand power, and global recognition of reaching beyond the shores of the U.S. When I stuck my toe in foreign waters, I quickly realized the magnitude of undertaking franchise development away from my home turf.

It requires comprehensive strategic planning and a specialized program to conquer the international journey to growth.

I asked Kay Ainsley, managing director of Michael H. Seid & Associates, to share her expertise with franchisors considering expansion into additional countries. She assists companies in creating programs for international growth that can successfully meet their objectives. An experienced franchise professional, Kay was previously director of international development for Domino's Pizza International and for Ziebart International, an automotive aftermarket franchise.

It can start simply enough. You check your email and there it is: a message from someone in the Kingdom of Saudi Arabia. It reads, "Dear Sir, Please allow me to introduce myself. I represent a member of the royal family here in The Kingdom. During a recent trip to the United States, the prince and his family ate at several of your restaurants and were very much pleased with the quality of your food. He believes that your restaurant would do very, very well in the Kingdom and would like to inquire about the Master Franchise Rights."

You're flattered, curious, maybe a little of both. So you respond to the email and the next thing you know you've dug out your passport and you're on your way... but to where? Is this the first step on the road to building a strong, internationally recognized brand, or are you heading down a path to disaster?

What to do? Smart franchisors will begin the journey by standing still for a moment and taking stock of where they stand in the United States.

There are many good and valid reasons for expanding your franchise system into international markets, but receiving an email isn't on the list. This email could be fortuitous, however, if you have:

- *A well-established brand at home and are close to achieving your desired level of market penetration. Strong regional brands sometimes choose international expansion over further domestic growth.*

- *A product that is truly hot but that could be fairly easily copied. The long-term success of some concepts depends upon establishing a strong foothold before others can enter the same space.*

- *Competitors who are entering international markets. While you don't want to be first, you may not want to be last either. Why let your competitors establish brand recognition?*

- *The resources, both people and money, to commit to long-term development and operations support.* No matter how much you plan, it will cost more and take longer than planned.

- *The strong commitment of executive management. Without the strong commitment of those at the top it is too easy to pull the plug on "international" when it costs more and takes longer (see above).*

- *Realistic expectations for growth and performance. To realize any benefit from international operations, you have to be in it for the long haul. The big up-front payment evaporates quickly when it comes time to get the new country going and provide support.*

Expanding beyond your home borders through franchising provides many benefits lacking in other forms of expansion. For this reason, even companies that do not franchise domestically choose franchising as they enter global markets. These benefits are not totally unlike those franchising delivers at home, but perhaps yield advantages to a greater degree:

- *builds worldwide brand awareness and bolsters your brand at home;*
- *provides local market expertise, knowledge of business and social customs, and often political and business connections;*
- *provides capital for development;*
- *franchisee has strong vested interest in the success of the brand;*
- *lessens the need for you to provide direct support; and*
- *leverages the talents of your corporate staff and provides new and exciting career paths.*

Franchisors should also be aware that international franchising has changed dramatically over the past 10 to 15 years:

- *Legal—More and more countries have enacted disclosure laws and relationship laws that affect franchising.*

- *Increased competition—In the past, "international franchising" translated into U.S. companies expanding into global markets. Today companies from any number of countries are using franchising to expand beyond their borders.*

- **More sophisticated franchisees**—*Foreign investors are no longer willing to pay the huge initial fees of the past. They are looking for a more reasonable sharing of risk and increased support from the franchisor.*

When considering international expansion, set your sights on foreign markets with characteristics similar to those of your current successful markets. Look at what drives your business model at home and apply those metrics where possible. This will enable you to target those international markets that offer better opportunities for returns on your investment.

Once you understand the drivers of your business it's time to develop a strategic plan. This can build a framework for international development with the flexibility to take advantage of opportunities that come your way. It is not, however, a one-size-fits-all plan for expansion and development. Each country must be analyzed before you make the decision to develop that marketplace.

While every industry, sector, and company have their own issues that must be addressed in the plan, here are some of the more common elements you must consider:

- **Goals and objectives**—What are you trying to accomplish with international expansion? What are your expectations for a return on your investment in terms of both time and revenue?
- **Core business drivers**—What makes your product or service unique? What factors drive your business? What are you willing to change or adapt as you move forward, and what is sacred to your brand?
- **Timing and budget**—What benchmarks need to be set? What is the budget for lead generation, sales, and initial and ongoing support?
- **Resources**—What are your current capabilities for international sales and support? Can internal resources be developed or do you need to hire expertise? More specifically:

  - Can you adapt your product or service to different market requirements?
  - Can you adapt your training program to different market requirements?
  - Can you adapt your marketing and advertising to different market requirements?
  - Can you logistically deliver proprietary product or equipment around the world in an efficient manner?
  - Can you adapt your IT and MIS to international currencies and operating differences?

    – *Can you create and implement a plan for communicating with foreign franchisees?*

    – *Can you create and implement a plan for monitoring performance and enforcing standards?*

    – *Can you structure a deal that enables a win-win for both you and the franchisee?*

Once you have developed the plan and understand what you are looking for in a market and franchisee, it becomes far easier to evaluate an opportunity. Below are some general considerations that can be set up as a matrix to conduct a market assessment:

- *trademark and intellectual property protection*
- *economic stability and projected growth*
- *political stability*
- *taxation rates and treaties*
- *ability to repatriate funds*
- *labor availability, skill sets, and restrictions*
- *recognition of contract law*
- *restrictions on franchising*
- *language and cultural barriers*
- *crime and corruption*
- *level of consumer disposable income*
- *availability and cost of advertising and promotions.*

Once a market passes the initial test, you will want to look more closely at specifics. Here are some of the questions you must answer:

- **Concept**
  - *Is the concept accepted?*
  - *Is there local competition?*
  - *Are changes required to meet local demand?*
- **Market**
  - *How strong is market demand for your product or service?*
  - *Does your name "work" in the market?*
  - *What is the consumer's ability and desire to purchase?*
  - *How many units are required to establish critical mass and market penetration?*
  - *How acceptable are your marketing materials, advertising, and promotional techniques?*

- *Economics*
  - *What are your costs?*
  - *What is your income potential?*
  - *How do you structure the deal?*
  - *Product sourcing and distribution*
  - *How will franchisees be supplied?*
  - *From where will franchisees be supplied?*
  - *What effect will duties and tariffs have on profitability?*
- *Support*
  - *What support will you provide?*
  - *How will you provide support?*
  - *How will you support any product or operational adaptations specific to the market?*
  - *How will standards be enforced?*
- *Technology*
  - *What adaptations are necessary to work in international markets?*
  - *What information do you need?*
  - *How do you provide valuable feedback in real time?*

Perhaps the most important element of an international plan is flexibility. You never know when an unexpected email will present an opportunity too good to pass up. However, the path around the world is littered with the remains of broken franchises. Having a plan, understanding what it takes to achieve success, and committing the resources to make it happen will keep you on the road to building a strong international brand.

(My thanks to Kay Ainsley of Michael H. Seid & Associates for her contribution of the preceding section.)

Keys to building a robust franchise program

Think beyond the box when examining your franchise opportunity. Don't fall into the trap of automatically structuring your franchise to follow traditional business models that 95 percent of franchises incorporate within their programs. Attorneys who initially counsel you use these benchmarks in developing your franchise formula, as they should. It isn't their role to consider creative alternatives. But it is your job to challenge yourself as you design and periodically assess your franchise system. You hold the complete, universal picture of your program and need to examine all avenues that may ignite or reignite your franchise offering and business model.

Consider nothing sacred, and dispel all preconceived notions. Free up your ideas and you just may discover epiphanies that can work for your program. Franchise visionaries have achieved successful system growth by implementing these nontraditional ideas:

- no franchise fees;
- no franchise fees for multiple stores;
- no royalties;
- preferred franchise fees for industry-specific experience;
- territories designed by franchisees for approval;
- guaranteed franchise buy-backs;
- customer selling provided by corporate staff; and
- national accounts programs.

Franchisors are breaking old standards

Innovative franchisors seeking to expand their offerings and attract a new pool of franchisees are breaking with tradition and instituting new ideas. Here are a few ideas that have proven effective for the systems that have used them to achieve specific goals as they developed:

- *No franchise fees for expansion.* Grow Biz, a Minneapolis-based multi-brand franchise system, at one time waived additional franchise fees for interested owners who qualified for expansion. Why require an additional fee from a trained, successful franchisee whose new store development brings more royalty income to the company? With these experienced, successful franchisees, the returns are high and the risk minimal.

  Some franchisors, such as GNC, have discounted initial franchise fees for new franchisees in certain markets to accelerate development there. In 2008, Papa John's Pizza was targeting experienced franchise operators with "no franchise fee" required in six of its markets. Merle Norman Cosmetics, manufacturer and retail franchisor of skin care products, charges no initial franchise fees or royalties to its franchise operators. The 77-year-old company has built a successful business model for 2,000-plus franchisee units and for the company.

- *Multi-unit, semi-absentee packages for qualified prospects.* Great Clips, when it was a modest-sized retail service franchise, did exactly this in a traditional mom-and-pop industry. The company spurred explosive growth by successfully attracting savvy, high-net-worth buyers looking to build a business organization through store managers. New franchisees initially were permitted to keep their current job while launching their store, an unusual business model that attracted additional prospects. Aggressive marketing that targeted their prospect profiles through media sources and brokers paid off. Within a few years, this innovative franchisor became a top player in the industry.

- *Conversions.* Once considered taboo by many, conversions are finding success with strong multi-unit independents who recognize the value of franchising in growing their business to the next level. With 41 cents of every U.S. retail dollar spent in a franchise, these owners are more receptive to compromising their independence to increase revenues and build equity. When Sears Carpet & Upholstery Care launched its new franchise, the brand targeted larger, successful independents to convert to their program. These savvy operators saw the business benefits of trading their independence for brand power. They could enjoy immediate savings in their advertising and purchasing power, and greater customer opportunities through the brand's national reputation.

- *Co-branding.* Setting up franchises within franchises presents an opportunity to share real estate expenses and staffing resources. Gas stations and convenience stores continue to incorporate franchise food brands into their business models. Wal-Mart centers and grocery chains have postal franchises and framing concepts, to name a few. There certainly are challenges to overcome in these partnerships, but they are worth the effort when both brands are compatible and can generate additional profits from their alliance.

- *Express franchises.* Scaled-down or "mini" versions of franchises have become more popular through the years, particularly within the food segment. Coffee, drink, and food kiosks and "drop-off" stations also have been incorporated into franchise concepts as a market extension of a franchisee's operation, or even as small stand-alone businesses.

Presenting earnings claims in your FDD

Amazingly, while more than 700 of all active systems make earnings claims today, this represents only 29 percent of all active franchise brands, according to market research company FRANdata. This means that 7 of 10 franchisors dish this responsibility off to franchisees, telling buyers they don't provide any financial information. This boggles my mind.

We all tout the compelling benefits of the franchising model, praising its value as a "blueprint for success" and "proven business system." Yet the overwhelming majority of franchisors won't divulge any financial performance data to support this. Savvy companies that do show results gain greater credibility over their competitors. I certainly had fun presenting earnings claims when I was involved in franchise sales because it provided a powerful selling tool that all buyers wanted and looked forward to during the recruitment process. *"There must be some reason why other companies you mention won't give you the information we do. You know, the FTC encourages franchisors to provide you with earnings claims to help buyers like yourself make more informed decisions. We agree."*

Companies through the years like Aaron Rents, Molly Maid, Jimmy John's, Cottman Transmission Centers, GNC, Church's Chicken, and CertaPro Painters have provided earnings claims benefiting prospective franchisees with financial performance data. Consequently, these responsive companies have strengthened their buyer attraction over competitors that don't divulge them. In fact, one franchise broker organization requires earnings claims from franchise companies seeking their representation. I congratulate them for this. Their brokers can assure clients that any franchise they represent will provide financial information in their franchise disclosure document.

What about liability concerns in presenting financial data? I've asked several attorneys this question. They report that lawsuits involving earnings statements are mostly with companies that don't present them in their FDD! Makes sense, since prospects hound and sometimes finesse sales representatives into providing earnings claims information they shouldn't.

How can I make earnings claims?

To best address the issue of how franchisors can present earnings claims within the context of the FTC's Item 19 regulations, I asked experienced franchise attorney, Lane Fisher of Fisher & Zucker LLC, to share his opinions. The following material consists of excerpts from his published articles (the first part co-authored with Rocco Fiorentino, CEO of United Financial Services Group, and the closing material with F. Joseph Dunn of Fisher & Zucker).

Is it unreasonable to ask a franchisor, which receives royalties based on unit gross sales, to report gross sales information for similar units over some period? You can't help wondering if providing this information could actually generate more qualified leads and potentially shorten the closing process.

State and federal regulators want you to give prospects this information so badly that they make it easy to report earnings if you apply accounting principles uniformly and consistently with generally accepted accounting principles (GAAP) and maintain the required substantiating data. Even if you believe that you are better protected from liability through a policy of making no claims (since virtually every complaint filed by the FTC contains allegations of improper earnings information), franchisors have not been entirely effective in policing and enforcing a "no disclosure" policy.

Earning claims defined
Earnings claims may include any statement of the following:

1. *average unit revenues, income or expenses;*
2. *average costs of goods, labor, or occupancy;*
3. *differences in revenues, income, or expenses based on location, market, or type of unit;*
4. *potential return on investment;*
5. *average annual "break-even"; and*
6. *opinions concerning any franchisee-prepared pro forma financial statements.*

Normalizing data
Earnings claims can show sales, costs, profit, or other industry-specific measures of unit performance. Seeking to motivate franchisors to make earnings claims, state administrators have shown substantial flexibility in allowing franchisors to register documents containing earnings claims that normalize data by limiting claims to units that have been open for some period of time, permitting classification by state or region (including sub-regions defined by advertising co-ops or media-efficient markets); type of unit (kiosk, inline, pad site, or mall/food court); those of a particular size or shape (by building design or layout); those with a particular capacity (number of seats, desks, customers, or students); units with a particular volume of business

(number of rooms, vehicles, students, volume of checks cashed, or any other measure of unit performance), which have been open a particular length of time (sometimes defined as mature versus ramping up); or which have been open during a recently concluded period (the last year).

Claims can state the results of specific franchisee-, company-, or affiliate-owned units expressed in terms of averages or ranges, and report the results of multiple-unit operators separately. Claims can involve historical results or projections of future results and can be based on results of franchise units, company-owned units, a combination, or data other than operating results.

Specific industry performance standards

Over the years, certain specialized, industry-specific measures of unit performance have evolved. In the hotel industry, average room and occupancy rates have long been disclosed by competing brands. In service businesses, including the automotive aftermarket, the volume of business is often expressed in terms of number of vehicles, number of jobs, gross profit per job, and break-even gross profit per job. Restaurants often disclose food or labor costs, usually as a percentage of gross sales.

Measures of productivity/frequency

There also are measures of productivity that can constitute earnings claims:

1. *achievable work day per technician*
2. *average annual revenue per sales day*
3. *average revenue per van or kiosk*
4. *average commissions or co-op advertising credits*
5. *value of national accounts*
6. *sales closing rates*
7. *vacancy/occupancy rates*
8. *yield from a particular amount of product or service*

Getting a competitive edge

These days, the competition for good, well-capitalized franchisees is fierce, with new and novel means of franchisee recruitment being developed every day. If your competitors disclose earnings information to franchisee prospects, there is competitive pressure on you to provide such information. An industry-by-industry analysis supports this proposition, as the use of earnings claims has been more universally adopted in certain industries.

Limiting liability

The irony surrounding earnings claims is that most franchisors don't make them for fear of liability to franchisees who do not achieve the stated results. In my experience, franchisors that use earnings claims are far less likely to get sued for common law fraud for making an illegal oral earnings claim than those franchisors that use a "negative" disclosure at Item 19. Why is that? Because federal and state law have created an incredibly expansive definition of conduct that could constitute an earnings claim.

For example, earnings claims can be based on sales or income, but also by stating that you can send your child to the University of Pennsylvania or afford an elegant vacation home. Using this expansive definition, franchisee litigators scrutinize the sales process until they find some act, statement, or omission that could arguably give rise to a claim. In an informal poll of a select number of franchisors that use earnings claims, each reported substantially no claims based on failure to meet stated earnings, and of course no claims that they made an "illegal" earnings claim outside of Item 19. By giving sales people the only information that prospects want to know, franchisors avoid all of the "salesmanship" undertaken to avoid the question—and all the energy consumed in channeling prospects to alternative sources for the information.

Amended FTC Rule provides even greater flexibility

The push for earnings claims gets even better. On January 22, 2007, the Federal Trade Commission approved the Amended FTC Rule. For franchisors providing earnings claims in Item 19 of their FDD, the rule became effective on a voluntary basis on July 1, 2007 and mandatory on July 1, 2008. According to attorneys Fisher and F. Joseph Dunn, "While rendering 'The government won't let me tell you' excuse for not making an earnings claim patently unusable, the [Amended] FTC Rule makes significant changes to the original FTC Rule, which are designed to make it easier and more attractive for franchisors to make an earnings claim. This will increase the competitive pressures on franchisors. However, the end result is that the regulators have again made it even easier to make a legally compliant earnings claim."

(My thanks to Lane Fisher of Fisher & Zucker for his contribution of the preceding section.)

So wake up franchisors, and stake your claims! If your business model is totally upside-down, it's quite understandable why you have no Item 19 in your FDD. But for the rest of you, make the move and show some financials. There are umpteen ways the government will allow you to do it. You'll help your franchise prospects make better decisions and build greater credibility for your opportunity.

Ready, set, grow!

To stand out among the 2,900 active franchise opportunities in today's market, you must seize your buyers' attention with benefit-driven programs and systems. Stay tuned to the cycles of the economy, your industry, new competitive influences, and buyer interests. Savvy franchisors do what it takes to maintain compelling franchise programs, remain sensitive to their buying audience, understand what those buyers want, and know how to package their opportunity to successfully recruit them.

- ✓ Evolve your franchise program to ensure that it is attractive to today's buyer. Listen to your franchisees and monitor the pulse of the marketplace. Businesses that remain the same eventually get left behind.

- ✓ Recognize that unexpected crises can occur during the life of your franchise system, and be aware that how you respond and adapt to these events will determine the level of success and longevity of your system.

- ✓ Challenge yourself. Consider alternative growth models. Is traditional single-unit development the best way for you to grow, or is there a place for expansion through conversions, master franchises, area development, or multi-unit programs for experienced franchisees? What about international development? Global markets may represent exciting growth opportunities for your brand, or on the other hand could present too many challenges to consider.

- ✓ Rules were made to be broken, so are royalty fees necessary for your revenue stream? Should you charge successful, high income-producing owners additional franchise fees to open more units? What if new franchisees designed their own territories based on your guidelines and approval? How about co-branding or express versions of your concept? However "out there" these thoughts may seem, they have worked with certain concepts. Keep the doors open and think beyond the walls of tradition.

- ✓ Earnings claims (now called financial performance representations) provide a competitive edge, helping buyers evaluate franchise opportunities that could satisfy their financial goals. The Amended

FTC Rule further encourages franchisors to share performance results in Item 19 of the FDD. If you're still holding back, don't ignore this option too long, or you'll lose ground to the growing number of companies jumping on the earnings claims bandwagon.

Chapter 4

Success Driver IV:
Successful Lead Generation

If you lose sight of your buyer,

you can no longer grow to the greatness you aspire.

Success Driver IV:
Successful Lead Generation

I confess, I am still guilty. I bet you are, too!

Ever wish for a marketing miracle, hoping to discover the "magic bullet" that creates stampedes of buyers begging for your franchise? How about fantasizing that your $300 newspaper ad just generated 50 leads, and your franchise Internet ads deliver 100 percent qualified candidates who return all your phone calls? Then suddenly, media reporters call you in sheer excitement about your press release, promising feature coverage in the *Wall Street Journal, Newsweek,* and on the major network channels. And just a second! Your phone light is flashing fiery red with 40 urgent messages from prospects you met at this weekend's franchise show! Just think, if we could all leisurely ease out of bed, stroll to work, and piled on our desks find stacks of outrageously qualified applications anxiously awaiting our response…

Then the dream turns into a nightmare and we wake up screaming, still facing the elusive, changing, and unexpected challenges of franchise lead generation. Frustration still haunts our calculating minds as we search for answers to find the perfect plan for attracting sensational candidates to our franchise opportunity.

Learn the secrets of recruitment marketing

Questions echo constantly throughout our industry: *"What kind of ads work the best?" "What's the most successful source for getting sales?" "Where shall I spend my ad dollars?" "How much will it cost for me to bring in new franchisees?" "What are the best ways to attract buyers?" "What's new and different in lead generation?"*

Great news! Answers to all of these marketing questions lie right in front of you. Sometimes you just don't realize it, or are trying to shortcut the process. Don't bypass sacred direct marketing principles, because you will suffer. Investing time in systematically evolving your lead generation campaign will pay off in greater leads and sales. With some research, digging, and testing, you'll shape your own prospecting bullets for lead generation success. But you must begin with self-discovery before you can construct surefire marketing successes. Once you learn the science of franchise lead generation, recruitment becomes a predictable process you can control and improve.

All franchisors quickly discover that an effective step-by-step selling process is essential to their growth. But many continue to chase windmills with their marketing, not realizing that effective lead generation also demands an effective, step-by-step process! Implement the principles described in this chapter and you can increase your prospecting success by 30 percent or more within 4 months.

Welcome to high-performance marketing

The material in this chapter is designed to boost your leads, reduce your costs, and accelerate your franchise sales. It reveals the four benchmarks to successful lead generation that high-growth franchisors use to expand their brands. More than 40 franchisors have each invested thousands of consulting dollars to help them implement this marketing process. Engage your resources to embrace these principles and you'll have the opportunity to produce more qualified buyers at lower costs. You'll learn to:

- Better target your ideal franchise candidates.
- Promote the key "wow" factors that can attract your buyers.
- Design your ads and website to trigger greater responses.
- Generate more prospects through free and low-cost sources.
- Develop a realistic budget to achieve your marketing goals.
- Build a better lead generation program for your concept.
- Drive greater qualified leads from your online recruitment.
- Implement marketing follow-up tools to increase applications.
- Gain marketing intelligence to effectively respond to changes in the marketplace and buyer attitudes.

How to achieve success

Actually, the principles of high-performance marketing are simple. I hope this doesn't disappoint you. But it's always the execution that grows the champions, and this is no different. Franchising is a blueprint for success, built on truisms such as "if you work the plan the plan will work" and "follow the system and you can be successful." It's no different for jump-starting a powerful lead generation program. Here's the time-tested, four-part formula to fuel explosive marketing performance for your franchise expansion:

- Define your market of qualified prospects
- Create your message that motivates buyer response
- Determine the lead sources that reach your buyers
- Measure results to improve performance

1 The Four Steps to Lead Generation Success:
Step One–Define your market of qualified prospects

Who is your ideal franchise buyer?

Let's begin with knowing your market. Producing quality prospects starts with understanding who your franchise candidate is. Marketing efforts will be disastrous if you don't! It's like being in a boxing match blindfolded with the lights out, with no clear target to punch. You'll be working with the wrong prospects and wasting a bundle of money and time. Worse yet, you'll award franchises to unqualified owners, a painful mistake not easy to resolve.

For superior marketing, craft your franchisee success profile first, before you even think about how to promote your franchise opportunity. If you ever lose sight of your buyer, you can no longer grow to the greatness you aspire. (For methods to help you identify your most desirable franchisee, review Chapter 2.)

2 The Four Steps to Lead Generation Success:
Step Two–Create your message that motivates buyer response

What motivates your buyer?

Once you know who your market of prospects is, how can you influence their thinking to take a look at your franchise concept? Approaching key buyers with a misguided message is a recipe for failure. *Selling Power* magazine published a landmark survey of 445 top sales executives representing 31 different industries. The research was conducted by sales experts and scholars from leading business schools. After polling participants on the marketing challenges of their companies, the study revealed an astounding fact:

"Only 56 percent of the sales organizations say their marketing collateral is designed the way their customers buy."

Franchise companies are often guilty of building lead generation programs without defining what successfully prompts their buyers to respond. Some dump big bucks hiring ad agencies to develop gorgeous-looking ads and glitzy marketing campaigns, only to discover they missed the mark and have to re-engineer their materials. The best way to drive leads? Know what drives your buyers! Find out how to court your prospects. The more attractively and convincingly you market your concept, the greater opportunity to attract the right people to your franchise family.

People buy opportunities, not businesses

Young franchisors frequently stumble launching their franchise marketing programs. They over-promote their products and ignore featuring their business opportunity. Show the benefits of owning your franchise! Market what your buyers are looking for as owners—not as retail customers. It's more than showcasing big, juicy hamburgers, beautiful display racks, colorful service trucks, or shiny, high-tech equipment. Thank you, but prospects aren't interested in eating your food right now, or purchasing your custom service truck. *"Tell me what your business can do for me!"* Focus on what they want, seek, and can aspire to achieve through your program!

Even Blockbuster, the established industry king, made this mistake in the late '90s. Their "Madison Avenue" agency wanted to create an aggressive marketing campaign that would ramp up their franchise sales. Because the agency wasn't schooled in franchise marketing, the understandably nervous franchise exec tried to hire a franchise consultant to assist. Unfortunately, politics dictated moving forward with the agency, and their first beautifully produced ad hit the streets. "Own your own Blockbuster, the hottest ticket in town," was the message, focusing on the huge inventory of selections and great store layout. That was it. Nothing about ownership benefits, lifestyle attractions, exploding market statistics, or purchasing clout. Nothing. Just another retail image ad, not response-driven. I called to console the frustrated executive knowing the ad campaign bombed. That ad never ran again.

Sell your opportunity and save your merchandise promotions for your consumer advertising. You'll attract interested prospects!

What are business buyers looking for?

So what is it entrepreneurs are seeking in owning a business? What is it that is important to them and their families? Why are they disturbed with their current situation, and what attracts them to your franchise offering? Decades of experience at thousands of franchise organizations has uncovered the basic needs and desires shared by business seekers. Here are some of the common motivators for owning a business:

- Being my own boss
- Controlling my own future and security
- Tired of company politics
- Flexible work schedule
- Family participation in the business
- More time at home with my family
- Building equity in my own business
- Opportunity for new challenge and growth
- Greater financial opportunities and rewards
- No more traveling or long commuting
- Being part of my local community
- Having fun operating my business
- Free weekends, daytime business hours
- Personal fulfillment, enjoyment, and satisfaction
- Make a difference in the lives of my customers and employees
- Unable to find employment, so I need to buy a job

What are franchise buyers also looking for?

The phenomenal attraction of franchising centers around its business format for success. It can be bought, learned, and replicated by aspiring business owners. Certainly, franchising isn't for everyone, but it does afford a blueprint for business without many of the risks, expenses, and frustrations of "going solo" as an independent. Here are some of the most common benefits that motivate people to buy a franchised business:

- Owning a business with a proven system of success
- Brand recognition and reputation of a franchise
- Opportunity to acquire better site locations
- Professional start-up training and ongoing programs
- Buying advantages of group purchasing
- Competitive advantages of research and development
- Increased equity and resale value of a franchise
- Marketing benefits and discounts of group advertising
- Profit from experience and networking with other franchisees
- Save time and money with a tested business plan
- Avoid costly mistakes the franchisor has already made

The market pioneer vs. the "me too" buyer

Start-up franchisors often attract franchisee leaders, not followers, with their initial marketing efforts. Leaders are more self-starters, take greater risks, embrace new challenges, and look for first-to-market opportunities that can offer higher financial and personal rewards. Speak to these movers and shakers. The critical key in awarding these first franchisees is gaining their total commitment and buy-in to follow your business blueprint, policies, and procedures. They have to understand their role is to execute your success formula, not to rebuild or change it!

New franchise concepts can be ideal for these higher-risk buyers who want to be the "first on the block," bringing a better service to the community or a first-of-its-kind to the consumer. Young franchisors need to recognize and focus on this slice of the market during their start-up phase. Their marketing and sales presentations should paint a picture of their extraordinary new opportunity, while convincing the buyer of the credibility of their system and providing realistic assurances of its future success.

On the other hand, big brand buyers are the "me too's," whose security needs require they join franchises familiar in their local marketplace. They are more conservative, needing franchise track records and consumer recognition before taking the entrepreneurial leap.

If you are a start-up franchise, don't fall into the common trap of trying to compete for these cautious logo buyers. Let 'em go, because you just can't win the race with them. They want to be part of the crowd, not the leader. They may be a great catch for your concept, but you're a few years too early for their tastes.

In rare instances, victory is just a matter of time! Two years after a new retail food franchise lost an interested multi-unit operator, he came back and bought. The franchise had grown up and now met his performance and credibility requirements.

What owner benefits will attract buyers to my franchise?

Here's the good news! Most buyers won't find what they want in your franchise concept. Your challenge is to stay away from these millions of opportunity-seekers who aren't the right match for you. Start-up franchisors need to weed out the misfits quickly and establish their ideal candidate profile to ensure healthy system growth. (For a refresher on how, refer to Chapter 2.)

Your success depends on your ability to attract highly desirable candidates to your franchise, candidates who will appreciate and embrace the ownership opportunities your business concept offers. You must clearly identify, define, and promote your outstanding points of distinction in your franchise recruitment program. Turn on the hot buttons of qualified buyers and your recruitment marketing takes off!

Billboard the "wow" factors your buyers want

Promote your top attractions in every way you can: in your sales collateral, presentations, public relations, and by educating staff employees. These "wow" factors, or benefits, will drive qualified candidates to join your system.

Survey your top producers to find out what it was about the business that attracted them. Often you'll discover some key motivators that you didn't realize were so important to your franchisees. Your existing owners will help you be more successful in approaching future owners.

Several years ago, I worked with a regional concept that wanted to expand nationally. The brand was a retail storefront that prepares standardized legal documents for half or a third of the price an attorney would charge. Surprisingly, in interviewing the successful franchisees, we found a strong element of personal reward from owning the business. This business benefit was noticeably absent in the brand's recruitment approach: *the owners' satisfaction in helping a huge market of extremely appreciative customers who couldn't otherwise afford the service.* The franchisor discovered that personal fulfillment was a strong selling point with franchisees and added this marketing motivator—with customer testimonials—to their recruiting materials.

In polling the better franchisees of a mobile service concept, we discovered their business was ideal for family participation: *the franchise was home-based, and provided part- and full-time opportunities and flexibility for parents, sons, and daughters.* Another great "wow" factor to market to their targeted owners!

So ask your good franchisees what they like about the business, what attracted them to your franchise, how it has benefited them and their family, and what it has done for them personally and professionally. Incorporate these buying motivators into your marketing and sales materials and you'll deliver a more powerful and convincing message to desirable prospects. Your credibility only grows as franchisees reinforce these "wow" factors during the validation process.

Start-up franchisors may know 60 to 80 percent of the key benefits of owning their franchise business. That's a good start! It does require adjustments until you know who your ideal franchise owners will be. Once you identify your first successful franchisees, package their positive experiences and testimonials into your recruitment messages. You'll notice the improvement in presenting your franchise concept to more qualified prospects.

For interested franchisors, franchise research firms can help you develop your franchisee success profile through profiling tools and satisfaction surveys. (See Chapter 2.)

Do your homework, or you'll pay the price

Years back, executives from a young franchise approached me in a state of total frustration, complaining about the poor quality of candidates they were attracting and the few qualified ones who weren't buying. Their entertainment rental concept "had legs," but it just wasn't promoted properly. Their marketing program featured semi-absentee ownership, promoting owners in t-shirts, sandals, and taking vacations. This hobby-type approach turned off serious business buyers and attracted dreamers. Too much emphasis was placed on lifestyle, with little focus on the business model. The executives simply didn't do their homework in advance and needed to reposition their message to get back on track. This was an expensive lesson, costing thousands of dollars in recruitment advertising and turning off qualified buyers who could have been royalty-producing franchisees.

Five cornerstones for building a successful franchise ad

Business buyers evaluating a prospective purchase want answers to key opportunity factors. If you don't provide these answers, their relatives, CPA, attorney, or armchair advisors will! During my career I've had the enviable position of gaining insight into these major decision-making criteria, which could make or break the attractiveness of a franchisor's concept with discerning buyers. I've listened to, learned from, and consulted with hundreds of print and Internet advertisers seeking ways to accelerate their response rates. This included providing in-house creative services to increase lead generation performance. What we discovered were the critical factors that attract prospective franchisees—whether you're a $50,000 cleaning franchise or a $1 million restaurant concept.

After developing and measuring hundreds of ad campaigns, it became clear what franchise buyers respond to, whether through print, electronic, trade show, or PR efforts. These "attention grabbers" must be showcased in your advertising. Otherwise, you'll lose their eyeballs in 2 seconds to the 10 competing franchises next to your ad.

Buyers need answers to five decision-making questions. Address these with a motivating message and you can take away more prospects from your competition!

1. *What is your opportunity?* Your opening copy must define in a compelling statement what owning your business is all about: *"We are offering a professional, proven automotive service now available for interested entrepreneurs in several states "* certainly isn't going to arrest my attention! Sounds boring, and where's the sizzle? Please, get me excited as I scan 200 franchises in nanoseconds on the Internet.

   Now let's transform this opening paragraph into an opportunity statement for the reader: *"Our high-demand safety technology has revolutionized the automotive industry! We are now offering in limited markets an executive management opportunity for qualified individuals seeking a low inventory, patent-protected product endorsed by the U.S. Automotive Safety Council and National Automotive Association."* Now we have grabbed their appetite from the get-go with sizzle and meat that can motivate prospects to read further!

2. *Is there a market?* In today's fickle marketplace, businesses must have staying power to survive. Buyers need to know about you. Does 75 percent of the U.S. population use your service annually, or is it a specialized product targeting the booming health and fitness market? Are you recession-resistant, and why? Prospective owners want facts about the success, acceptance, and sustainability of your franchise concept. Does it have a future, or is it just another fad? Tell me up front to satisfy this fear.

Why in this competitive world don't franchisors broadcast compelling industry research about their businesses? It's a must, and great way to get a prospect's attention. For example, many buyers mistakenly think gourmet coffee is a saturated business, so one franchisor tells them, *"The specialty coffee market continues to explode in an underserved market, with 77 percent of Americans now drinking hot and cold coffee beverages, according to the Specialty Coffee Association."* Many buyers don't realize the magnitude of the picture framing business, so another franchisor tells them, *"Everyone is a potential customer! The average U.S. household owns 14 paintings and pictures in closets, under beds, and in garages waiting to be framed and hung."*

3. *How will I benefit?* Here's your key opportunity to grandstand what's special about your franchise. This doesn't mean making meaningless, generic statements about *"providing high-quality products and great support for our franchisees."* Showcase your "wow" factors, those outstanding four to six advantages that will excite prospects and catapult you into their top picks for investigation: *"24/7 on-call franchisee help line"; "customer accounts provided through our national marketing system"; "daily customers averaging 20 visits per month; "70 percent of our new franchises are purchased by existing owners"; "keep your full-time job starting up this business; "free weekends and holidays"; "you can produce income within 45 days"; "no royalty fees."* Sears Carpet & Upholstery Care aggressively leveraged their "wow" factors. The company promoted some extraordinary benefits they

offered prospects: *"Franchisees can access extensive local mailing lists of Sears customers and can offer zero percent interest when they use their Sears credit card."* Sears headlined its brand power in their ads, stating, *"Two thirds of households in the U.S. have done business with Sears."*

4. ***Are you credible?*** Buyers need assurances about your business successes, capabilities, and health as a franchise system. Brag about your achievements: *"Ranked in the top 10 retail franchises in the U.S. by* Entrepreneur *magazine"*; *"Recognized as 'Business of the Year' by the state of Colorado"*; *"Servicing 550,000 households since 1976."*

Ad testimonials are essential for establishing credibility with your prospects, yet more than one third of franchise websites don't include them according to Franchise Update's Annual Franchise Development Report. Who do you think buyers believe more—you, or franchisees who have invested their lives into your business? Always feature owners with their photos and franchise locations in your ads. Their experiences and advice carry far more impact than your sales pitches. Customer testimonials are also effective, especially for new concepts.

5. ***Do I qualify?*** Prospects want to know if they meet basic qualifications so they don't waste their time responding to your franchise advertising. And if you don't at least list initial financial requirements, they're also wasting your time. Flurries of emails and phone calls from individuals who can't afford your $300,000 franchise make little sense. In addition, let the interested reader know up front if your success profile requires strong management or sales skills, an engineering or mechanical aptitude, or prior food service experience. Remember, buyers want to be pre-screened so they can investigate franchise opportunities that are the right fit for them.

Creative treatment must grab buyers' attention

Your creative approach must grab your prospects' interest and motivate them to respond! Engage buyers by painting verbal and visual pictures of your opportunity, creating emotional and logical connections that draw them closer to your franchise using the following techniques:

- ***Attention-getting headline or theme***—Two seconds is all you have to grab your prospects' attention so they will stop and focus their eyes on your message. It's a tall order but remember, you need only one in hundreds scanning your ad to hit pay dirt with the right candidate. Check out Internet and print ads and see which headlines catch your attention. Then test your own by alternating your headers to see which ones pull the best. You can increase leads at lower costs with this easy exercise.

- **Compelling graphics**—What a difference a well-designed ad makes. Invest in creative! Particularly if you don't yet have a strong brand, your ad is who and all you are to the buyer. Your image certainly changes with a full-color professional ad rather than a black-and-white piece designed on your personal computer. However, depending on your buying audience, your most effective ad may be the simple two-color ad! For a Hallmark franchise, the high-end graphics approach matches the audience and image they are pursuing. But then I never understood why Color Tile used to run plain, two-color ads promoting their floor and wall decor franchise.

- **"Hot buttons" sales copy**—Your first impression will definitely be your last if you don't immediately engage a prospect with your message. There is no tomorrow. Sales copy must sizzle, excite, and romance your opportunity. Entrepreneurship is the American Dream, and it's your mission to sell your franchising dream. Tailor your copy to conform to your ideal buyer's character traits. If you seek analytical owners for your accounting service franchise, prospects are more logic and fact-driven, so speak to them in their language. Provide examples, industry statistics, testimonials and limit the fluff and fanfare, which isn't what motivates this group.

- **Call to action**—This may seem obvious, but prompt your prospect to respond before they turn off the computer or put your magazine ad on the shelf! *"Contact us now for full details about our extraordinary opportunity"*; *"Take our 2-minute virtual tour at our website www.legofunfranchise.com"*; *"Call about our next free seminar coming to your city"*; *"Free 10-page industry growth report now available."* Make sure to include your phone number! Though email has become the dominant communication tool for buyer response, don't miss those valuable cell phone calls—especially for those on-the-go "road warriors" who may not have the convenience of a laptop when they're ready to contact you.

Tips for greater ad responses

1. *Test, test, test.* Especially with Internet's instant feedback, measure different creative to determine which bring the greatest response and run with it. Advertising is a science, so experimentation often pays off in additional franchise prospects. Did you know the headline "business opportunities" draws greater response than "franchise opportunities" does? Or that "businesses for sale" outperforms both of these recruitment titles? Test, test, test!

2. *Develop opportunity-driven ads.* Focus on ownership benefits and rewards, market potential, product demand, lifestyle, unique advantages, and growth opportunities. Franchisors too often get caught up in retail-oriented ads, forgetting that their products are secondary to the business opportunity their programs offer. This mistake presents a huge challenge costing franchisors millions in lost deals.

3. *Make earnings claims.* Only 29 percent of franchisors today provide Item 19 earnings claims in their disclosure documents. When you have a strong financial story to tell, showcase it! Teaser claims in your promotional material will whet reader appetites about your success and motivate them to respond.

   AlphaGraphics proudly advertises its $1.1 million average annual store sales. Aaron's prominently promotes the average $371,527 pre-tax cash flow of its top-performing stores. Heavenly Ham (now HoneyBaked Ham) used to feature the system's 12-year growth record, which averaged a 9 percent year-to-year increase in store sales. Such impressive figures turn heads toward these franchise concepts when potential buyers are scanning through the sea of available opportunities.

   Twenty years ago, our direct marketing franchise, American Advertising Distributors, promoted an 82 percent repeat client base, a major "wow" factor for candidates considering a sales franchise. And congratulations to Molly Maid, which emphasized on its website that more that 13 percent of its owners generated more than $1 million in revenues. This dispelled misconceptions that there isn't money in cleaning homes!

   Buyers earnestly embrace franchise financial data and are frustrated because most franchisors won't provide it. Impressive ticket averages, profit margins, customer counts, same-unit sales increases, customer retention percentages, and other financial facts can make the difference, especially when your competitors refuse to publish their numbers!

4. *Avoid the empty store syndrome.* Franchisors continue to create ads with beautiful photos of their store, or of custom vans without any owners or customers in sight. Better yet are the midnight shots of lighted structures, which unless you are a 24-hour service, tell prospective owners they will be working every hour on the clock.

5. *Recognize the "I" problem.* Being ranked number one, winning awards, and listing press articles is great for establishing your credibility. But without emphasizing how these achievements translate into business benefits, they have little value for the potential buyer. Don't forget the direct-response principle: "What's in it for me?"

   Molly Maid won the prestigious Microsoft Windows World Open two years in a row for the software scheduling technology they developed for their franchise owners. Quite an accomplishment, this certainly was a "wow" factor for recruiting franchisees... if they knew how it would benefit them. Unfortunately, the company proudly showcased this new acclaim in its advertising, but forgot to translate the achievement into an owner benefit. Shortly afterward they added the missing "wow." It read something like this:

   "Two-time winners of the Microsoft Windows World Open, Molly Maid created a proprietary management program that helped existing owners build million-dollar businesses by saving countless hours in employee scheduling, administration, and paperwork."

6. *Why do prospects respond?* Ask each candidate in the initial conversation *"What was it in the ad that prompted you to contact us?"* I guarantee it will help you refine your ad approach to really connect with your buyers. You'll be surprised at what unexpectedly triggered a response.

   Ralph Ross, founder of several franchises, was a stickler about gaining buyer insights that could strengthen his franchise marketing. He mandated his sales execs get ad feedback from every ad respondent so he could continually perfect his lead generation.

7. *Invest in direct-response creative.* The cost will pay back several times in higher responses. Avoid agencies with no franchise recruitment or lead generation experience. Their institutional and image campaigns may win advertising awards, but could deliver you the golden goose egg.

8. *Advertise without a website.* If you are a new franchisor, you can start generating leads even before you launch your own site! Franchise recruitment websites will create your promotional page, copy text, and request form and email all prospect inquiries to you. In fact, some analysis reports indicate that more prospects prefer the convenience of responding initially to a commercial franchise site, rather than transferring to the actual company websites. They appreciate the convenience and ease of selecting potential opportunities.

9. *Make the media provide solutions.* Tap the media for new ideas and ad techniques that are working. They are involved with hundreds of franchise recruitment campaigns and gain valuable, up-to-date response information. When leads dwindle, immediately share your dilemma with your ad reps. Press them for solutions. Does your ad message need changing, and how? What other franchise ads are doing well, and why? What headlines, banners, copy, and graphics are prompting the greatest responses?

Encourage and empower the media to actively share responsibility for your ad success. One sharp media sales person conducted a comprehensive lead generation analysis for his client and increased responses 25 percent simply by recommending the franchisor rerun a high-performing ad from three years prior. Another savvy rep had her creative department completely rework a franchisor's ad with new graphics, format, and copy and boosted leads by more than 50 percent.

Building your franchise recruitment package

Dynamic, high-quality presentation materials are critical to your lead generation and sales performance, especially for buyers who have never seen your concept in their market. Franchisors spend $5,000 to $100,000 annually producing these sales aids to showcase their opportunities with prospects. When your opportunity information arrives at a buyer's doorstep, it must win first or second position in the stack of other concepts they are considering. Pay attention small franchisors, because you can compete! It's not about the money you invest, but the creativity and execution of your message that make the winning difference!

The quality of your marketing materials reflects who you are

Unfortunately, most franchise organizations aren't household names yet. Perception is reality, and the image you project heavily influences whether you win or lose that prospect's initial response to your opportunity. Online, buyers usually choose the most attractive, professionally presented concepts when quickly surfing unfamiliar franchises. They're overdosed by the thousands of franchises they see and edit as they go. I know, because prospects typically selected our start-up concept over the competition because our site was *"dynamic, and a more impressive presentation than the other guys!"* This certainly isn't the most prudent way for buyers to make initial decisions, but first impressions do push you to the top—or sink you into oblivion. So, invest in designing, packaging, and presenting your print, online, trade show, and press materials. You'll get your money back tenfold!

Check out other franchise promotional kits

This is the fast track for creating your own material. I keep my favorite 25 franchise packages in my office, which earned shelf space with their compelling presentations. I also keep a few "humdingers" that have been disasters in franchise development. The best of these disasters is from my days at *Entrepreneur* magazine. We generated volumes of leads for a franchise service seeking grants and special funding programs for college students. The founder complained the leads were 100 percent unqualified and never returned his follow-up calls. Because we had some successes with competitors, I asked him to send me his mail-out package for review. I received a plain white envelope containing eight photocopied pages explaining the program and asking the recipient to return the detailed application with a refundable check, if turned down. There wasn't an ounce of excitement in the material motivating a buyer to take action on his franchise. The sales literature was plagued with misspelled words, cold copy lacking ownership benefits, no graphics, photos, or student testimonials. Double thumbs down, this was the worst franchise presentation I have ever witnessed.

When I called the franchisor and offered recommendations, I slammed into a stone wall. He hyperventilated, yelling that his program worked and there was no reason to romance his service with expensive artwork and fancy copy. In disbelief, I kept his incredible package. Until this day it's a great reminder that you can't assume everyone will follow the elementary principles of marketing.

Competitive intelligence dictates that you periodically study recruitment materials from other franchises. They can be in totally different industries, it doesn't matter. Put your head inside of the prospect's and ask yourself these key questions: Is the material well-organized? Are you impressed by what they say and how they present it? Does the material convey a strong brand image for their target buyers? Is too much information shared too quickly? Or is the package full of fluff, failing to address basic prospect questions? Are you more or less interested in the program after reading about it? If you were a prospect, would this presentation compel you to return their application form for more information?

Here's a reference check of primary content and items included in franchise recruitment packages. Naturally, how you present and deliver this material will vary depending on your concept and franchise sales process.

Franchise Recruitment Package Materials	
Content Checklist	**Design Elements**
Franchisee and customer visuals	Mailing envelope
Opportunity description	Pocket folder
Mission and values statement	Brochure
Industry growth potential	Page inserts/step sheets
Earnings claims (FPRs)	Retail pieces
Points of differentiation	Business card
Ownership benefits	CD/DVD presentation
Products and services	Integration with website
Initial and ongoing training	
Support services (operations manuals, site selection and construction, marketing, intranet, conventions, R&D, etc.)	*Multi-Purpose Mini-Brochure*
Franchisee and customer testimonials	Use for:
Press and special recognition	Franchisee referrals
Corporate history	Direct mailings
Discovery Day highlights	Trade shows
List of locations	Handouts
Investment, royalty, and advertising fees	Soft leads
Start-up costs	
Questions and Answers/FAQ sheet	
Qualification process	
Qualification response form	

3 The Four Steps to Lead Generation Success: Step Three–Determine the lead sources that reach your buyers

Lead generation programs that work

Successful franchise recruitment requires building a marketing plan that produces qualified prospective buyers at acceptable costs. This isn't an easy task, especially in our new media age, where franchise buyers now access multiple recruitment and educational sources to research franchise opportunities.

During the 1980s, the majority of franchise buyers had a few sources for finding franchise opportunities, similar to how TV viewers were captive to the major networks. *Entrepreneur* magazine, the *Wall Street Journal*, major city papers, and national franchise shows composed 90 percent of media budgets. Developing lead generation plans was the easiest part of the recruitment process. No longer!

How to build an intelligent lead generation budget

Years ago I recall the terror in my franchise client's voice when he returned from his annual meeting. *"My CEO was ecstatic with our 40 sales this year. But then he announced we need 70 more franchise sales for next year, with only a 10 percent increase in the marketing budget! How can we make this happen without the necessary funding?"* He was right! Their service company couldn't ratchet up sales from 40 deals one year to 70 the next with the measly budget increase the CEO allocated for the new, accelerated goal.

All too many companies shoot in the dark when it comes to establishing franchise goals and corresponding budgets. There's a common misconception that if a successful sales team gets more aggressive and works harder, they'll catapult sales performance through their innate talents. Not so.

Over the past two decades misdirected planning practices have thrown some franchises into tailspins because of unrealistic development expectations.

If you know what you're doing, building an intelligent lead generation budget isn't that difficult. Shockingly enough, the Annual Franchise Development Report once again reveals that 43 percent of franchisors still don't know how effective their marketing dollars are in producing franchise owners. This is due either to inexperience in knowing how to determine what really works, or to the franchisor not caring enough to invest the time and energy to discover the answers. Here's how to find those answers:

- *Use sales performance history*—What was your cost per sale for your various lead generation sources over the past year? The current overall median is $7,000 per franchisee sold, according to the survey results. This figure often varies by industry and/or size of investment. Some low- and mid-level investment opportunities surprisingly do require higher budgets. I've found that sales-driven systems, such as direct mail franchises and temporary personnel services, require significantly higher budgets. If you are a new or misguided franchisor groping for benchmarks, purchase Franchise Update's Annual Franchise Development Report (go to www.franchiseupdate.com/afdr or email sales@franchiseupdatemedia.com). And ask savvy franchisors what they are experiencing. You have to budget an average cost per acquisition to know where you are going.

- *Track costs by advertising categories*—How many sales have you generated from your $20,000 spent on various Internet advertising? How many deals from your $10,000 invested in two franchise shows? What about the $2,500 you spent in promotional mail-outs and posters to franchisees and employees about your internal referral incentive program?

- *Track costs by individual sources*—Years back, mass newspaper advertising was a home run in producing sales for the five franchise concepts owned by Grow Biz, the successful franchisor of recycled retail merchandise. Yet a Connecticut newspaper grabbed $30,000 of their budget before the marketing director discovered that publication never generated a single qualified lead, let alone a sale! Tracking is particularly important in measuring the cost-per-sale figures of your Internet advertising, which requires more diligent tracking through a lead management process; and quizzing new franchisees about how they found out about you on your franchise application, phone calls, and the Discovery Day visit.

- *Time-to-sale ratios*—Measuring your average number of days to closing from initial inquiry is essential when a special recruiting campaign is launched for a limited time. I remember the 60-day bonus program a founder wanted to implement with a franchise broker organization. I had to remind him that his franchise sales cycle averaged 75 to 90 days! If you don't know your closing cycle, start measuring now. On another note, if your sales are averaging six months or more, this is usually a red alert that your sales process or sales personnel need drastic correction ($1 million-plus investments requiring large real estate commitments are often the exception). For reference, the average sales close takes 12 weeks from initial inquiry.

- *Multi-unit ratios*—What is the average number of franchise units a new franchisee usually purchases? One? Two and a half? This is easier to calculate for established franchisors. Factor this ratio into your budget so you can project the unit and cash expectations for each sale.

Choosing the right media plan for you

Carefully review each media's program in your selection process. You may want to ask other franchisors what works for them, as well as asking media reps for examples of franchisors generating quality prospects from their lead programs. This is valuable information, but not always a "surefire formula" for selecting productive lead sources for your franchise. As franchise sales veterans know, a good media plan with one company doesn't mean it will work with another, even within the same industry. Countless variables affect results, such as differences in candidate profiles, franchise programs, investment levels, qualifications, sales processes, corporate philosophies, etc.

One franchisor's celebration of results often is another's commiseration. I certainly experienced this as a franchise consultant, customizing more than 30 different media plans for franchisors, a few for directly competitive concepts. There simply are no magic bullets, because each of your franchise opportunities is not the same. You may be attracting similar audiences, but not the same audiences!

Building your successful lead generation program

The good news for franchise recruitment is there are key lead generation sources that will work to various degrees of success.

1. *Base your recruitment budget on cost per sale*—If you don't yet have this information, contact Franchise Update Media Group for the latest Annual Franchise Development Report (go to www.franchise-update.com/afdr).

2. *Non-paid media sources*—Include referral programs and networking opportunities in your lead generation plan, with related expenses budgeted accordingly.

3. *Use multiple media sources*—Using only one medium confines your message to just a portion of your buyers, limiting awareness and consequently the potential of your sales growth. Betting your success on a single source can be dangerous. "I only use the Internet" or "Brokers are the only way to go" or "PR is 100 percent of our recruitment budget" puts your franchising expansion in a vulnerable, high-risk position.

4. *Increase winners, dump losers!*—Beef up what's working, get rid of what isn't, and try alternatives. Ride the winners as long as they continue to produce franchisees, upgrading your presence while the going is good.

5. *No annual contracts to start*—As a rule of thumb, commit only to 3 to 6 month contracts when signing up with a new media source. You need to find out if the new source works!

6. *Say "yes" to conditional annual contracts*—Once you discover a source is working, you can save by committing to a long-term agreement. But do so only if there are reasonable terms that allow you to drop out. Most media have a 30-day notification clause that allows you to opt out with prior written notice, provided you pay the frequency rate you have satisfied at the time of your cancellation. I often signed annual contracts with this stipulation, since it provided greater savings while reducing financial risks in the event of poor performance. With the dynamics and complexities of lead flow in today's multi-media environment, your top sales source today may become tomorrow's turkey soup.

7. *Test, test, test*—To conserve experimental dollars, run smaller ads on a limited frequency schedule and you'll produce better results. Build on the winners, get rid of the losers and watch your ad costs drop and your sales rise!

8. *Don't forget trade media*—Franchise advertising should be tested in your industry publications, websites, and shows, which may also produce good franchise prospects, sometimes at a much lower cost!

9. *Create an opportunity fund*—Budget some money to take advantage of special editions, activities, or new media programs that arise during

the year. A special fund for this purpose helps prevent missing out on special opportunities.

10. ***Quarterly adjustments to your plan***—The best performing media plan is constantly evolving. Analyze your lead generation activities at least every three months. What you don't measure, you can't improve. Continually keep track of your advertising performance. Companies that review their recruitment programs only once a year are making costly mistakes—especially considering how volatile website marketing, broker leads, PR, referrals, or most any of your sources can be at any given time. Changes in buyer interests have been triggered by hurricanes, election years, war, and booming and busting economies.

11. ***Only results count***—Recruitment advertising has one primary mission: generate qualified prospects for franchise ownership. Branding, image, or any other marketing objective really has no value if your advertising isn't generating e-mail responses, or better yet ringing your phone. Recruitment advertising is response-driven and demands continual sensitivity and adjustments to maximize your success.

Free and low-cost lead sources

Grassroots marketing works in recruiting franchisees. It's the bread and butter of successful area developers and master franchisees, who often must employ local guerrilla marketing to capture a majority of their franchisee owners.

The good news is that lead generation costs for these sources (see table) can be significantly lower than costs for national ads, Internet websites, and PR firms. But unlike picking up the phone, placing an order, and giving your credit card number, this is proactive marketing that requires more planning, personal involvement, and time commitment. For start-up and "bootstrap" franchisors with minimal recruitment budgets, it's the only way to grow. For mature franchisors targeting unsold local territories, it's the only way to complete their growth.

Referrals

Today, savvy franchisors with good validation are jumping their referral sales 25 percent and more by developing aggressive, well-planned referral programs. Yet many franchise systems don't capitalize on the full recruitment potential within

Free and Low-Cost Lead Sources

- Franchisee, employee, and supplier referrals
- Trade journals
- Business brokers
- In-store recruitment brochures
- Franchise opportunity signs in site locations not leased
- Packaging materials seen by consumers
- Local newspapers and business journals
- Regional opportunity magazines
- Direct mail and email to organization members and employees
- Direct mail and email to prior prospects
- Business and financial planners
- Bankers
- Attorneys
- Politicians
- CPAs
- Business lead exchange clubs
- Franchisor lead exchange groups
- Entrepreneur clubs and associations
- Company personnel departments
- Chambers of Commerce, Jaycees, Rotary, Junior League, other civic and fraternal organizations
- Outplacement centers
- Early retirement groups
- Military centers
- Speaker services for organizations
- Industry spokespersons
- Columnists and bloggers who write about franchising
- Radio programs
- Career counseling
- Small Business Administration
- Small Business Development Centers and SCORE offices
- Economic development and urban redevelopment programs
- Universities and vocational schools
- Starting a business/franchise seminars
- Adult education classes
- Business and investment consultants
- Press releases on franchisees and community contributions
- Team and event sponsorships

their networks. They appreciate the leads they receive, but don't actively promote what is the most valuable lead source in franchising. Referred prospects are as precious as gold, just waiting to be discovered in your own backyard!

Money Mailer's system-wide enlistment of franchisees to help recruit new franchise owners was critical to re-energizing the company's development throughout the United States. Buy-in from their advisory council, combined with a multi-channel referral campaign to franchisees contributed to a 600 percent increase in new franchisee sales over the prior 18 months. (For more details on Money Mailer's remarkable turnaround, see Chapter 1.)

Higher quality, higher closes

Studies validate the power of referral sales. Close rates for direct referrals are typically three times higher than for other leads. According to the Annual Franchise Development Report, referrals continue to be a top franchise sales producer every year. Quick analysis of lead costs and sales ratios provides a compelling message to all: maximize your referral sales potential!

Expand your referral sources

Franchisees are logically your prime resource, but don't overlook your employees, suppliers, and business associates. Tapping these secondary referral sources can also produce qualified prospects. One East Coast sales executive launched an upscale quick-service café by extensively prospecting his industry network. He sold his first 8 new franchisees for the new concept by aggressively soliciting the food operators he had built relationships with over the previous 15 years. Ask all your vendors for franchisee referrals. As your "partners," suppliers should be expected to refer your opportunity to individuals they know are looking for a business.

Developing a successful campaign

Include a budget for referral marketing in your media plan. Producing special promotional materials and incentives will spur referral activity, at a selling cost often substantially lower than for other lead generation activities.

High-growth companies with referral campaigns stress that recognition, reward, and repetition are keys to a successful campaign. Sending a once-a-year memo announcing referral fees for new franchisees is only the start of what should be a year-round effort. (If you don't have a referral compensation program, run it by your attorney first.) Every two weeks, put your recruitment effort in front of your franchise network with scheduled mailings, website postings, meeting announcements, group emails, newsletter updates, and other communications.

Create an 8½ x 11-inch, tri-fold recruitment brochure with a referral space on the back panel to identify franchisees, employees, or business associates. This handout piece makes it efficient and easy for the referring individual and informative for the inquiring prospect. The same brochure also can be used as an inexpensive mailer to "borderline" franchise inquiries and as a handout at seminars and trade shows.

Get the word on the streets

How many of your franchisees' customers and acquaintances realize that you offer franchise opportunities? I guarantee most will be unaware… unless you tell them! In one instance, a friend of the founder of a $1 billion temporary employment agency was looking at a competitor's franchise. To his surprise, he happened to read an article about his friend's company. This prompted him to buy into his friend's system. How fortunate that the founder's friend saw the article. Never assume everybody knows about your opportunity!

Consider providing franchisees with retail posters, ads, stationery, invoices, and other tools that let potential prospects know you are a franchise. Window signage saying "Franchises Available" should be in any retail, office-based, or mobile franchise. Some franchisors tag their retail TV and radio spots with "Franchise Opportunities Available" where appropriate. Simply put, broadcast to your customers that you have franchises and you will sell more franchises!

When I sold for a three-year-old franchise system, customer referrals were the top recruiting source, producing 46 percent of our sales. The national average was 24 percent that year, according to Franchise Update's annual report. When a customer is already a fan of your concept, half the battle is won. They see themselves owning your business, a positive experience they know firsthand as a patron, and now are interested in pursuing as a proprietor. Closing ratios should be three to five times higher for qualified customer applications than for non-customer applications.

Your operations staff is a key contributor to referral sales. The quality of their training and coaching abilities is a testament to the number of enthusiastic brand customers who not only want to purchase your product but believe in it so much that they want to own and market it as well. Recognize your operations team for the role they play in building the franchise system. An excellent support system builds happy franchisees, employees, and customers… who will continue to fuel your franchise growth!

How to increase participation

Some franchisors aren't generating any significant referrals. If their problem is triggered by poor system support and struggling operators, this is very understandable. But some franchise systems with good validation still lack referral activity. This is often the fault of the franchisor. Sometimes franchisees haven't been asked for referrals. In some cases, they weren't educated about the advantages of having franchise neighbors and national growth. Consequently, these owners may be reluctant to refer prospects, concerned only about potential territory encroachment by a new franchisee.

Savvy franchisors recognize they must communicate the direct benefits to their franchisees about how franchise growth can increase branding and equity, reduce costs, provide greater competitive strength, expand research and development, etc. Ironically, some franchisors emphasize this powerful message when they recruit new franchisees, but then stop spreading the word once they join the system. Promoting the growth benefits of franchise development is a year-round effort.

Put it in your agreement

The best time to introduce your referral program is when your franchisee signs the contract. Include a clause that requires franchisees to participate in promoting franchise opportunities, with an agreement to display corporate brochures in their operations, and acknowledge that "franchise opportunity" taglines can appear in their retail pieces. I know of a sign franchisor that incorporates a franchise brochure rack into all store designs, clearly specifying that its exclusive use is for recruitment material and that it must be stocked at all times.

But how can franchisors get some of its older, less enthusiastic franchisees to actively contribute to a referral campaign?

Create a VIP referral program

Develop a special referral program providing additional recognition and rewards for franchisees who embrace franchise development with their full participation by validating your system success, displaying and distributing franchise materials, and producing qualified candidates through their efforts. The greater incentives in such a program can prompt other franchisees to join in, especially when they see a higher referral fee for the VIP participants.

Recognize your top franchisees

Tell your franchise system who your franchisee builders are. Recognition is a powerful motivator. Applaud those who champion the expansion of your brand.

At your annual convention, consider referral awards as part of your franchisee presentations. Individuals assisting in the growth of your franchise system deserve special recognition. Illustrate the important contribution of referrals, asking franchisees in the audience who were introduced to your system through other franchise owners to stand up. What a powerful impact this can make.

What does your plan look like?

If you haven't yet, build a referral plan into your recruitment program for next year. The costs are minimal and the long-term payoffs can certainly be rewarding!

Internet

The Internet has revolutionized franchise selling

Twelve short years ago, many of us could have mistaken a URL for an electrical code! The Internet's impact on the franchise community has been nothing short of astounding. It certainly has changed the way we do business in franchise communication, commerce, and recruitment. For many franchise sales departments, the Internet is now the primary lead source for bringing new franchisees into their programs. It was the marketing phenomenon of the '90s and the anointed king today. Why, and how, has this happened? To think there were only 130 websites in 1993, and that today with a click of the mouse we can choose from among tens of millions!

The new marketing frontier

In the 1980s and earlier 1990s, franchise advertising and sales were straightforward. There were standard lead generation formulas for print, PR, and trade shows with clearly defined results. It was pretty much a "no-brainer." The selling challenges we faced were 1) developing effective brochures, print ads, direct mailings, and handout materials, and 2) fine-tuning our sales presentations and follow-up to franchise inquiries.

But in early 1996, six visionary franchisors paid money to run ad banners on Entrepreneur.com, igniting a new franchise medium called online recruitment. From that day forward the Internet has grown into an integral part of most franchisors' marketing plans. Hats off to Computertots, Mail Boxes Etc., Molly Maid, Money Mailer, PostNet, and Stained Glass Overlay for pioneering the way into this unknown marketing frontier!

Today's low-cost leader

Online advertising has become the leading media source for franchise leads, according to the Annual Franchise Development Report. This inexpensive recruitment medium is driving volumes of email inquiries to our in-boxes from around the globe. The ad playing field has been leveled, with small companies now competing with large companies for prospects. Franchise advertising on the web is quick, convenient, and easy. Even before building a website, a start-up can launch their opportunity on commercial sites that will develop their promotional pages and response forms. Within 24 hours, a newborn franchisor can solicit responses worldwide.

The 1-800-DryClean franchise launched its franchise growth through the web. The company sold more than 15 franchises through the Internet before producing a franchise brochure or using any print or other advertising sources.

Embrace the Internet and win

Certainly the Internet may not be your strongest recruitment source, and in the case of some franchise concepts may not even be part of their lead generation efforts.

But every franchisor must respond to the reality that every day more business buyers use the web to research, respond, and buy businesses. The number of active franchisors that have sold new franchises on the Internet has catapulted from 5 percent in 1996 to 70 percent today. The Internet selling leaders have invested the time, dollars, and experimentation necessary to stay ahead of the curve and improve their cyber-recruitment success. Every new franchisor must diligently test the Internet. Chances are it may very well be a good recruitment source for qualified franchisees.

Start-up companies can now compete

Internet marketing is the least expensive ad source for leads, according to the Annual Franchise Development Report. This is great news for start-ups and, as noted, has definitely has leveled the playing field. Now a young, sharp franchisor with a limited budget can build a modest yet effective website and buy Internet advertising that can be viewed around the clock from anywhere in the world.

Thanks to the web, franchise buyers are discovering smaller start-up franchises they may never have come across 10 years ago. Have you ever marveled at a small franchise website that downloads quickly, is easy to navigate, and provides a simple, compelling message to prospective buyers? And how often are we surprised by a major franchise site that is confusing, difficult to navigate, and prompts us to bail out because of impatience and lack of interest? Large or small, all franchises now enjoy the opportunity to compete for the same buyers.

Multi-media planning

So how has the Internet affected our industry's lead generation and sales efforts? Does its ascendance mean that traditional franchise advertising will eventually die, replaced by cyberspace? Let's take a close look at what savvy franchisors have experienced in their online journeys, and how they are integrating the Internet into their sales programs.

Smart franchise marketers caution us, *"Don't ever think that the Internet will become the answer to franchise recruitment."* Sales for most companies are still generated through referrals (see above), and traditional media sources are still major contributors to attracting quality franchise candidates. Savvy franchisors will continue to leverage the proven success of publications, shows, direct mail, and other media to drive additional buyers to their websites.

Years ago the vice president of franchising for a multiple-brand company explained it this way: *"A buyer came to our booth at a franchise show, recognized our brand, saw we were busy with other attendees, picked up our advertising brochure, read it at home, saw our URL on the page, went to our website, was more impressed, and contacted us."*

Always spread your risk, even when you believe you've found the perfect recruiting source. What if your Internet leads start drying up? What if your newspaper ads stop generating the buyers they used to produce? Dependency on any one source places your sales future in a vulnerable position—not a good position to be in.

Online visitors require fast follow-up

High-performing franchisors drive technology to facilitate personal contact as quickly as possible. They profit from online communications by converting email inquiries into "live prospects."

Internet prospects demand fast response to their inquiries. Waiting two or three days for a media kit after they contact you by phone is okay, but waiting more than 24 hours for a response to their Internet inquiry is death. We must initially communicate with the online prospect in multiple ways. Instant automated emails and phone follow-up are necessary to further engage and turn prospects into serious candidates. Internet responses cannot be treated the same way as print or trade show follow-up. They require more effort, but the rewards are worth it, considering the frequently lower sales costs compared with some other sources.

Internet efforts can generate many more inquiries than traditional media, but initial prospect interest typically isn't as high as with a direct phone response, referral, or press lead. Sales people must spend more time diligently digging through these greater volumes of Internet responses to find the qualified buyers. Therefore, marketing response tools that help keep you in front of prospects are critical.

Streaming video clips, dramatic store photos, testimonials, voice emails, and e-news bulletins are some of the tools available to achieve this. For companies seeking assistance, there are technology services that specialize in providing recruitment tools to help improve your Internet marketing success.

In-depth lead tracking

Before the arrival of the Internet, identifying lead sources was quite simple, and consequently determining your best lead generation efforts was pretty much a "no brainer," as noted above. Franchise buyers would get information about your opportunity through the *Wall Street Journal,* magazines such as *Entrepreneur, Venture,* and *Success,* local newspaper ads, the IFA's Annual Directory, and a few other publications; by attending franchise opportunity shows; or by reading PR stories. Monitoring your best advertising was straightforward. But when the Internet explosion hit the franchise community in the mid-'90s, monitoring lead flow became a huge challenge for many stunned marketing departments.

Since then, poor media tracking has cost franchisors thousands of dollars every year.

Did a lead originate on the Internet, or was it just the transmitter from a print ad, show, or in-store brochure? Which franchise website, portal, search engine, strategic link, print piece, or radio interview should get credit for generating traffic to your own website?

Specific media measurement systems must be installed and all personnel in the sales process carefully trained to ask the right questions and properly credit which media contributed to the sale. The stakes are too high for making mistakes. Too many franchisors still struggle with effective lead tracking. If you are in this group, contact management solutions are readily available such as ACT! , Salesforce, Outlook, and GoldMine. Franchise lead filtering and tracking systems are readily available through eMaximation, IFX, FranConnect, MyBruno, and other vendors. And don't neglect the site analysis programs and other data collection tools available from your web host that will provide additional marketing intelligence.

Poor lead monitoring is a major challenge plaguing franchise development today. Most franchisors still don't have a good grip on sourcing exactly where their leads are coming from. By no means is it easy, as it requires an aggressive effort by both marketing and sales departments to constantly probe candidates for this information. But it's too costly a problem not to fix.

Drilling for answers pays off

Smart Internet recruitment requires knowing how prospects get to your site. Buyers themselves may not remember their course to your home page, so your tracking assistance is critical. Identify these lead sources and you'll build a high-performance lead generation program. To further sharpen your analysis, here are some simple tips:

- Connect all your website links for your franchise development directly to your franchise page, and create a special URL for all your recruitment marketing and advertising. One great way is simply to keep your ".com" address for your main home page, and create a new ".net" or other address to send buyer inquiries directly to your franchise recruitment page. For example, www.moneymailer.net and www.greatclipsfranchise.com are the recruitment site pages for these two franchisors and are separate from their consumer or retail home page. Using this dual approach allowed a savvy marketing franchise to solve the tracking challenge of sifting through their home page traffic to identify recruitment visitors.

- Continually record a prospect's response source(s) upon their initial inquiry, on your application, at Discovery Day, and in new franchise training classes. Use a multi-source system that can credit two or three different media for the same sale. Was the Internet the originator or communicator of the lead? After suggestive probing, a seasoned sales person at a retail franchise learned that his buyer saw a local story promoting a franchisee, visited his store, and contacted his franchise broker to pave the way for joining the system. Three sources contributed to make this sale!

Working with web techies

High-performance recruitment companies build successful relationships between their franchise development and Internet technology personnel. Techies can make or break you if your site isn't performing the way you want. Web developers may have intranet, e-commerce, and other technical expertise, but without direction from management they will fall short in building response-driven recruitment sites. Franchise sales must guide techies in developing their cyber-tools. The techies' role is to build and activate technology solutions to best communicate your message to your world. Don't allow them to take control of you or your process. And certainly don't let their techno-babble throw you off, which at times is simply a smokescreen to sidestep issues.

Working as a team with your Internet engineers is critical to successful online recruitment. As one experienced technology officer advises franchisors, *"Stick to your fundamental principles of direct-response marketing. Don't let web developers intimidate you into deviating from the rules."*

A frustrated development executive called concerning his company's new recruitment site for their collectables franchise. Online responses had plunged, so he asked me to review his Internet efforts and identify any problems. After reviewing his website, I assured him that he could instantly elevate his inquiry flow by shutting down the new website and reactivating the former one! The techies had transformed a highly effective website into a picturesque piece of commercial art that was slow, hard to read, hard to navigate, and difficult to respond to.

Three Keys for E-Recruitment Success

E-recruitment has its own set of rules and its own benefits. With the Internet overwhelmingly acknowledged as today's number-one source for franchise leads, knowing how to work its lead generation magic to maximum advantage is essential to franchise recruitment. The three keys to success in this realm are:

1. Build a response-driven website
2. Market your website effectively
3. Convert inquiries into sales

Here's how to do it!

Key #1: Build a response-driven website

The goal of Internet marketing is to generate quality prospects, no different from magazine, newspaper, trade shows, or referrals. The only purpose of online recruitment is to connect qualified franchise buyers with franchise sellers. Buyers checking out websites are overwhelmed in a jungle of confusion. They become impatient, their attention span wanes, and they zip from site to site until they abort their research and move on.

Your website is your Broadway stage. The curtain goes up as each interested visitor comes to see your franchise. Your performance must engage, motivate, and compel the audience to stand up from their seats and contact you. How well you design, build, and script your recruitment website will determine the success of your online lead generation. You may excel in driving visitors to your website, but if you can't convince them to respond, you'll be another Broadway flop as online buyers storm out of your theater to preview another franchise showing.

How you design your website and promotional pages can make or break your online lead generation success. If you're not first or second best in your business category, you'll lose deals to your competitors. That's how influential your web presence is in today's market. In the eyes and minds of the potential buyer, your web presence is "who you are." Invest the time to do it right! Research the competition and pump up your online presentation to stand above the crowd.

First recognize that producing websites and producing franchise recruitment kits are worlds apart. Communication, design, and direct response techniques are different. Confusing the two can cost you big sales. Websites are interactive and dynamic, so duplicating your recruitment package online will lose your buyer audience. Check out these guidelines for building a response-driven website:

1. Your website must be fast and responsive

- *Directly refer all franchise inquiries to your franchise page*, not to your home page. This sends prospects straight to the information they want.

- *Maximum eight-second download* per page with few graphics or single images. If pages are slow downloading, fix or eliminate them before your prospect eliminates you.

- *One click access to every section* with sidebars, buttons, and drop-down menus to facilitate speed and ease of use.

- *"Micro" content copy* that is quick and concise. This is an electronic media, a miniature TV screen that must tell your story in as few words as possible.

- *Your response page* should always be one click away. Place response buttons readily in sight on every recruitment page so visitors can request information at any time, and include an 800 number for the passionate buyer who wants to speak with you now.

- *Post the statement* *"You will be contacted within 24 hours,"* which will encourage interested visitors to complete your inquiry form. Prospects are often frustrated by slow or no responses from websites.

- *Display an instant "confirmation screen"* when a visitor completes and sends their form. This acknowledges that you received their request and reaffirms you will contact them within 24 hours.

- *Use an auto-response system* that triggers an email/video message to the inquirer, providing engaging information about your franchise and what the next step will be in investigating your opportunity (usually personal contact with a franchise development executive).

2. Your website must be simple

One sales executive at a retail franchise stresses that websites and emails should not be used to sell prospects, but to spark their interest. Keep your franchise site simple. If you provide too many specifics online, buyers may use or even misinterpret that information to reject your opportunity. Compel the prospect to contact you by teasing them with just enough information to make them want more. An effective website is:

- *Easy to understand*, not confused with information overload and design clutter choking each page. I'll never forget the complicated home page of a franchise website developer, with complicated navigation bars jammed across the top and side of their home page. Not a confidence builder for franchisors seeking design help for their sites!

- *Easy to read*, using legible, dark type on a light background, using reverse-out copy only for headlines and sidebars. Use contrasting colors with type large enough for 50-year-olds to read. Stay away from stylized type fonts that make it difficult to see. This is electronic media, not print.

- *Easy to use*, with navigation tools that allow your visitor to effortlessly skip about between sections, and to change course or back up at any moment. Never try to trap your visitor so they can't leave your site easily. Franchisors tried this trick in the early days, which infuriated prospects. And don't assume every online user is totally intuitive or web-savvy. When in doubt indicate "Click here" next to a key link that may be more subtle on your page.

- *Easy to focus on*, providing one central theme per page so readers can process information simply without distractions and confusion. Many websites are far too complicated, and often plagued by information overload. "Superior Training" should be the focal point for one page, "Award-Winning Marketing Program" for another. Segment and departmentalize rather that try to cram it all into one section or screen.

- *Easy to respond to*, with your request form one quick click away from any page a prospect is visiting. Use check-off boxes or buttons so prospects can easily click qualifying answers, limiting fill-out information and typing wherever possible.

3. Your website must be informative and motivating

- *First impression is everything* in the battle for qualified candidates. The presentation and quality of your site must exceed or at least match the impact of your other promotional material. Think of it this way and you can only increase your website effectiveness: Your website is a dynamic movie screen, and your audience is wondering where your story will lead. Engage the viewers and you'll win their acclaim!

- *Showcase your opportunity*, featuring your "wow" factors. Refer to the "Five cornerstones for building a successful franchise ad," earlier in this chapter.

- *Make prospects want more*, teasing and touching their interests with program attractions that will compel them to respond.

- *Make your site interesting* to the prospect so they will enjoy their experience and respond accordingly. Animation and special effects are attention-getters—but don't use too many or you'll slow down site speed and scare (or bore) away your prospect!

- *If appropriate, offer an incentive* for the prospect to respond, such as a free industry report, franchisee newsletter, coupon discount for using your retail services, etc.

- *Review and update your website* at least every six months to ensure your message remains fresh and effective, and that it is using technology that maximizes the impact of your franchise opportunity with prospective owners.

4. Your website content must deliver what buyers are seeking

Franchise buyers seek meaningful information to determine whether they will pursue your opportunity. Responsive, buyer-driven websites address your prospects' interests by grouping relevant content into easy-to-use sections (see below).

There's no need to build the watch for them, just show them how it works. Too often well-meaning franchisors induce prospect overload on their home pages by delivering "TMI" and "TMC" (too much information and too much confusion). Prospects don't want the whole story at this preliminary stage. Avoid this temptation, or confuse and lose visitors. Provide a simple, intuitive "dashboard" so they can easily drive your site and complete your inquiry form for more information.

Less is more. Don't try to sell through your website. Just whet a prospect's interest with enough highlights to contact you. Then your sales pros take over!

So, what critical information do franchise buyers want? I admit making several mistakes learning the answers. It took years of developing and evaluating hundreds of franchise websites to discover the universal content motivators. The results are plain and simple. Here's one effective approach that satisfies prospect interest for online information. It provides the key content that prospects expect to see on your home page navigation tabs:

- The Franchise Opportunity
- Ownership Benefits
- Training and Support
- Publicity and News

- About the Company
- Questions and Answers/FAQs
- Discovery Day
- Request for Information

Drop-down menus from these tabs should provide one-click links to key information pages that present your marketing programs and ad samples, franchisee and customer testimonials, corporate culture and mission statement, available territories, franchise qualifications, Discovery Day, etc.

Key #2: Market your website effectively

It doesn't matter how impressive, informative, and compelling your website is… unless the buyers you are looking for know how to look for you! It's like being located in the state of California without a phone directory listing or a map available for prospects to find you. Qualified traffic is everything, so invest the time and money to drive these prospects to your website. Here are some effective tips for marketing your website:

- *Print your website address* on all and every material you can think of: print ads, brochures, menus, service order forms, window signs, vehicles, napkins, TV and radio promotions, press releases, grand opening banners, t-shirts, etc.

- *Optimize your search engine positioning* for your business category and opportunity by contracting your website host or another service provider to continually drive your presence on different search engines and directories. However, don't expect much response unless you successfully secure first-page positions.

- *Keyword buys.* More franchisors have "gone direct" and invested money to purchase keyword phrases specific to their opportunity on Google, Yahoo, MSN, and other search engines and directories. Results have paid off for some, offsetting the high costs with increased sales. For example, if you are a dry cleaning franchise you can purchase ads at the top of Google's first page for the keywords "dry cleaning franchise," "dry cleaning business," and "dry cleaning opportunities." Inquiries you receive will be highly targeted from people focused on starting up a dry cleaning business. Again, it's a pricey marketing investment up front, but it may reap rewards on the back end. At the time of the last Franchise Leadership & Development Conference polling survey, the majority of the 200 participating franchise brands had purchased keywords on search engines to recruit franchises. Of this group, one third said they found it worth the investment.

- *Cross-link your website* with complementary websites that share visitor demographics that fit your candidate profile. The price is right (free!), but it does require a time commitment to aggressively contact potential site partners to create the reciprocal agreements.

- *Test ad banners.* You have two seconds to grab a prospect's attention. Your banner is an online freeway billboard that Internet users scroll past as they drive. Grab your buyer's attention with a compelling, easy-to-see message that will make them pull over for a better look.

You'll increase your results if you periodically rotate and monitor three to four different ad banners on advertising sites. Try a series of "teasers" that will motivate visitors to click through to your opportunity. By testing logo banners against message banners, I found that opportunity-driven banners invariably outperform banners that only promote your name. Sears Carpet & Upholstery Care and Spring-Green Lawn Care discovered up to 50 percent differences in responses when testing their ad banners. Savvy commercial websites are certainly cooperative in testing what works best for you, because greater ad performance ensures a more loyal customer. In 1996, PostNet was one of the first franchisors to test banners. The up-and-coming franchise outperformed the giant Mail Boxes Etc. by three-to-one in prospect inquiries. Rather than creating a logo banner as MBE had, PostNet created greater traffic with the attention-grabbing banner "Business services are booming!"

- *Test your message.* You'll also increase your responses by analyzing your ad performance on a website portal. How many visitors that come to your "webmercial" are requesting more information? Ask the sales rep for the ad portal to provide the percentage of your page views that produce leads. If your conversion rate is currently 2 percent, can the right ad changes jump performance to 5 percent or more? You bet! I've witnessed impressive lead boosts by changing ad messages without spending a penny more. Doubling your lead flow for the same investment dollars is a huge marketing achievement. Unfortunately, most franchisors don't take the time to make this happen, so they spend more marketing dollars to make up the difference.

- ***Write all of your descriptive copy*** for online listings and banners as a sales message. Weave your opportunity statement or "wow" factors into your Internet listings. Include keywords for greater search optimization. Take note of those websites that publish your basic information for free, and edit their copy to "jazz" it up where possible. These listings are just as much a commercial as your promotional copy bites are on franchise advertising sites.

- ***Buy space on franchise advertising websites***, which in most cases will be your greatest traffic sources. They spend the money and do the marketing to bring franchise buyers to their portals, offering the collective attraction of hundreds of opportunities for their visitors to peruse and the educational know-how to help guide prospective buyers in their investigation of franchising opportunities. (For tips on how to best evaluate and negotiate with commercial websites, see "How to buy online advertising" below.)

Key #3: Convert inquiries into sales

Handling Internet inquiries effectively requires a rapid response process that incorporates high-tech and high-touch. You snooze, you lose. We are all impatient when our own emails aren't answered within an hour. Franchise buyers are no different, and are quickly turned off by slow or no communication.

Here are some follow-up techniques franchisors use to capture and reinforce prospect interest:

How to buy online advertising

There has never been a greater media challenge for franchisors than selecting website advertising. From bedroom-based to 25-employee companies, franchise recruitment websites are springing up daily. Industry experts estimate there are now well more than 150 online advertising companies pushing for your franchise marketing dollars. And every salesperson has a great story about how their website is the best, and how they'll generate more qualified prospects than the online rep who's going to call within the next hour.

Bridging the communication gap between advertising sellers and buyers compounds the confusion. Our heads spin with definitions and data concerning hits, impressions, page views, unique visitors, links, search engine positions, click-through counts, and demographics. Buying decisions at times are prompted by the selling ability and persistence of the rep, by the website's attractive design, or by the great deal you just cut.

Weeding through the Internet jungle

If you are not experienced at effectively analyzing "tech talk," take the shortcut to better buying and zero in purely on sales results. Conduct your research on various websites using direct-response questions. The sole purpose of your online franchise advertising is to generate quality prospects to sell your franchise to, just as you normally do. If you can't get satisfactory answers to the following questions from a website in business six months or longer, hold on to your wallet!

1. *"What franchisors have made sales from your website? Any with similar investment levels or business categories I can speak with? Email me names of clients I can call."*

2. *"Do you have any top 10 keyword search engine positions with Google, Yahoo, or MSN? Give me specifics."* (Nielsen Online continually rates these three search engine giants, which together produced almost 90 percent of all online searches in June 2008, with Google by far the traffic leader at 59 percent).

3. *"How many qualified online inquiries can I expect per month from your site for my business category?"*

4. *"What is unique about your site that can produce more prospects for me?"*

5. *"What audit reports can you provide that will help verify information you have provided to me?"*

Test buys on new websites

Marketing plans are always evolving and should never remain static. Throwing a recruitment plan in the drawer to use next year throws you out of touch with the current lead generation environment. Therefore I always budget an "opportunity fund" to test and measure different and new media, including a few newborn websites that catch my interest.

Since start-up websites don't have performance histories, carefully consider lead generation factors before you get romanced by fancy graphics or bells and whistles. Unfortunately, a few new websites have misled franchisors with inaccurate or exaggerated claims. If you don't think you have enough Internet savvy to make an informed decision, call a few of their initial advertisers and ask what marketing information motivated them to participate. Second, ask the vendor these key questions before making any financial commitments—and personally check to validate their response:

1. *"Is your website on the first page(s) of Google, Yahoo, or MSN, and if so, which ones and where are you positioned?"*
   "How many unique visitors are you bringing to your site, and where are you getting them?"

2. *"Give me two major reasons why I should consider you over established franchise sites that have been in the industry for years."*

3. *"How many thousands of dollars are you spending every month to promote your website, and exactly where are you advertising? How about franchise keyword positions on search engines?"*

4. *"Since you don't have a track record yet, what is your best introductory offer and what is my shortest advertising commitment? I have more than 100 websites to choose from, so to take a risk with you I need a deal to motivate me. If your website can bring me quality candidates, you will have a long-time advertiser."*

Remember, even if you don't speak "tech," you're still in the driver's seat with these fledgling ad sites. They need you much more than you need them! Offer to be a "beta test" advertiser who can help champion their great recruiting abilities to other franchisors… that is, if they perform well and generate buyers for you like they claim.

Print

How to buy print advertising

Magazines, newspapers, direct mail, billboards, and other print media have been the backbone of business-to-business and consumer marketing for centuries. Kicking back and reading a magazine in the comfort of our home, office, or a coffeehouse or on the beach, airplane, train, or bus is a personal experience that can never be replaced. We aren't interested in skipping about on a computer, or we just don't have one at our fingertips. Print is portable, tangible, and easy on the eyes. The convenience of print and a more captive mindset provide strong advertising opportunities to reach franchise prospects, opportunities that should never be abandoned for the flash of electronic media.

Here are some quick tips that will help you make better decisions when purchasing print advertising:

- *Ask about readership profiles and circulation audits*—Make sure the medium reaches the profile of your ideal buyers. Here's the good news! Print media are light years ahead of the Internet in identifying and documenting who their readers are, how many they have, and knowing their demographics, lifestyles, and purchasing habits. Publishers conduct surveys and focus groups to better understand their audiences. Larger, high-profile publications such as the *Wall Street Journal*, major daily newspapers, or *Entrepreneur* magazine provide you with ABC or BPA industry audits and comprehensive reader profiles. Franchise industry trade publications such as Franchise Update's *Multi-Unit Franchisee* magazine, and the IFA's *Franchising World* also provide valuable marketing intelligence to assist in your decision-making.

- *Different ads for different audiences*—Adjust your graphics and message for the readership. I've seen ads with male franchisees featured in a women's business publication; copy written for white Middle America appearing in a magazine serving Hispanic readers.

- *Frequency over size*—You'll get much greater bang for your buck if you run a quarter-page ad four times rather than a full-page ad once. Agencies are notorious for buying a full-page one-time run for a franchise recruitment ad, rather than smaller ads over several issues for the same price. Just say "No" if you run into this. Franchise recruitment is direct-response advertising, which requires frequency. Magazines in particular have long "shelf lives" and additional "pass-along" readers, which will continue to generate responses months after the issue's original publication date. At *Entrepreneur* magazine, we discovered a 67 percent renewal rate with franchisors on first-time frequency schedules, and an 18 percent renewal history with "one-shot" advertisers.

- *Run consecutive issues*—People sometimes don't notice you the first time they read a Sunday Business Opportunity section, or perhaps they aren't interested that week in looking for a franchise business. But then the shoe drops and they're informed of a pending layoff that week, or a cut in pay, or a job transfer to another state, or another motivating reason to seek their own business. Second, we typically don't read every issue of our favorite magazines, and read only certain ones when we travel. You should place a minimum three-time test for any print publication to produce results. If you plan on running an ad just once, you'll be flushing your money down the drain. Repetition sells deals.

- *Format your ads for maximum response*—In magazines, not only does size matter, shape does too. Specifically, one-third-page vertical ads typically produce more leads than one-third-page square ads, since they read from top to bottom; half-page islands (floating on the page surrounded by text) usually outperform half-page horizontal ads; two-thirds-page ads can be as effective as full-page ads since editorial copy wraps around the two-thirds ad, creating more reader attention; and a half-page horizontal spread that spans two pages can increase results over a full-page ad, because the adjacent editorial allows readers to spend more time reading and seeing your franchise opportunity.

- *Ask about remnant space*—When a magazine or newspaper is formatted prior to printing there are always "holes" that need to be filled. These open spaces either are sold at the last minute by the sales people at preferred (discounted) rates or, failing that, are filled with "public service" ads or duplicate ads, which is typically the case in newspaper classified sections. Find out the remnant space policy at different publications. Although last-minute deals are usually reserved for veteran clients, here's how you'll increase your opportunities to grab a leftover space at a reduced price: prepare a lineup of your franchise ads in the different shapes and sizes that fit the various ad sizes of the publications you use. Then let them know you can have artwork in their hands the same day should a remnant space become available!

- *Four-color ads aren't necessarily better*—Lead generation is direct-response driven, so don't spend the extra money for full-color advertising unless it makes sense or doesn't cost more. Four-color ads are always a wise choice if you are promoting a visual concept such as Stained Glass Overlay, Carpet Sculpture Gallery, and food-related franchises. When considering a black-and-white ad, take note: studies reveal two-color ads are higher response generators than black-and-white ads, since headlines and major points can be highlighted to attract greater reader attention.

Tricks of newspaper advertising

Good news. If you find the magic formula for classified advertising, it can be a great selling source that is easy to monitor, as well as easy to control costs. When I sold SpeeDee Oil Change & Tune-Up in Southern California, classified was our winning media for recruiting 80-plus owners into our system. But later, at a different service franchise I represented, classified bombed.

The key to classified is understanding how to use it to optimize results. Whether on a national, regional, or local basis, franchisors must test and re-test this medium, which produces noticeably different results in different markets during different cycles. The Tampa newspaper produced three sales for our direct marketing franchise during one year, yet Orlando and Miami papers came up empty. Newspaper advertising has its own set of marketing rules, just as with Internet and magazine advertising. In today's digital world, you can also run ads in their online classifieds.

- *Consider a newspaper ad placement agency*—If you are going to run ads in more than two papers and plan to grow from there, newspaper classified specialists can definitely make life easier, helping you to effectively write and format ads, advise when and where to place them for greater responses, and save you time and manpower by collecting, checking, and sending "tear sheets" of each newspaper ad run.

- *Request sample pages to review*—Because different newspapers are not formatted alike, it's helpful to get a look and feel for how ads appear in each publication. This can assist in how you design your message and approach.

- *Special attention-getters help*—Stars, boxing of ads, color headlines, bold type, and other highlighting techniques can increase readership. Check each publication to see what special effects are available to showcase your ad.

- *Compelling, concise message*—Readers are bouncing about, scanning business ads every two seconds, so your message must grab their eyes with engaging copy that instantly invites interest.

- *Call to action*—Newspapers are the news of the day, so give phone numbers with time-sensitive instructions such as *"Call now,"* or *"Calls accepted on Monday and Tuesday."*

- *Line ads can be most effective*—Smaller in-column ads run on successive Sundays is a smarter buy than placing larger display ads on a less frequent basis… unless you have larger budgets and are aggressively blitzing local markets for rapid development.

- *Consider "rate holders"*—Rate holders are inexpensive one-line ads that run every day, offered in combination buys with Sunday ads. I once sold a mobile check cashing franchise to a multi-unit owner who had missed the Sunday ad but responded to the small rate holder ad during the week.

- *Stay away from holidays*—People are typically traveling, focused on family events or celebrations during these special occasions. Their minds are on vacation, miles away from buying a business.

- *Test, test, test*—Rotate headlines and copy from time to time and you'll discover the ads that delivers the best responses. Too few franchises bother to take the time to do this, but as with other media, monitoring your marketing approach will pay off in more franchise sales every year.

Direct mail does work

Years ago at a West Coast franchise, we regularly purchased mailing lists from select publications targeting business executives who matched our ownership profile. We also ran ads in these magazines, creating a multi-touch campaign. Boom! We hit a home run through our cross-marketing, generating highly qualified responses. Our return rates were ordinary, but our prospect close ratios were extraordinary.

An East Coast restaurant franchise with a $1 million-plus investment, sold franchises by blasting a group mailing to its database of inquiries from the previous two years. Each mail piece included a four-color brochure from the company's vice president highlighting newsworthy developments in the franchise program. Encouraged by this success, this franchisor also purchased a list of multi-unit franchise restaurant owners and again made sales.

Years ago, Servpro, a home and commercial service franchise discovered its more successful owners came from close-knit families with strong core values. Management was frustrated with mass media ads, which weren't attracting this candidate profile. Direct mail answered their prayers! The company struck pay dirt by mailing franchise opportunity letters to church membership lists and other like-minded organizations. This became their best recruitment source for the next few years.

In summary, direct mail marketing is certainly part science and part art, and requires trial and error in discovering each franchise's formula for success. Patience and testing are keys to getting it right. This means reaching the ideal audience, creating an attention-getting package that gets opened and read, and delivering a compelling presentation that prompts buyers to respond.

Conversion campaigns in real estate and pharmacy franchises also have enjoyed sizable success with direct mail campaigns, which directly solicit independent owners to join their systems. Sears Carpet & Upholstery Care also cashed in when launching its franchise program. Identifying potential buyer lists is definitely not an issue; the challenge is attracting qualified conversion prospects and avoiding the failing independents.

Trade Shows

Investing in trade shows

Franchise shows were the champions of recruitment during the 1980s and early 1990s. Franchisors effectively sold owners throughout the U.S. by "working the circuit" 40 weeks a year. Buyers flocked to these events, excited to meet franchise executives face-to-face and get the direct scoop about their opportunities. These convenient showcases provided entrepreneurs with a great personal experience to learn, evaluate, and buy a franchise business in their own backyard. For franchisors, these events were an ideal recruitment tool for building target markets.

Then, a combination of events shattered the marketplace and threw trade show selling into a tailspin for several years: over-saturation of franchise shows and the discovery of Internet for investigating franchise opportunities. Buyers could now kick back, fire up their computer, and get instant online access to franchise information in the comfort of their own home. The Internet became the "remote control" for franchise shows! Why battle traffic, parking spots, travel costs, and admission prices, if you didn't have to? Consequently, attendance plummeted and U.S. franchise shows faded away, with the exception of the annual IFA show in Washington, D.C.

Then bang, shows rallied back into the limelight. As the year 2000 approached, entrepreneurs rediscovered these franchise events. Consumers began turning off their technology as franchise shows returned to town. They once again embraced the power of this live venue, which offers personal experiences and interaction with the people behind the franchises. It turned out that the bricks-and-mortar show environment could never be replaced by online commercials and automated emails.

Which trade shows are right for you?

Not only are franchise opportunity shows productive, but industry-related shows can also work to increase sales. A cleaning franchise successfully recruited additional operators by exhibiting at their industry's expos. An advertising service also struck pay dirt at a major marketing exhibition, recruiting industry candidates considering their own business.

Since the early 1980s, I've exhibited in numerous franchise trade shows and seminars with both service and retail concepts. Results ranged from great to bad, depending on the quality of the shows and attendees, the markets where the event was held, and the concepts I was selling. Overall it was worth participating, as we awarded more than 100 franchises as a result of exhibiting at these events. When selling an automotive franchise, we sold multiple new owners at almost every event.

Are you ready to exhibit yet?

Caution! Make sure you are well prepared to exhibit at a show. If not, you can make critical mistakes that will cost you sales opportunities. First, attend a show before you participate. Walk the aisles, note the better booth designs and props that are attracting attention, observe how sales people are approaching visitors, how they ask questions and present their concept, and how they get interested candidates to complete inquiry forms. Pick up any handout materials to get a sense of what may be appropriate for your business. Check out the food franchises that offer samples of their sandwiches, ice cream, cookies, smoothies, and other products. Will it be worthwhile for you to display or pass out some of your products? Should you bring your service van as some do?

Every year, over-anxious franchisors pull the trigger too soon, signing up for a trade show without proper preparation. Occasionally start-up franchises participate before their franchise program is ready to market. Results are usually disastrous. This is your "coming out party" for your concept, so make sure you are at your best when you hit the stage. Bad reviews spread fast.

How to buy trade shows

Get as much information as you can before investing the time, staff, and money in a trade show event. If you haven't yet experienced exhibiting at a show, here are telling questions to ask before you decide to sign up:

1. *"How many years have you been producing shows?"* If the show group is new to the business, stay away until they have a track record, or put down only a very minimal deposit up front. You may not get your money refunded if they fail to get enough exhibitors and never hold the event. As I am writing this, several franchisors have just "been taken" by a new show producer who failed to open his first two events.

2. *"How many years have you been producing franchise shows?"* If they are new to franchising, also be cautious… producing a franchise expo is much different than producing an auto show.

3. *"What is the average attendance of your shows?"* Franchise shows should generate between 2,000 and 6,000 attendees to be considered; and seminars from 30 to 100 attendees. Anything less is usually money wasted.

4. *"How many dollars are you spending on promoting this show, and what specific media will you be using?"* If you don't get a clear answer, don't sign up! Franchise opportunity shows typically spend $50,000 to $150,000 for local market expos, and in the millions for national and international events. Small seminars sponsored by participating franchisors should spend at least $10,000.

5. *"What other ways are you marketing this show?"* Better show groups often will get key organizations within the market involved who will support and promote the event to their audiences and customers, generating more attendance and credibility for the show. This may include the local SBA office, Small Business Development Center, the city's business or economic development department, local newspapers, business journals, magazines, banks, etc.

6. *"What are the demographics of your show attendees?"* Be sure to ask the sales person this question before they find out your qualifications, otherwise they'll tell you what you want to hear! Professional show groups know the entrepreneurial interests and financial profiles of their attendees, carefully tracking this information through sign-up questionnaires. Vague responses to this question should trigger a red alert about the potential quality of the show.

7. *"What franchisors have exhibited at your show? Which ones have made sales? Who in similar business categories and investment levels have done deals? Please provide me with contact information for some of these companies."* If getting franchise references is a problem from an experienced show group, then abandon your discussion and, again, shove your wallet back in your pocket.

Public Relations

Discovering the power of public relations

Twenty years ago I first witnessed the magic of great PR. Dan Dorfman, a renowned investment advisor, wrote an article praising our small business-to-business franchise, which had 100-plus owners at the time. Immediately afterward, our phones were ringing off the hook for three weeks! His syndicated column, which ran in 300 newspapers throughout the U.S., named us one of the "top 10 best franchise investments in America." Eleven sales later, I sat down and realized what had happened—and what can happen for franchisors with excellent PR reaching the right buyer audience at the right time. Simply put, PR sells franchises. Since then, I have discovered these general truths about using public relations as a recruitment tool.

- *Success stories featuring your franchise owners* are very powerful in generating buyers. They excite prospects reading about real people like themselves, who through your franchise, are achieving their dreams, making money, and enjoying your business and what it's provided for their family. I once asked an owner of a Once Upon A Child franchise, *"How did you hear about this opportunity?"* She exclaimed, *"What happened was bizarre. I just returned from their competitor's headquarters and was about to sign their franchise agreement. That day by sheer coincidence, I read a wonderful article about a local Once Upon A Child franchisee close to where I live. I visited the owner and was so impressed by her business, I changed my mind and joined her franchise system instead. I'm thrilled I saw the article!"*

- *Top rankings by the press*, business publications, research groups, and other organizations certainly boost your credibility and hence your lead flow. *Multi-Unit Franchisee* (formerly *Area Developer*) magazine's Top 50 Multi-Unit Franchisees, *Entrepreneur's* Franchise 500, the *Wall Street Journal's* 25 Franchise High Performers, the *Franchise Times* Top 200,

The *Inc.* 500 list of fastest-growing companies (as of 2007, the Inc. 5,000), Nation's Restaurant News awards, *Franchise Business Review*'s Top 50 Franchise Satisfaction Awards, and other industry rankings present great PR opportunities to enhance your marketing efforts.

- *Franchise events* that attract media attention can create significant payoffs. It's A Grind Coffee cashed in on a press invitation to reporters inviting them to learn the secrets of becoming a "coffee barista." Sure enough, a major St. Louis news channel filmed its excited reporter making lattes at a new franchisee's coffeehouse. The impressive five-minute broadcast was posted on the company's franchise website and shown at Discovery Days to prospective owners. Watching them watch the video on a 50-inch plasma screen, you could see prospects' eyes widen and smiles grow as they immersed themselves in the coffee business. You could read their thoughts: *"Wow, this is a newsworthy, fast-growing national brand I can be part of!"* The power of PR strikes again.

- *Franchisor features* at times have produced extraordinary buying interest, depending on the franchise concept and story line developed by the reporter. Krispy Kreme, Chuck E. Cheese's, and Boston Chicken catapulted into multi-media blitzes that triggered tremendous franchising interest. The press fell in love with the story of California Closets, which ignited the company's growth. It had all the right angles: from the Oprah Winfrey Show to numerous national magazines, founder Neil Balter became a prime-time celebrity as the college kid who transformed his school project of fixing up messy closets into a major industry.

- *Industry speeches and participation* sometimes prompt buying interest from attendees. I was on a speaker panel with the founder of a men's grooming franchise, who was seeking a business for his son. Three months later, his family bought our direct mail franchise. Another franchisor met the chairman of an international multi-franchise company at a prayer breakfast during an IFA conference. Several months later the firm purchased the master rights to develop his U.S. franchise in their country.

- *Charitable and community campaigns* often bring press attention and local appreciation. The Franchise Emergency Action Team (FEAT), started by Dick Rennick, CEO of American Leak Detection, is a national franchise support group that provides on-site assistance to families and businesses victimized by national disasters. Participating in concert with the Federal Emergency Management Agency (FEMA), Dick and other participating franchise networks have been recognized for their tremendous efforts in helping ravaged communities in need. Molly Maid has sponsored counseling programs for battered women. SuperCoups (owned by ADVO), has sponsored its corporate owner's America's Looking for Its Missing Children program for years.

- *Advertorials* are paid advertisements that some media publishers provide. They include editorial and interviews designed to look similar to feature articles. Keep in mind these are not the same as a PR story, since many buyers recognize them as an advertisement, not a third-party endorsement.

Hiring a PR agency

Public relations is a business and a world unto itself, and most franchisors should consider outsourcing their publicity efforts when they can afford it. Good agencies have established ongoing relationships with editors of key media and know how to package and present your franchise with story angles they are seeking. They understand which TV, radio, print, and Internet venues have target audiences you need to reach, and they can create special events and activities that will garner live and positive coverage for your franchise.

Unlike what we may think, public relations is a very tough, fiercely competitive business. Successful PR agencies are professional "boiler room magicians," constantly pitching your franchise to hundreds of media people every month through phone calls, letters, PR kits, email blasts, personal visits, trade show events, lunch meetings, etc. To get the media coverage you expect (or want!), they must be smooth, engaging, creative, persistent, convincing, aggressive, and tough in the trenches.

Selecting the agency that's the right partner for you is similar to choosing an ad agency. Provide a Request for a Proposal (RFP) to a minimum of three firms, outlining your requirements and expectations in employing their services. This is particularly important when contracting a PR agency. Monitoring and measuring the success of their recruitment efforts must be understood and agreed upon up front, otherwise your relationship can erode quickly. For me it's quite simple: if PR produces or contributes to additional franchise sales, it works. Building brand, image, and market awareness are certainly great benefits. But for companies seeking aggressive growth, generating additional franchisees is what great public relations is all about.

Contact small and larger franchisors with good press coverage for their advice when considering potential PR agency partners. Focus on those that may be similar to you in size and ask about their experiences, both positive and negative. What factors do they believe are key in selecting the right PR firm?

Should only local PR agencies be considered?

Absolutely not, unless you are interested only in local market coverage. National PR has no geographic boundaries that will limit the performance of your agency. I once found out the hard way, selecting an area-based firm in the belief their local expertise would compensate for their less-impressive track record when compared with an out-of-state agency. And the convenience was great: at a moment's notice their account executive was at our doorstep. Unfortunately, we had to fire the company after nine months. They couldn't deliver the bigger stories in the bigger media!

Preparing your proposal

Your RFP should provide performance requirements for 1) "recruitment PR" that will build more franchise sales, and 2) "retail PR" that will build greater branding and sales at the franchise unit level. Provide agencies with your promotional, sales, retail, and other material that will give them a sense of your business. The sample proposal on the next page may help in preparing your RFP.

Generating your own press

As a bootstrap franchisor, there certainly are ways you can gain public attention through your own personal efforts. Ask some franchise PR firms for general advice on how to stir up some publicity on your "franks 'n' beans" budget. They can often help out with suggestions. Their valuable direction may help accelerate your initial PR successes and avoid costly mistakes, so you can use their services in the not-too-distant future! Let's take a look at three franchisors who triggered extraordinary media attention through their personal PR efforts.

1. Margaret McEntire, founder of Candy Bouquet International, is a walking news story. She had the instinct, business savvy, and selling skills to crack into the news scene through her engaging, entrepreneurial determination. The media loved her spirit, the values she instilled, her rags-to-riches journey, and the international franchise business she had created from her garage—and which, by the way, had failed the first two times!

PR: Sample Request for Proposal

Dear Mr. Mulligan:

Our Domidums Are Fun Factory is currently accepting proposals for public relations services. We are actively seeking a professional team who can develop and launch our new PR campaign this coming January. Our company is a specialty game franchise with 99 locations nationwide. Our national franchise support center is based in Tampa, Florida.

Enclosed are samples of materials for both our franchise recruitment program and our retail stores. Check out our website at www.domidumsforever7.biz. We have also included our FDD and a fact sheet about our company.

All interested firms must respond with your Proposals by December 8, 2008 to Groucho Harper, Marketing Director. Your proposal must recognize the following requirements and requests:

- The fee structure should be based on a retainer plus expenses (please identify what your additional expenses would include).
- The public relations activities proposed should support our franchise sales efforts, as well as our retail locations and promotions.
- Please include any franchise experience, client lists, and samples from your firm.
- Do you have PR experience within our industry? If yes, what results and insights can you share with us?
- Explain any quantifiable results obtained for franchise or other retail clients as a result of your placements and programs.
- Include a projected timeline that shows when we should expect to see results once we hire your firm.
- What is the structure of your firm? How many people are on staff? Who would be the key contact representing our account? What is their experience and role within your organization? What other accounts would this person be handling? Who would be assisting their efforts in working with us?
- How would you propose to service our account and how much time would be dedicated to us?
- Why should we choose your firm?
- What are the two greatest strengths your firm is known for?
- How do you recommend we measure the success of a PR firm's efforts?
- What reporting and communication system will you use in working with our staff to ensure a responsive, successful relationship? Please elaborate with specifics.
- What is one idea you would implement for our company right away?

Thank you for your time in reviewing this request. On December 15, we will contact you concerning your RFP. The two public relations firms we believe can best accommodate our needs will be invited to our Tampa offices to deliver a one-hour presentation to our executive team, which includes our vice presidents of franchise sales and operations. If you should need additional information, please contact me at 800-123-4FUN x77.

2. Neil Balter, the college kid who started California Closets, hit it big with national news shows from the start. Oprah Winfrey, Good Morning America, radio interviews... you name it, he was in demand. He was a publicity event in the making, the engaging and inspiring story of a student who had created an entire industry based on his senior class project.

3. Dale Young, founder of the Perma-Glaze franchise, definitely used his creativity to foster media attention. Refinishing bathtubs is not the sexiest news item of the day. But this didn't stop Dale from personally taking on the challenge. He created a riveting visual for the media that would arrest any reader's attention—which is what reporters thrive on. For his "dream photo," he donned his classic tuxedo and strutted into his warehouse surrounded by hundreds of refinished bathtubs. Elegantly poised in an antique beauty with engraved claw feet, he raised his crystal champagne glass to the skies, as a photographer shot the scene from 40 feet above. The franchise media went nuts! Full-page four-color stories, brand recognition, franchise calls, and industry buzz abounded. This picture was worth more than a thousand words. The image was dazzling, and it showcased the value of his Perma-Glaze franchise service: transforming worn-out, ugly bathrooms from embarrassment to beauty that every homeowner can appreciate.

PR tips for do-it-yourselfers

If you aren't ready, willing, or able to afford an outside PR firm, a common situation among start-up franchise companies, don't despair. There is plenty you can do to get the word out on your franchise opportunity. Here are some of the tricks of the trade:

- *Wait until you are ready*—Sometimes opportunities come faster than expected, before you really have your act together. It's tough to resist the exposure, but your wisest decision may be to pass at the time. If you are a young franchisor and don't yet have a successful franchisee, readers won't get that excited about your opportunity. It's still just a concept without any franchisees who can rave about your business. You must have testimonials to profit from press. It's critical to wait until you have an inspiring message to deliver. Once that city paper or TV station runs your first story, it will probably be a year or two before you can get their attention again.

- ***Develop a newsworthy angle***—It's not what you think is a great story, it's what the media considers newsworthy! What is it that they want? Study each media source carefully. What kinds of stories do they like to write? What regular sections and columns may be the best opportunities for approaches you can develop? Read the press religiously. You may have a franchisee who's an avid hang glider and you discover the local Business Journal features business owners with unusual interests. Maybe your franchisee of the year was a U.S. Army general and a franchise magazine is seeking military vets who made it big in franchising. Or perhaps your industry publication is spotlighting "innovative start-ups" and your company is the first to franchise a segment of the business.

- ***Never say another publication is running your story***—Old news is no news, and editors are easily irritated by that comment. Be careful. *"Just because another media outlet picked up on your press release, how does that have any relevance for us?"* What you may think will get you into the news, in this case may do the reverse. Remember, writers and reporters love to "scoop" a story before their competition does.

- ***Order editorial calendars***—Get a schedule of feature stories planned for the next year. The media publishes them 6 to 12 months in advance, so get the lineups now and you'll increase your press potential by 30 to 50 percent. How often have you read an article or watched a local news broadcast that was a perfect fit for your franchise? Most franchisors miss out on these great press opportunities because they don't prepare. Knowing what's coming down the media road is like securing real estate sites in new shopping centers... the prime-time locations are locked up long before the "For lease" sign is planted in the ground.

- ***Follow their rules***—Ask each media source or outlet for tips on how they prefer your press releases; who to send them to; and in what format they would like to receive them. Sometimes these instructions are published on their website or provided through recorded instructions for you to follow.

    During the 1970s, I was a part-time press aide for Joe Garrubo. The New Jersey Assemblyman paid a former Associated Press reporter, who was a master of news coverage, to train me. He taught me the ins and outs of getting Joe into the media, including into the powerful statewide newspaper, *The Star-Ledger*. We met with the paper's satellite reporters at the state capitol in Trenton, rather than at their Newark headquarters. The reporters showed me exactly how to prepare my submissions: write a top sheet with a paragraph summarizing the attached press release, and highlight in the upper right-hand corner the legislative bill the story was about. *"You need to submit releases to Trenton on Wednesdays, because it's our slowest day so you get the most attention. Also, never send anything again to the Newark offices. Too much red tape, too much competition for space."* My news mentor also taught me how to get TV coverage, which paid off later with a three-minute piece featuring Garrubo on the ABC evening news.

Each media company has its own sacred system for identifying and selecting editorial candidates they deem newsworthy for their readership. Learn how to cater to their process and you can score more with press opportunities.

- *Submit powerful photos*—The media are always searching for dramatic and interesting professional photos that will grab their audience. They are selling their viewers with each story they present, and visuals can greatly enhance a story. Invest money to create powerful photos and you can blow away the stack of other press releases. Retail and restaurant businesses have more "glamour appeal" for creating photos with pizzazz. What can service and home-based franchises do?

   As Perma-Glaze's bathtub photo shows us, they can do a lot. American Advertising Distributors was searching for an extraordinary photo that would command front-cover space and a feature story. An industry publication was going to write about advertising franchises and include the most successful owners from several systems. The magazine had not yet selected a cover photo for that issue. American Advertising was determined to trump the competition for the cover and hired a professional photographer to conduct a shoot featuring the successful lifestyle of their top franchisee. Mission accomplished: the magazine published a four-color cover featuring their franchisee Dan Rosen, fishing on his private lake with his beautiful lodge towering in the background. The editor had embraced the "castle that coupons built" theme. The inside story featured more photos of Dan in his chateau. What about the other franchisees in the article? The amateur snapshots of their owners were dwarfed in the feature article.

What benefits were realized from this cover story? Reprints of the feature photo spread were displayed in the company's franchise packages for several years, impressing many franchise prospects. Second, Dan got tremendous mileage in strengthening his market dominance through this national publicity. What's more, he was most grateful for the major recognition and thanked headquarters numerous times for making it happen.

- ***Burn those "grip it and grin" shots***—As a lead generation tool, there is nothing less imaginative and more boring for the public media than flash photos of franchisors and franchisees receiving awards. They are great for in-house newsletters, post-conference publications, and recognition for franchisee achievements in their local hometown papers. But for the professional media, these shots of handshakes are just another pile for their "round file." Their audience, unless they happen to be a relative or friend, could care less.

How to optimize your online press

Press releases can produce franchise publicity and lead generation online. Yet many concepts don't optimize PR opportunities for franchisee recruitment by using search engine tactics to produce coverage on news sites, media e-newsrooms, blogs, and business and social networks. First-page PR positions on Google, Yahoo or MSN can generate franchise prospects for franchisors. And whether you're doing this or not, your competition is.

Press releases may be distributed through wire services that push releases to online media outlets, and/or through services that post releases online through RSS feeds to search engines and news agencies. One service, Franchising.com, embeds inquiry forms into franchise press releases, directly generating online leads for their clients.

One of the critical factors for successful e-releases is your keyword selection and placement within your news story. Print editors personally read your content for relevancy. However, search engines electronically "read" your keywords for relevancy. This means newsworthy stories for the print world must be reworked to include multiple keywords that can increase your placements on search engines, portals, directories, and blogs.

Here are two simple techniques that can help increase your online placements among the millions of franchise prospects who read news on the Internet.

1. ***Headlines:*** Always use your business category and the word "franchise" in your headlines, as in the following headline: "Duckie's Child Learning Franchise Reveals Ground-Breaking Study."

2. *Body Copy:* Lace your story with popular search words and phrases for your franchise business, as well as for general searches of franchise opportunities. As you know, there are endless combinations, so pick the most popular in describing your concept. In addition to its name, Duckie's Child Learning could optimize their online press by selecting from among these keywords:

Business opportunities	Childs learning franchise
Business opportunity	Child's learning franchises
Business ownership	Child franchise locations
	Childs franchise locations
Childrens franchise	Child's franchise locations
Childrens franchises	
Children's franchise	Franchise
Children's franchises	Franchises
Child/kid franchise	Franchising
Child/kid franchises	Franchise business
Childs/kids franchise	Franchise businesses
Childs/kids franchises	Franchising business
Child's/kid's franchise	Franchising businesses
Child's/kid's franchises	Franchise opportunity
Child development franchise	Franchise opportunities
Child development franchises	Franchising opportunity
Child's education franchise	Franchising opportunities

4 The Four Steps to Lead Generation Success: Step Four–Measure results to improve performance

Audit your advertising and increase results

What you don't know, you can't measure. And what you can't measure, you can't improve! Successful recruitment programs invest in marketing intelligence and monitoring tools to 1) determine their most productive selling sources; 2) create compelling, direct-response advertising for each media source selected; and 3) stay ahead of or in step with the competition.

Good news for you smart execs! More than one third of franchise companies still don't track their marketing performance—which provides competitive advantages for those intelligent franchisors who do successfully monitor, measure, and modify their lead generation programs. By knowing where you are and where you want to go, you build the shortest road to get there. Not so for the shotgun advertisers who stumble along an aimless, winding path wasting marketing dollars. They have difficulty setting realistic budgets and franchise goals, and continue to lose opportunities for achieving greater growth.

Not analyzing media results is extremely costly. After monitoring their group newspaper advertising, a multi-brand franchisor discovered they paid one newspaper $30,000 for producing two inquiries over a three-year period. To make matters worse, neither lead was qualified. After an audit, another franchise organization realized the few thousand they thought they were spending in "cheap" secondary publications had become quite expensive, totaling more than $40,000 annually!

Closing performance gaps with the sales department

Recently I reviewed the lead generation performance of a retail food franchisor. We discovered a costly disconnect between marketing administration and the sales team. The company was on a half-dozen online ad sites and had recently dumped the lowest lead producer. In checking sources for each deal they closed that year, wouldn't you know the website they axed was the top sales generator? The problem, of course, was that they were looking only at leads and buying advertising based on their lead activity flow. They made the all-too-common error of equating marketing success with number of leads delivered.

How can franchisors effectively track their leads?

"It's easier than many think," according to Chuck Fuller, former vice president of Interactive Media for Entrepreneur, who says the technology is already in place. Matt Alden, managing partner of Kiekenapp & Associates, advises franchisors to ask the prospect to identify the lead source as they are responding. Find out while it's fresh in their mind, whether they found you through a website, another advertising medium, or both.

- Include *"How did you come to our website?"* on your online response form, and provide a drop-down screen or check-off boxes listing all the recruitment sources you use for online, print, shows, referrals, PR, and other venues.

- You can measure your click-through traffic from other sites and search engines by instructing your web host to set up special address links for each of these locations and providing you with summary reports.

- Use a franchise lead management system to organize your lead activity, and to identify candidates who progress through the various stages of your sales process to the final close.

Emotional buys are no longer affordable

Recruitment advertising has one primary mission: generate qualified prospects for franchise ownership. Branding, image, or any other marketing objective really have no value if your advertising isn't generating responses. Only results count. However, some companies that recognize this still hesitate to aggressively address their lead challenges.

A franchisor in the Southwest was spending $50,000 a year in an industry publication because they believed it should work and that they should have a "presence." Another service franchise invested $100,000 annually with a major ad source that used to produce qualified buyers. Even though their sales steadily dropped and the medium was no longer effective, the franchisor felt guilty about breaking the long-term relationship and continued to advertise.

Is it your marketing that's not working?

Sometimes an advertising source takes the fall for underlying weaknesses stalling franchise development. I have seen one franchisor sell qualified franchisees through brokers, while a direct competitor failed miserably; a service franchisor dump a print publication claiming "poor and unqualified leads," yet two similar companies ranked it as their leading sales source; one franchise executive get caught hiding international leads in his drawer, after the media source furnished duplicates to his suspecting management; and a franchisor stop advertising because none of the inquiring prospects responded to his five-page, photocopied follow-up letter plagued by misspellings and bad grammar. The lesson in these extreme examples is to monitor performance in all areas of your recruitment program.

Start now and profit

Enjoy added recruitment rewards by aggressively auditing your advertising this year. If you are in the group of franchisors who don't know their specific lead and sales costs by media, or that haven't analyzed the effectiveness of their marketing program, now is the time. The payoff in reduced costs, greater lead activity, and sales can be significant.

Ready, set, grow!

✓ Embrace the four successful lead generation principles that high-growth franchisors use to expand their brands:

    1. Define your market of qualified prospects.
    2. Create your message that motivates buyer response.
    3. Determine the lead sources that reach your buyers.
    4. Measure results to improve performance.

These are the steps to achieving marketing success. Stray from this formula and your lead generation will suffer.

✓ People buy opportunities, not businesses. They are motivated largely by what the franchise can help them achieve, not what the franchise does. Ownership advantages, lifestyle benefits, and self-fulfillment drive decisions that buyers make in selecting the franchise program that suits them. Don't second-guess the answers: interview existing and new franchisees, as well as new prospects, and you'll strengthen your recruitment approach.

✓ The five cornerstones of a franchise recruiting message are instrumental in attracting your ideal prospects:

    1. What is your opportunity?
    2. Is there a market for your concept?
    3. What are the ownership benefits?
    4. Is your company credible?
    5. How can I qualify?

Carefully craft the answers to trigger your buyers' hot buttons, and the quality and quantity of your prospects can multiply. Invest the time, research, and energy to get it right. It's the fuel that will drive your marketing campaigns.

✓ The quality of your marketing material reflects who you are. Your presentation must win first or second position with your qualified prospect, whether it's your recruitment website, at a trade show booth, or in your franchise brochure arriving at their doorstep. Competition can be fierce, and only the best prepared are in the running.

✓ Recruitment advertising is the direct response business. You'll achieve greater success by employing the principles of buyer motivation and testing and measuring ad results. Quality lead generation is all that counts. Find out what works best by changing ad approaches, running different headlines, and experimenting with your visuals. You can improve your lead performance by leveraging today's online technology, which allows you to monitor prospect activity on website pages and banners, and track the percentage of visitors who convert into leads.

✓ Build an intelligent lead generation budget based on your lead and sales performance history. If you know your acquisition cost per sale, and which lead generation sources are producing these buyers and for how much, then budgeting is a simple matter of metrics. The problem for many franchisors is that multi-tracking of sales sources does require technology and management diligence. According to Franchise Update's Annual Franchise Development Report, 43 percent of franchisors still don't track their sales costs, and even more don't track their sales cost per media source. Those of you who do measure performance are saving money, increasing sales, and beating up on your competitors who don't.

✓ Grassroots marketing works in recruiting franchisees. For start-up and bootstrap franchisors with minimal recruitment budgets, it's the only way to grow. For mature franchisors targeting unsold local territories, it's the only way to complete their growth. It's the bread and butter of successful area developers and master franchisees. But it does require more planning, personal involvement, and time commitment. An aggressive franchisee and customer referral program can produce 30 percent or more new franchise owners.

✓ The three keys for e-recruitment success are:

1. Build a response-driven website
2. Market your website effectively
3. Convert inquiries into sales

In today's environment, the Internet strongly influences how franchise prospects research and respond to franchise opportunities. Consequently, the marketing function has expanded dramatically. Marketing execs have to attract prospective candidates, trigger responses, and provide systematic follow-up and analysis to support the efforts of the sales staff.

✓ Buying advertising is a systematic process. All media purchases require frequency to test their success. No two lead generation plans are the same, so copying competitors is not the answer. Monitor ad results at least quarterly. Dump the losers, boost the winners, and test additional options. Never use one lead generation source, however tempting. If it unexpectedly turns sour you're out of the recruitment business.

✓ Media monitoring is a multi-sourcing task. Document all the marketing venues that push a buyer to your concept. Continually ask, *"What source(s) prompted you to find out about our franchise opportunity?"* on your initial inquiry forms, applications, at Discovery Day, and in training class. Credit four lead sources if a new franchisee initially saw your magazine ad, attended a trade show, read a success story about a franchisee, and then inquired online. Remember, the Internet is often the transmitter, not the originator, of a prospect inquiry.

Chapter 5

Success Driver V:
High-Performance Sales Program

The best close starts with the opening…

take the lead or your buyer will.

Success Driver V:
High-Performance Sales Program

Our business of franchising starts with selling franchisees. You can prepare your Franchise Disclosure Document (FDD), operations and marketing manuals, professional décor, and logo design packages all to perfection, but the cold truth is: *"Nothing happens until somebody sells something!"* Franchise recruitment is what makes sales happen, fueling the engine that transforms our franchise concepts from dreams to reality.

Franchise development has skyrocketed in recent years. According to the International Franchise Association, 1 million franchises now populate the U.S. landscape, with a new one opening every 8 minutes. Franchising is the world's most successful growth model for small business expansion, and new unit development is the catalyst for system growth. And with nearly all of today's 2,900 franchise companies seeking additional market expansion, adding new units is essential to achieving their goals.

Welcome to the world of franchise recruitment

Franchise selling is serious business in the franchise world. Young franchisors have bet the ranch on building their empires, spending a lot of up-front money preparing their franchise opportunities for launch. I recently read an overly anxious franchisor's email: he wanted to jump-start his development by raffling off a free franchise in each of his planned markets. Wow! This is extreme, but it does reinforce the franchisor's need to get franchises up and running in their marketplace or risk failure.

The job of recruiting franchisees lies in the abilities and leadership of the franchise development department. When sales are up, everyone celebrates and shares the fame. When recruitment is down, heads roll and the development team takes the blame. And they should, when you consider the high incomes development professionals command. Franchise selling is a science and an art, not easily learned or mastered. The sales department is highly accountable for the future growth of the company, carrying an enormous responsibility for the organization's success.

Be prepared for a surprising transition

Franchise recruitment is unusually specialized, employing principles and techniques foreign to most other business development strategies. The process itself is counter-intuitive, not adhering to selling fundamentals we have successfully practiced in prior lives. Naive newcomers to franchising are blindsided and bewildered by this rude awakening, unprepared for the challenges of franchise sales. Woefully, fledgling franchisors are shell-shocked when so many "interested" candidates don't buy their franchises. And they don't have a clue why, nor know how to fix the problem. I'll never forget a frustrated start-up franchisor who was at his wit's end:

"Joe was ecstatic about my opportunity. I spent three intense hours with him in my office, showed him everything about my business, answered all of his questions, and gave him my franchise disclosures. Man, was he excited! I was sure he was going to come aboard as my first franchisee. Joe just needed to go over our meeting with his wife, and then run the documents past his accountant. Why didn't I hear from him again? I can't believe it! He disappeared from the face of the earth, never returning my phone calls."

Successful corporations have stumbled

Large corporations have tripped and fallen just as hard when they have franchised their products and services. They contract a franchise law firm to prepare their legal documents, and frequently turn to their business development division to implement their franchise marketing and sales program. Not understanding that corporate and franchise sales are universes apart, disaster can strike... except at savvy corporations that employ franchise sales consultants from the start.

I saw ignorance hit hard when a major U.S. service company with more than 75 years in business fell victim to buyers snubbing its new franchise opportunity. The rejection had nothing to do with their business. All of America knew their powerful brand and respected their enormous history of success. People banged down their door to find out about the new franchise, but only a few bought. The rejection had everything to do with their horrible franchise process! When prospects initially requested general information, sales materials—including the FDD—were mailed to them, sometimes without even a phone call.

Steer clear of the big guns

Here's a quick tip to the thousands of young "no name" franchisors: don't get lured into hiring consultants or former executives who have worked only with large, mature franchise brands. Unless they have worked with start-ups, they probably can't help you. The McDonald's, Subways, KFCs, and Dunkin' Donuts are in a different development world, experienced at addressing recruitment challenges that don't relate to your growth needs. Their name recognition is so powerful they're approached constantly by thousands of brand fans seeking their opportunities. Unlike you, they don't beat every bush just to get a few good prospects to listen to their story. Big brands are in the business of greater market penetration, non-traditional franchising opportunities, resales, and carefully screening and rejecting masses of inquiries to grant franchises only to candidates with the "right stuff." Basic concept repositioning, mass lead generation, and opening multiple new markets are no longer primary. Emerging franchisors should seek franchise development pros who know how to ramp up systems that can't play off national branding.

Recently I met with three executives from "household name" companies. We discussed revitalizing development for a new franchise company that demanded immediate attention. I quickly realized we were born in two different worlds. They applied performance objectives not achievable by 99 percent of franchise companies. They were seasoned experts in organizational management, operations, brand building, and business modeling. But these execs were clueless about the realities of ramping up start-ups and young franchise organizations. I still chuckle about a sacred moment at a sales and marketing conference in Chicago, when an attorney from one of the national burger franchises was delivering his keynote address on franchise selling. The audience shook their heads in total bewilderment, the overwhelming majority unable to relate to the much-larger world of the well-established food giant.

What franchise recruitment is not

So what is so tricky about franchise selling? Are most young franchisors stupid? Of course not. They simply don't realize the peculiarities of effective franchise recruitment. This isn't anything like selling cars, real estate, insurance, technology, or advertising, and it's a 90-degree turn from selling employment opportunities. Convincing families you just met to invest $50,000 to $1 million or more in your franchise requires special training, terrific people skills, perception, and professional dedication to your practice. You are creating new worlds of hope for aspiring entrepreneurs, who often commit everything they own into your franchise opportunity. To this day, I constantly remind myself of the paramount role franchise development executives play in helping entrepreneurs achieve the American Dream of business ownership.

Who will sell your franchise program?

There's good news, so if you're a fledgling franchisor reading this chapter, don't panic. You have several options for orchestrating a high-performance franchise sales program. I don't promote one avenue over another, because there simply is no single "best way" for all concepts. The type of business, franchise program, corporate resources, leadership philosophies, and other personal and company-specific circumstances will influence which road to take. Here are your choices:

- *Do it yourself*—For start-up companies, founders often are the best sales person for their concept. Their personal success stories, burning passion, and visionary leadership can excite potential owners to want to be part of their ground-floor opportunity. Recruiting the first franchisees also is a valuable learning experience for the founder and certainly keeps overhead down. But this is obviously a temporary role. As the company grows, founders must shift their focus to organizational and strategic demands that will require more of their time-pressed attention.

- *Hire an employee*—Through industry referrals or franchise headhunters, there is some great talent available. Depending on your needs, concept, and budget, there are three tiers of franchise talent available at corresponding salary ranges. Sometimes potential talent may be right in front of you, in an existing employee who may possess skill sets that can grow into this role through professional coaching and attending industry sales training programs.

- *Outsource to a sales professional*—"Hired guns" frequently can get you off the ground much faster than doing it yourself. There are, on occasion, freelance sales pros who take on a few franchise clients and represent them on a temporary or long-term basis. This immediately provides you with a seasoned, talented individual who should produce sales for you once they build a pipeline of prospects. You also retain the flexibility to eventually bring sales in-house should circumstances change.

- *Outsource your sales department*—Specialty franchise sales organizations can take over your recruitment program, doing everything from developing your sales materials and lead generation plan to closing deals. The better firms are highly selective, so don't be surprised if you don't happen to qualify for their services. Your concept must "have legs," a good support team, and a high level of franchisee satisfaction. Your recruitment budgets and goals must be reasonable, and your management team committed to supporting their sales efforts. Sounds like a tall order, but with the right representation, these professional firms could catapult your franchise into the industry spotlight.

- *Contract franchise sales brokers*—Franchise brokers or "consultants" have successfully spurred dramatic franchise growth for both new and mature concepts. These firms generate and screen qualified prospects, educate them about franchise ownership, and introduce them to your concept. If needed, many brokers will help improve your sales process so you'll be more successful in closing deals. You pay a fee only when you sell one of their client candidates. A quite hefty amount I may add, but it could be worthwhile since you risk no money up front. No deals? Then you don't pay a nickel. *(For in-depth-information, see "Selling deals through franchise brokers," later in this chapter.)*

1. Quick-Start Training for New Franchisors and Sales People

You'll recruit new franchisees much faster if you initially understand, prepare, and learn the best methods for selling franchises. Working smarter shortens the race to the finish line! Here are some triggers that will help accelerate your pace.

Learn the three key selling skills. Effectively selling franchises demands *1) following a successful sales process; 2) strong relationship-building skills; and 3) effective closing skills.*

1. The first key requires your commitment to *follow a successful sales process*. This can be extremely mind-bending for some franchisors,

since the franchise recruitment process is an odd duck with its own rules. Some of you may require the "detox chamber" before you get it right. Don't feel bad, because franchise sales pros initially suffered through these same challenges. The key is going in with your eyes open, knowing that if you aren't coachable and willing to change habits you'll drown. Many development consultants concur that only one in four new franchise salespeople will be successful recruiters. Often the challenge isn't a question of intelligence. It's the inability to adapt, the regression to old sales techniques that don't work, and second-guessing and short-circuiting the principles of the franchise process.

If you don't have an effective sales process now, get one in place ASAP before you lose more qualified buyers. Employ a sales consultant, attend franchise development workshops, and/or implement the time-tested sales process revealed in this chapter. Sixty percent of your success is the process, 40 percent is the execution. A CEO contracted me to retrain a former auto sales whiz who was striking out awarding his franchises. First I reviewed the steps of his recruitment process, which had delivered quality operators until the new sales guy took over. The system in place was effective; the problem was his new sales person. I recommended three times that the CEO fire him, before he finally did. We spent hours training this rep, shopped his presentations, and gave him how-to solutions with homework to correct his mistakes. He simply couldn't shake his former selling techniques. I sent him to "reform school" a few times to see if he could change. He was a personable, persuasive guy. But he was slave to his old habits. The new twist to franchise selling was too painful and too far from his comfort zone. The CEO finally kicked him out and sales took off once again.

2. The second key to recruitment selling is ***strong relationship-building skills***. Franchising is a family, a partnership, a journey, and an experience that changes the lives of the people you bring into your system. Successful sales execs are genuinely sincere, interested, and engulfed in their prospects' worlds. They relish their role in counseling candidates and opening doors of opportunity that can help them realize their goals. They have deeper insights and sensitivities to a buyer's personality, motivations, hesitance, and family situation. Buyers quickly see this personal dedication. I once had the pleasure of hiring John, a sales executive who is truly a master in connecting with his franchise

candidates. They often raved about him and wrote letters about his valuable counseling and friendship in guiding their decision-making process. One of his fans was visibly upset at a Discovery Day because John was unable to be there. *"We were so thrilled, thinking we would finally meet John. You can't believe how he helped us with his coaching and caring about our future. It's such a disappointment he couldn't make it."* Fortunately the couple did sign, although there was a fleeting moment I thought John's absence would jeopardize closing the candidate.

Relationship-building can't be emphasized enough in franchise recruitment. Perhaps money-driven "sales predators" can initially manipulate a buyer with a powerful recruitment process, but their insincerity eventually gets the best of them. I asked a new retail food franchisee why he didn't select another concept he had seriously considered. *"I realized they were more interested in my franchise fee than in me. Their franchise exec was a 'shmoozer,' mouthing all the buzzwords and ignoring my feelings. He didn't care about me. He was interested in getting his commission. I loved their concept, but I wasn't comfortable about their motives."*

This reminds me of an experience in my 20s, when I worked for the Prudential Insurance Company. I asked a Prudential sales person to show me life insurance options for my young family. Wouldn't you think I was a slam dunk sale? The agent was late for the appointment, talked at me, never took the time to listen, and got huffy when I didn't write him a check. Two weeks later, I purchased from a professional agent from a competitive company who showed interest in the welfare of my family. He asked a series of questions and explored several options before making his recommendations. I never felt I was being sold and actually felt good buying from him. Ironically enough, Prudential conducted a consumer survey that addressed my buying experience. One question was *"What has been the greatest factor influencing you in purchasing your insurance policies? The company name, product, or the sales person?"* The sales person won first, then the product, with the company name last. So it is in franchise recruitment: If you can't get close to your buyer, you can't close the buyer!

3. The third key in franchise selling is ***effective closing skills***. In working with a quality candidate, your franchise recruitment builds to a crescendo signaling the final step in the process—when the buyer must

make the life-changing move, cash out bank accounts, and leap into your franchise world placing total faith and trust in your hands. "Closing the close" is an art and a science. It requires confidence, leadership, and a clear perception of who that franchise buyer is and what they are thinking. It's knowing what behavior and influences will comfortably steer the candidate to, rather than away, from your franchise. The closing event distinguishes the masters of franchise recruitment from the ordinary. Pros "ink more deals" because they can adeptly uncover and overcome the hidden objection, unmask unwarranted fears, and reaffirm the decisive steps that initially led the buyer to choose your franchise opportunity.

Frequently, franchise sales people struggle at the final close. They dance through the first four to five weeks and crumble when it comes to check-asking and check-cashing time! These are what I call the "professional visitors." They know how to follow the process and they do boast strong people skills; they are likeable, responsive, and empathetic. But they just can't get the contract signed. They make excuses for their candidates, unknowingly making excuses for themselves. It could be one or more of many reasons: their own insecurity, a lack of belief in the franchise concept, an inability to read their candidates and provide assurances, thinking "commission" rather than "right fit" for the buyer, or straying from a proven closing process. Now don't get me wrong, even the best of the best sales pros loses a few deals now and then. But not very often!

- *Visit with franchise owners.* Franchisees are a wealth of information, stories, encouragement, tips, and experiences for the new sales person. I was a successful franchise owner before I sold franchises. But I had no clue what to do in marketing a franchise opportunity. However, I did know firsthand what it took to run a rewarding franchise business, which was a great introduction to recruitment selling. I shared with prospective owners the joys and frustrations of building our franchise business into the top franchise in the system, and I replayed success stories of other prosperous owners. Buyers always were most interested in what franchise operators were doing, how they were doing it, and what the challenges were. Today, I still share how my direct mail business profited from the power of the franchise network: *"We failed miserably trying to develop a successful marketing program for builders.*

Hearing this, our headquarters referred us to franchisee Dave Evans in Atlanta who had cracked the code for success. Dave shared all the details of his program with me. The next year my partner and I wrote $80,000 in additional revenue, and more thereafter!" This valuable information put significant cash in our pockets. And this wasn't the only time we profited from consulting with other franchisees. (Thanks again Dave— Frank and I are still indebted to you!)

Most franchise sales people are not former franchisees. But calling, visiting, interviewing, and soaking up as much of their world as possible can pay off handsomely with your franchise buyers. They want you to paint a picture of people like themselves who are successful in your business. Leverage these personal experiences of your franchise owners from the start. If prospect Joe is a sales engineer and your franchisee Bill once was, talk about Bill and how he just opened his third location. If prospect Mary has a concern about the competitive environment in Chicago, share how franchisee Julie took customers away from the competition through her grand opening and introduction of your superior products.

There's nothing more powerful with prospects than case studies and anecdotes. Remember, franchise buyers are investing their savings to achieve their entrepreneurial goals and dreams. Providing real success stories from owners transforms their dreams into reality. Have a new sales person visit with franchisees and pick their brains, asking why they joined the system, what ownership benefits they are enjoying, as well as what challenges they're facing and how they are addressing them. Owners welcome your interest in their business lives and can share feedback worth its weight in recruitment gold.

- *Shop the competition.* As in any business, if you don't know what your competitors are doing, you'll flounder in ignorance. Contacting direct and indirect competition is smart business, and quickly provides marketing intelligence you can apply in strengthening your sales presentations. For instance, emphasize your outstanding training programs if you discover other franchises can't match the extensive training and technology support you deliver.

  Collect FDDs, recruitment packages, and learn from a competitor's sales presentations and techniques. Observe what they do well and where their weaknesses are. Don't worry about researching this public information, because smart franchisors do the same to stay on top of their game. But don't even think about going beyond this point. Some overly aggressive franchisors have crossed the ethical line in past years. Never, ever, attend a Discovery Day under the guise of a prospective buyer. This is clearly a violation of business ethics and could be cause for legal action.

Shopping a competitive sales exec, Hal, paid off big-time for me when I was recruiting franchises for American Advertising Distributors. When I had a prospect who wanted to take a look at our competition, I graciously referred candidates to him. You see, I discovered Hal was my best sales person. He was a nice, older gentleman, but hard-of-hearing and yelled when he spoke to me as a potential buyer. It was obvious Hal struggled to close any deals. He really appreciated the prospects I sent him for comparison shopping. I really appreciated that he helped close more deals for me. I finally got together with Hal at an industry event and treated him to a night of drinks, which we both really enjoyed together. I was crushed when I heard he retired.

- **Role-play for refinement.** Most sales people dislike role-playing. It puts them under the microscope, with someone (or a group of "someones") critiquing each presentation point, eye twitch, and probing question they make. It's not fun. But it's an accelerated learning technique that forces them to better prepare, practice, and present your great franchise opportunity. Once you have a sales process in place, recruit a staff member to role-play with your sales reps, so they can sharpen their delivery and get it right. These mistakes don't cost you anything. Contacting prospects without role-playing may cost you a franchise sale and its 10-year royalty stream.

- **Shop yourself to get it right.** Ralph Ross, founder of American National Fidelity Group, was a master of franchise selling. He taught me the self-learning process of recording your sales calls so you can listen to the playback and perfect each step of your sales presentation. If you haven't tried this, do it because it works! It's a Berlitz-type technique for faster learning. Ralph instructed me: *"Tape your sales calls on a microcassette during the next week. When you feel comfortable with your performance, give me your two best copies."* After reviewing the material, the founder would call me into his office, where we replayed notated segments. He praised me where I did well and offered guidance in areas I needed shaping up.

What you discover when you shop yourself is that mistakes leap out at you that you instantly correct, such as talking too much and not listening enough; not probing with open-ended questions; repeating yourself; allowing your prospect to take control; forgetting key benefits; pushing rather than leading the candidate; or not closing the call effectively. I strongly recommend that both new and experienced franchise sales people use this taping technique to self-monitor. It's self-improvement on steroids.

- **Get shopped to get it better.** The final tune-up is to have third-party mystery shoppers contact your sales people (or you) so you can evaluate their recruitment approach, relationship-building skills, closing techniques, and overall effectiveness in moving them through your recruitment process. High-performance franchise companies contract outside services to periodically shop their sales personnel. Let them know from the start that you are doing this and investing the money to help the team grow and increase their sales results. It's amazing how sales people immediately brush up their prospect presentations and lead follow-up when you implement a shopping program.

  When I conducted a mystery shop for a franchise, I had my client tell the sales team to get ready because the program was starting that week. But actually it wouldn't begin for another three weeks. Why would I do that? Because this prompts the reps to immediately sharpen their presentation, thinking they will be contacted soon. It also catches them off guard when they eventually are contacted and evaluated. Interestingly, some sales people will tell you they were shopped before it happens! Random timing gives you a more accurate picture of a sales person's ongoing performance. It provides a sensitivity to delivering consistency and maintaining a higher level of professionalism. It also serves as documentation when you need to terminate a sales person who isn't coachable or performing to your standards. For those interested in this, shopping services are available through some franchise development firms (find out more at www.franchiseupdate.com/gtg).

  To take performance training to a new level, some franchise sales managers are implementing phone technology that allows them to listen in on their sales personnel's calls. It measures the call time, records the conversations, and includes a "whisper feature" that allows you to coach the sales rep during the presentation without the buyer hearing. Some industries have been using this tool for several years to monitor customer service and quality control.

- **_Learn one step at a time._** When you establish a new sales process, don't try to learn it all at once. Focus only on the first step until you get it right; then on the second and successive steps. Franchise selling takes time, practice, and feedback to master the details, variables, and nuances within each stage of the process. There are no shortcuts; if you try, you'll fail and pay for it big-time. Only after you have successfully learned to pre-qualify inquiries and book them for scheduled follow-up appointments should you dive into total preparation for the second stage of the process. This sequential learning will accelerate your command of the selling system. Some call this the "Swiss cheese method" of poking holes one at a time, rather than trying to swallow a huge chunk all at once.

  As you encounter the different buyer styles, motivations, and personalities, you will learn to more effectively evolve, organize, and structure your presentations. Without a doubt, start-up franchisors will save significant expenditures of time and money by attending professional sales workshops and/or hiring reputable sales development consultants to get them on track from the start.

- **_Contact the worst leads first._** First impressions are everything in franchise recruitment. If a qualified prospect who is ready to buy has contacted two other concepts and wants to know about yours, you'd better have your act together. I was working with a young food franchisor who immediately tried selling some of his good customers interested in owning his franchised business. What a disaster! The founder was like a shotgun, spraying information into these prospects' faces for hours. He was very excited to tell his story, but had no system in place to recruit these hot prospects effectively. I said, _"Tell me about these people, their financial situation, skill sets, expectations, and goals, and how they will operate the business."_ Silence reigned. He didn't have the answers and didn't recruit any of these initial customer referrals.

  If you are a first-time franchise recruiter, practice on your weakest leads first. Use these "throwaway" prospects as your training camp.

Work on overcoming objections. Try different ways of presenting your benefits. Ask the key questions and discover how to engage these leads through controlled, yet open conversations. When you gain confidence and get into a comfortable rhythm, it's time for Game Day. Be prepared before you take on the quality candidates. You want to have all the moves in place that will win them over to your franchise opportunity.

2. Implement a Compelling Sales Process: The Six Steps to Selling Success

The foundation of your successful selling program starts with your sales process. It's the anchor to embracing, guiding, and closing quality candidates who will help you build your system. It's the tightly honed script that ensures successful production from initial contact to closing. It's the Broadway hit performance that every night leads audiences from opening curtain to standing ovations; the World Series champions who mastered the execution of their game plan. Franchise development is no different: follow the plan, the plan works. This is the playbook to success for top-performing recruitment programs.

Every sales process must be refined to work most effectively for each franchisor's concept, franchise program, and franchise candidates. Establishing your sales process is an evolution that recognizes the changing marketplace, competition, buyer motivations, and current strengths and challenges within your franchise. For example, a company plagued by litigation two years ago should consider presenting their FDD later, rather than earlier in their sales process. This allows them to first focus on building relationships, credibility, and trust with candidates. The positive validation from current successful franchisees reinforces the strength of the franchise opportunity. Once that is established, the FDD can be addressed and delivered to the prospect, who is more confident and understanding of the company's former issues.

The Six Steps to Selling Success is my playbook for fueling high-performance selling. Inherent in every strong development process, this basic framework for recruitment has produced tens of thousands of sales for franchisors over the past two decades. There will be variations tailored to each concept, but the core approach remains the same. It's a quick-learn tutorial that breaks through the complexities of franchise selling. The principles are simple and highly effective. The execution is quite demanding, but when followed correctly can produce rewarding results.

The process incorporates self-qualifying and self-closing principles. The steps are:

The Six Steps to Selling Success	
1. Pre-qualification	Determine who your potential prospects are and sell the application.
2. Program Review	Conduct a program overview and interview to see if there's a mutual match of qualifications, interests, and expectations.
3. Disclosure Review	Educate your prospect about the purpose, benefits, and information in your FDD; clarify and answer questions.
4. Franchisee Validation	Require your candidate to speak with franchisees to gain greater insight and understanding of the opportunity through the owners' personal experiences.
5. Discovery Day	Attend Discovery Day at your headquarters for executive approval of the franchise.
6. Awarding the Franchise	Grant the franchise to qualified buyers based on your pre-determined closing schedule: during or shortly after Discovery Day.

1 The Six Steps to Selling Success:
Step One—Pre-qualification
Objective: Pre-qualify the inquiry and sell the application

Most young franchisors have their sales executive initially screen and pre-qualify prospects. This makes sense during the start-up period when dollars and people are scarce. As soon as feasible, however, I strongly recommend using a qualification specialist to perform the initial follow-up of inquiries. This person can be worth their weight in platinum! Thirty-six percent of franchisors now employ qualifiers, according to Franchise Update's Annual Franchise Development Report (to obtain a copy, go to www.franchiseupdate.com/afdr). You'll save time, money, and increase sales performance.

The qualifier focuses on timely follow-up of every lead, eliminating poor and mismatched inquiries and setting phone appointments for quality prospects to speak with your development professional. This frees your sales executive and staff to focus only on pre-qualified prospects, increases the number of candidates they can handle, and consequently provides greater opportunities to sell more deals. Using a qualifier as the gatekeeper also elevates the credentials and status of the franchise sales exec, who will speak only with individuals who have passed the initial qualification.

The initial conversation with potential prospects is critical. The mission is to pre-qualify, take control, and capture their attention in an engaging 5- to 10-minute conversation. (Anytime you realize an individual isn't qualified for your franchise, let them know. Don't waste their time or yours.)

Your closing objective is to motivate the inquirer to return their written application, the "Request for Consideration" (RFC), in the package they will receive. You must whet their appetite for your opportunity and create a responsive candidate hungry for additional information. Keep this first encounter brief. Too much conversation during your first personal contact leads to information overload and is counterproductive. It lowers the prospect's thirst for gaining more knowledge and often reduces their interest to move forward.

Start by taking or confirming the potential prospect's basic contact information. Screen them with six to eight key questions (see sample script). Present a benefit-loaded description of your business and opportunity. Describe the candidate you are looking for, the type of person who can be successful in your system, and the process for taking the next step. Deflect their detailed questions. These will be answered in the comprehensive information package they can receive by completing your RFC form.

Confirm their continuing desire by closing the discussion with, *"How would you like to proceed at this point?"* or *"Are you ready to take the next step?"* (If they're not interested, let 'em go because chasing is wasting!) For individuals wanting to move forward, instruct them to return, within five days, the RFC you are sending in your franchise ownership package. If the application is not received, wait one day and follow up with a call thanking them for their interest and wishing them the best of success in their future endeavors. Don't worry, those still interested will promptly get back to you, apologize for the delay, and return their completed RFC. Taking the opportunity away sets the stage for your qualification system, which expects serious prospects to respond and follow through with their commitments.

As mentioned, "TMI" (too much information) can be dangerous and counterproductive during the initial personal contact. Keep this step brisk, energetic, and general. If you give too much, you often lose the candidates who jump to a premature decision before seeing the complete picture of your opportunity.

<u>Length of conversation</u>: *5 to 10 minutes*

Sample Pre-Qualification Script

Name _____ Lead Date_____

Address _____

City _____ State _____ Zip_____

Phone _____ Cell_____

E-Mail Address _____

Hello Mr./Ms. _____, I'm Bill. Thank you for contacting us about Bow Wow Juice Bar's ownership opportunities. Juice is hot, and Bow Wow is the fastest-growing beverage bar franchise for dogs in the U.S. Our owners enjoy an easy-to-operate, strong cash flow business in a friendly, dog community café that requires no food preparation or cooking. Before we provide additional information, do you mind if I ask you a few questions?

How did you hear about Bow Wow? _____

What attracted you to respond to us?_____

When are you looking to get into a business? ❑ 1 year ❑ 3 – 6 months ❑ sooner

Why are you looking now? _____

Where would you like to open a business?

1st choice _____2nd choice _____

What is your career background?_____

For our franchise, our average investment is $275,000, which includes working capital. Upon qualification, you'll need a minimum $400,000 net worth with $100,000 in available cash. Do you have this? _____

CALL CLOSING

(If initially qualified)
It's been great talking with you. The next step is to review our franchise package, which you will receive by mail within the next two days. If you haven't, also review our website at www.BowWowJuiceBar.com. You'll find a wealth of information about our franchise program, how it works, and the multiple opportunities we offer. If interested, submit our 2-page Request for Consideration form within 5 days and we'll review your information. I'll then contact you to schedule an appointment with Ray Barker, our Director of Franchise Development. He'll want to know more about your business aspirations, answer your questions, and provide specific details about our ownership program. Okay?

Thanks for your interest in Bow Wow Juice Bar. We look forward to receiving your information. Good-bye.

Length of call: Start _____ End _____ Total Time _____

(Qualifier's Observations) _____

_____

Initially Qualified By:_____Date of Initial Qualification:_____

Initial Determination:

        ❑ Qualified: Follow up if not heard from by: _____
        ❑ Not Qualified
        ❑ They have no further interest
        ❑ Market not available

Database updated by: _____Database updated on: _____

2 The Six Steps to Selling Success: Step Two—Program Review
Objective: Qualify the prospect, build rapport, and establish the process

This meeting with your prospective candidate is the most important step in the recruitment process. It's your first real "date," the one that determines whether you two have what it takes for a serious relationship. Your prospect certainly is interested in your franchise. They responded to your franchise offer; were previously interviewed by you or your qualifier; reviewed your initial franchise package and website; and submitted their RFC, providing their personal information, work history, and financial statement.

This 30- to 45-minute session presents the opportunity for you to speak more openly with these motivated respondents. The vast majority have no reference point on how to buy a franchise. First and foremost, you must assume a leadership role, otherwise the consequences can be disastrous. Aggressive buyers will certainly take delight in assuming command. If you are a brand-new franchisor, you'll quickly realize this after a few "free-for-all" conversations with prospects that have no structure to follow.

It's your role to **take control and lay the framework for the Program Review.** This will include a review of their RFC, goals, and expectations; addressing basic questions and discussing your program; and, if they are interested in taking the next step, sharing the investigation process for your franchise.

First, review their RFC. If it's illegible, sloppy, or incomplete you probably don't have a very qualified or motivated candidate. If they can't take the time to fill out your application properly, that's a warning signal. They need to follow your process if they want to qualify. In these cases, bounce the RFC back to them, asking for their completed application if they want to be considered and receive proprietary information about your franchise. You may think that's harsh, but once you see the difference between candidates with well-prepared applications and sloppy ones, the light bulb will go on for you.

When reviewing a completed RFC, ask the prospect at least three specific questions to clarify and dig further into their information. Just telling a prospect their RFC "looks good" without further attention lessens the stature of your franchisee selection process. Focused questioning shows prospects you care about their ability to qualify for your program. It also tells them you want to know more about their personal interests. For example, *"Joe, I see on your application you spent time as a studio musician and operated a recording studio. How does that business work? How did you successfully compete in such a competitive industry? I also notice you take time to coach your daughter's soccer team. What motivated you to take that on?"*

Now **paint the picture of your ideal franchisee**, describing the skill sets and attributes of successful owners in your system (or for start-up franchisors, those you believe are the right match for your program). This is a great qualifier, often prompting serious prospects to "sell" their capabilities to fit this profile; or sometimes prospects will excuse themselves, realizing they don't have what it takes for your franchise.

Second, address general questions the candidate has about your program, deferring any specifics that will be answered in the FDD or later in the process. Next **ask some telling open-ended questions** (see below, "Winning Questions that Increase Your Selling Success"). Use these probes and you'll better understand the prospects' motivations and concerns, resulting in more effective presentations focused on their hot buttons. Too many sales executives don't probe enough, and then wonder why they lost a buyer to another opportunity. When you focus more on your prospect and less on your program, candidates will develop a stronger interest level in your franchise! If you ask the right questions, you'll also know the key drivers to their decision-making.

Now **involve your prospect by providing an assignment** that further engages them in your process, one that requires active participation to complete the task. These are great qualifiers that will provide clear signals demonstrating the seriousness of your buyer. These interactive assignments should be simple and reinforce the desirability of your opportunity. An inspection service franchise exec may say to their prospects, *"Check out local Yellow Pages and record the number of plumbers in your market. These can be prime customers for our inspection services. Let's discuss what your market opportunity is in our next conference call."* A coffee franchise exec may instruct their prospects, *"Go sit in a local Starbucks between 7 a.m. and 8 a.m. Count customers served during a half-hour period and multiply by the industry average of $4 per transaction. Let's see what you come up with in our next meeting!"*

Now's the time to **start pre-closing your prospect**. As franchise pros stress, "the best close starts with the opening!" This is the opportune time to set expectations and take control through leadership. Use this process to "establish the ground rules" and you will identify better candidates, build more credibility and confidence, and increase closing success:

1. ***Define your role in the process***—*"My role is to educate you about our franchise, and to explore this opportunity with you to see if we're the right fit for each other. This is a franchise partnership, and we're interested in candidates who can be successful, satisfied owners. I am not here to sell you. My responsibility is to facilitate the investigation process. Our executive*

review committee makes the decisions on offering our franchises to qualified candidates." (This helps puts your prospects at ease, knowing this is a mutual decision that has to work for both parties.)

2. ***Introduce the review committee***—"*If you want to be considered for our franchise after completing our investigation process, you'll attend Discovery Day and meet our review committee, the people who award our franchises to qualified candidates.*" (This further builds the credibility and importance of your approval system for screening qualified buyers.)

3. ***Require open communication***—"*Any time in the process you have a question, concern, or want to stop, let me know! Just wave the red flag and we'll address the issue. Out of respect for you, I will do the same. If this franchise isn't the right one, we certainly don't want to waste each other's time. Does that make sense?*" (This rule allows you to directly confront and "straighten up" or disqualify prospects who make excuses or break appointments.)

4. ***Agree to a time frame for decision-making***—"*Candidates we work with decide within three to four weeks whether this is the franchise they want and if they are ready to make a commitment. Can you?*" Most prospects agree to this timetable, since it is logical and they have no reference point on how long it should take. "*Okay. Now, moving forward, we'll schedule conference calls that work for both of us in our investigation.*" Prospects are looking for this guidance to decision-making, which you have now defined with a specific timetable. Disqualify individuals who can't commit to an acceptable decision time. If it's a military person considering a franchise down the road, ask them to contact you four to six months prior to discharge; or place them in a future follow-up file. Too much can happen in between for them to be classified as a "prospect."

5. ***Explain your process for reviewing the program***—"*We have five more steps for exploring our franchise opportunity to determine if we are right for each other. These are the Program Review, which we are conducting today; the Disclosure Review; Franchisee Validation; Discovery Day; and Awarding the Franchise. Discovery Day is a meeting at our headquarters where you'll visit with our support team, tour our operations and local franchise locations, and get final review committee approval for securing the franchise. Does this*

investigation process make sense for you?" (Most systems award the franchise after Discovery Day, while others award the franchise and sign agreements at the event. It can work well either way, depending on how you set expectations and what's most effective for your development program.)

Now it's time to **conclude the Program Review** by preparing your prospect for the next stage of investigation. Reconfirm their interest by asking, *"How would you like to proceed? Good, you say you want to continue. Then the next step is to send you our franchise documents, referred to as the Franchise Disclosure Document, or FDD. Have you ever read an FDD before?"* (If the answer is yes, gain additional insight by asking the candidate what they think an FDD is about, what they have learned, and what questions about the document still remain. If this is the first FDD your prospect will see, it's imperative to provide an overview in advance—how it came about, what its purpose is, and how to best review it. Set their expectations about the FDD from the start, or you are in for trouble! If you don't prepare your candidate properly for this large, complex document, you may shock them right out of the process. Here's one approach you might take:

"The Federal Trade Commission requires every franchisor to present an FDD to buyers interested in their franchise opportunity. An FDD provides a wealth of information and specific details about the franchise program. It's an extremely helpful document in understanding what the obligations of the franchisor and franchisee are in their relationship. It includes financial performance information providing you with earnings claims; itemized cost ranges for start-up; real estate assistance; our initial training agenda; reporting procedures; franchisee communication systems; annual conference and area meetings; and scheduled field visits.

"Most people are overwhelmed when they first read an FDD. They're thick, extensive, and repetitious. It's a great cure for insomnia, so brew the coffee and get comfortable when you read it! You may want to review sections in intervals, rather than all at once. Be sure to make a list of questions as you go through it, so we can address each one in our next phone meeting.

"You'll notice that these documents are tough, one-sided, and biased. They certainly are, and for good reason. They are designed to protect the brand. They're written to safeguard the quality of products and services that make our franchise system so successful. The disclosure document protects the 98 percent of good owners from the few rebels who can slip into the program. If Joe is a Cold Stone Creamery franchisee and he's serving his grandmother's fried chicken, he has to stop. It may taste great, but it damages the brand and creates confusion at the other locations. If Joe refuses to comply, the franchise agreement allows the franchisor to throw him out of the system.

"Ask yourself if this agreement is fair and reasonable, since it is non-negotiable. By law, special material changes can't be made for you unless they are unilaterally provided to all other franchisees in our system. You have to feel comfortable with it just as our current franchisees are.

"Some business buyers are intimated by a franchisor's requirements for uniformity of systems and procedures, and that's perfectly okay. It just means they are not a candidate for any franchise and, like Joe, should start up a business on their own. Does that make sense?

"Let's set our next telephone appointment now for our Disclosure Review. [Book this next meeting in six to seven days.] *I'll priority mail the FDD so you'll get it in the next day or two."*

(Note: Many companies now send FDDs electronically for instant delivery. FTC-approved electronic document services are available should you be interested. FranServices.com is one of the pioneers in providing this service.)

After scheduling next week's meeting, if the prospect is a "no show" for your appointment, wait a day and call thanking them for their interest and wishing them the best of success in their future endeavors. If they return your call with a sincere apology, let them know they will be disqualified if they miss a future appointment without prior notification.

Length of conversation: *45 to 60 minutes*

3 **The Six Steps to Selling Success:**
Step Three: Disclosure Review
Objective: Determine franchisability of candidate and pre-sell Discovery Day

Ask the candidate what they thought of the FDD, and whether the information it contains was helpful. Review the material, answering the candidate's specific questions. It is important that you provide accurate answers. When in doubt, get the right facts to your candidate later rather than winging an answer now. The legal consequences are too risky to play it by ear. Wrap up this discussion with, *"Now that you understand what our FDD is all about, do you feel comfortable with how our franchise program works?"*

Franchising isn't right for everyone, so make sure your prospect understands and buys into the franchise way of doing business. If not, wave the red flag and disqualify the candidate. If you bring mismatched candidates into your system, you will end up in constant battle.

Winning Questions that Increase Your Selling Success

Carefully designed probes presented throughout your sales process will bring a franchise prospect closer to you, and help you gain invaluable insights into their character, interests, and buying motivations. Below are some of the classic questions that have worked for hundreds of franchise sales executives. Pick your favorites and use them throughout your recruitment process. Your candidates appreciate that you want to know more about them and care enough to ask them these revealing questions.

1. Why are you looking now?
2. How long have you been looking?
3. What in particular was it in the ad that prompted you to respond?
4. What was it about our business that made you respond?
5. What other opportunities have you considered? What do you like and dislike about them?
6. How do you define success?
7. Are you really ready to own your own business? Why?
8. What don't you like about your current job? What do you like?
9. What has been your experience in managing other people? What are your strengths? Any areas perhaps requiring improvement?
10. How will you know when you have found the right opportunity?
11. What gets you most excited about this franchise? What are your biggest concerns?
12. What do you want your business to do for you?
13. What do you expect to gain by making a career change?
14. What does franchising mean to you? What are the advantages and possible disadvantages?
15. What are your strengths that will help you succeed in your own business?
16. What makes you believe you would be successful operating one of our franchises?
17. How do you see yourself in this business? What role will you play initially and long term?
18. How does your spouse or partner feel about this opportunity? What do they like? What do they dislike?
19. What contributions do you believe you can bring to our system?
20. What do you do for relaxation?
21. Tell me about some of your hobbies and activities outside of work.
22. What do you think about our opportunity so far?

If your prospect plans on using legal counsel to review the documents, strongly urge them to hire a franchise attorney. They'll save time, money, and be much easier to work with than a general attorney, whose ignorance of franchise law will drive them to try altering your agreement with a plethora of special exceptions and material changes. Your prospects will suffer the most, burning up their money on worthless advice. It's like going to a podiatrist for heart surgery. I'll never forget a candidate's expression when I tore up a family attorney's eight-page letter demanding lower royalties, no territory restrictions, and a few other choice changes!

After reviewing the disclosures, turn your attention to a much more exciting subject: your prospect. **Probe with more open-ended questions** to show interest and discover more about the prospect. This will help you more effectively guide their investigation. Knowing their hot buttons and where their interests lie is more important than rambling on and on about your products, policies, and programs. Find out what's key to their decision-making, and what their turn-offs have been in looking at other opportunities. *"What in particular was it you didn't like about the two other franchises you were considering?"* Get closer to what your prospects think and want. They appreciate your interest in them, which shows you care. This is what makes the difference in selling your franchise opportunity—not the cool-looking granite tabletops in your restaurant, or the super-suction, state-of-the-art mega hoses you brag about in your high-tech maintenance vans.

Now is the time to further build the value of the Discovery Day visit and what they will see and experience there. Let candidates know that before they can attend Discovery Day, 1) they must **speak with a minimum three franchise owners**, and 2) they will need **preliminary financing pre-approval**, if they will seek funding for the business. (See below, "How To Set Up Financing Sources.") Provide candidates with a list of owners to contact, and outside lending sources who have successfully financed your franchisees.

(Note: Start-up franchisors should promote Discovery Day as the time to reveal firsthand how your business concept is "the next McDonald's"; promote the extraordinary advantages in joining your system early, e.g., first-to-market and wide-open territories and expansion opportunities; strong one-on-one corporate support; and "first-in" fees, which traditionally increase for owners who join later.)

Set expectations and guide candidates before they make franchisee calls. Provide tips on how to make their interviews most meaningful, and what questions they may want to ask. (If you don't, you'll hurt yourself and your prospects, who sometimes get frustrated from lack of information, or leap to bad decisions because they didn't have a systematic approach for validating franchisee satisfaction.)

"Like any organization, we have three groups of owners: the star performers at the top; the mainstreamers who do well; and those few who are struggling. The critical question for you is, 'Which group will you identify with?' Which appear to have personalities, skill sets, and business characteristics similar to your own, and are the type of owner you see yourself being?' If you speak with someone facing difficult challenges, try to find out what the problems might be. If the owner says, 'I just don't have time to get out and market in my community,' or 'My employees keep quitting on me,' this tells you something doesn't it!"

Often your prospects won't know what key questions they should ask to get the most out of their conversations with franchisees. It's your role to provide suggestions that will make their validations most meaningful in doing their due diligence. Here's a sample questionnaire to offer prospects that will help them better evaluate the satisfaction and success levels of franchise owners they speak with:

- Why did you choose this franchise in searching for a business?
- What was your prior background?
- How was your initial training?
- How is ongoing support and marketing?
- How do you stand up against your competitors?
- What do you like about the business?
- What don't you like about the business?
- How are you doing? Are you meeting your expectations?
- How helpful was corporate in assisting you with site/territory selection?
- What are the keys to success in this business?
- How has your overall experience been as a franchise owner? Would you do it over again?
- What one piece of advice can you give me in considering this franchise?

Now your buyer has in hand a methodical validation process to compare, summarize, and evaluate their discussions with the franchisees. Set a phone conference one week later to review your prospect's conversations with owners.

Length of conversation: *40 to 60 minutes*

Conducting Successful Validation Calls

Franchisee validation can make or break the sale of your candidate. Pow!... Just like that and a once-supercharged prospect can deflate to nothing in 24 hours, bailing out of your process instantly. This is the most influential stage in the selling process. What franchise owners say means far more than what a corporate sales person tells them. Franchise operators are doing it, and it's their experiences that count foremost with cautious buyers.

Be sure to prepare your current franchisees for responding to prospective new owners. Recognize their efforts, follow up with them, and show your appreciation for taking their valuable time to speak with your prospects. They themselves once called to gain better perspective about the franchise program before they decided to join. Provide a required pass code your franchisee can ask for so they are assured the prospect isn't a competitor shopper or an individual who hasn't been qualified by corporate yet. This chases away any of these fishers.

If you're a growing franchise, here's a heads-up: The more aggressive your development efforts, the more prospects will be calling your owners and tying up their time. These are a few ways franchisors help relieve this common problem: 1) let prospects know when franchisees are most available and the busy times not to call; 2) periodically rotate overloaded owners off the list; 3) ask prospects what profile of operators they prefer to speak with—by career experience, success levels, length of time in the business, or markets they reside in; 4) promptly enlist new franchisees as validators, since their enthusiasm, availability, and evaluation of your start-up support will go a long way with prospects; and 5) provide top owners with advance notice of a highly qualified prospect who will be calling, so they know the importance of responding to that person.

I was fascinated by Aussie Pet Mobile's remedy for ensuring a fast, effective connection between serious prospects and franchisees. Aussie is the largest mobile pet washing franchise, largely "driven" by multi-unit franchisees. In their recruitment process, franchisee phone calls are now the last step before their Discovery Day visit. David Louy, executive vice president, said delayed responses and time-robbing phone calls had been eliminated, which benefited both qualified buyers and his busy franchisees. "You may think we lose deals by only permitting prospects to contact our owners after they have booked Discovery Day. Doesn't happen! It's all about setting expectations and establishing our well-defined process with candidates right up front."

How To Set Up Financing Sources

Establishing strong relationships with lending sources is integral to recruitment success. Most buyers do not have financing sources and look to you to for assistance. Work only with responsive franchise lenders who can build credibility and confidence with your candidates. If the loan executive doesn't have good relationship and customer service skills, don't do business. Also, stay away from the loan sharks that overcharge fees to package and place the loans. Take care to act in the best interest of your franchise buyers.

Seek reputable lenders who believe in your concept, know how to effectively work within your process, and provide buyer insights and feedback that can help you in qualifying and closing. I considered lenders a part of my sales team. They served an important role in the success of our recruitment process.

Typically, franchise candidates are naive and vulnerable when considering a business loan. They don't know what to expect or to do, since most have never applied for one before. Frequently they stroll down to their local banker thinking, *"Of course Joe will lend me the money. We've been his good customer for 25 years."* Cold reality dawns when banker Joe recoils at the mention of a business venture. He drills the prospect about your franchise and instructs him to produce a 50-page business plan. And this is just for starters.

Prepare your prospects with realistic expectations when you discuss funding options. *"A big benefit for owners joining our system is we have third-party lending sources in place. They have pre-approved our franchise business. It's a matter of you qualifying based on your credit record and financials. Naturally, you don't have to use these sources should you choose to finance the business elsewhere."* If candidates want to pursue their local bank, an interested uncle, or other money prospects, prepare them for disappointments so they won't spin into depression and disappear when doors slam in their face.

What are today's most attractive programs for financing franchisees? What's the story on SBA loans, conventional and non-conventional sources, 401(k) financing, leasing options, special minority lending, and inner city programs? Here's a general rundown of the lending market:

- **SBA loans**—Traditionally, franchisees have acquired funding assistance through the Small Business Administration. The SBA has been proactive in franchise lending, owing to the success rates many franchise businesses enjoy. The SBA Franchise Registry is a special national program of qualifying franchise systems, whose franchisees receive an expedited loan process when applying for financial assistance from the SBA. Their franchise agreements have been pre-approved by the SBA, thereby shortening the loan process and ensuring consistent eligibility decisions. The franchise candidate still must qualify with the participating SBA lender.

- **401(k) financing**—This can be ideal for individuals with available retirement funds. IRAs, 401(k)s, and other retirement accounts can be used to fund a franchise as an investment inside a candidate's retirement account. There are no distribution taxes or penalties. Companies specialize in structuring this financing for franchisees.

- **Leasing**—Lease options for furniture, equipment, and other assets are popular for certain franchise concepts, such as mobile franchises and food franchises. Franchise systems are an attractive market for third-party leasing companies. In addition, manufacturers will often direct lease to franchisees (e.g., for technology products or franchise service vehicles).

- **Home equity loans**—Ever-popular during real estate booms, home equity loans have been a fast and easy resource for financing franchises. In 2008, when home values had plunged, equity financing declined as well. For homeowners with no mortgage or a small one, it is still a very viable money source.

- **Family and private loans**—You often can't count on these deals materializing, but some franchise successes are a result of an uncle or friend stepping up to finance the aspiring franchisee. To save you time, also require any "angel" investors to complete the Request for Consideration with their detailed financial statement. This step will eliminate several donor prospects, now that it's their time to "show you the money!"

- **Non-conventional loans**—Creative financing is also a hit-or-miss option, and not readily available. It has served well in isolated instances, when a franchisor is enamored by an impressive candidate who falls a little short qualifying with traditional lenders. These financiers look at other assets and factors they may be willing to collateralize to fund that attractive franchise candidate.

- **Minority and redevelopment loans and incentives**—National and local programs do provide incentives and lower interest financing for franchisees who qualify as a minority business owner, U.S veteran, or owner locating their franchise within a redevelopment business zone. The most expedient resource for finding out more about current programs is the International Franchise Association.

- **Conventional loans**—This financing is generally available only to experienced franchisees with successful track records. Unlike SBA loans, conventional business loans are not backed by the U.S. government. Subsequently, it's extremely tough to secure this type of financing for new franchise owners. Occasionally, a funding company appears that has financed franchisee start-ups, but this is quite unusual.

4 The Six Steps to Selling Success: Step Four—Franchisee Validation

Objective: Candidate gains insights and understanding of the opportunity from owners

Review the results of your candidate's conversations. *"Tell me about the owners you spoke with. What did you learn from them? Any surprises? Who did you identify with? Who did you feel most comfortable speaking with? Why? Were franchisees satisfied with our support services? What were some of the benefits they were enjoying as owners? Can you see yourself achieving your goals in our business?"*

Know how to respond with assurance and conviction when a prospect dwells on a particular franchisee who is facing problems, unhappy, and falling short of financial expectations. *"As discussed, we have star performers as well as a few struggling. Unfortunately, this is the case in every business. There's no getting around it. Why do you believe the franchisee is having a hard time? Remember, the key is who you relate to. Is it this bottom producer, or the successful owners you spoke with? We provide the training, guidance, and tools for you to build a successful business. But it's still up to our franchisee partner to make it happen."*

(Note: If your system is dealing with issues affecting franchisee performance at the time, be straightforward and recognize the situation. Before speaking to owners, prepare the candidate if you are experiencing temporary product distribution problems, construction delays, or staffing shortages. Most important is knowing you have solutions in place so these objections are minimized should a franchisee bring them up.)

During this Franchisee Validation step, also **verify your candidate's status with potential lenders** to insure they've received preliminary pre-approval at this stage of the process. If they're working with one of your recommended financing companies, you'll already know this.

Their responses to your probing questions at this stage will help qualify your prospect's interest and commitment as a serious buyer. Mentally, they should be thinking as franchisees and be prepared to move forward. *"As you know, Discovery Day is the next step. Let's schedule you now and make sure you are well prepared for the event."* With their confirmation, let them know what opening(s) you have available and coordinate with their schedule.

You are now preparing your candidate for the close. If they hesitate, raise the red flag and find out why there's an issue. Didn't they fully agree to your timetable in the initial Program Review? Move 'em to the next step, Discovery Day, or move 'em out if their excuses are unacceptable. If they can't follow your investigation process, how well will they follow your system? Decision-making time is here, and now's the time to take the final step toward franchise ownership. It's your responsibility to properly prepare them for the event to ensure a successful outcome on their behalf.

Often new or mediocre sales people experience recurring problems getting people to Discovery Day. If your process works, they simply haven't executed properly, established the ground rules, or set the correct expectations with candidates. The process naturally flows to the Discovery Day event. Executed properly, it doesn't need to be sold. It just evolves. Remember, the best close starts with the opening.

Length of conversation: *30 to 60 minutes*

5 The Six Steps to Selling Success: Step Five—Discovery Day

Objective: Attend Discovery Day at your headquarters for executive approval of the franchise

Discovery Day is show time! Whether you have one franchise or a thousand, this special event propels your sales process to a crescendo. It's "Confirmation Day," where serious buyers come to you ready to join your franchise with the blessing of your approval committee. It's always my favorite stage of the process, when everything becomes real for your candidate and you. The journey of rigorous courtship has led both candidate and franchisor to your altar of consummation.

To ensure success, your Discovery Day must always meet or exceed the buyer's expectations. Anything less, and you must clean up your act quickly. Invest whatever it takes to make this event work.

There is wide variation in the preparation and professionalism of home office presentations for qualified franchise candidates. Some companies focus their entire recruitment process toward scheduling the Discovery Day event, while others view it as an optional trip for potential owners who want to know more about the franchise.

Surprisingly, a few franchisors have recently eliminated their Discovery Day. I know of an automotive franchisor who decided, *"It slows down our sales process because of travel preparation and scheduling. We now try to take care of this without the home office visit."* A food franchise executive explained to me, *"It drains our resources by tying up our executive staff for the day. We can't afford to take the time."* Wow, I thought, you can't afford not to take the time! I spoke to a successful founder of fitness centers in the southeastern U.S. who was trying to upgrade the quality

Preparation for Discovery Day

Companies schedule Discovery Days in different ways: once a month, once a week, or anytime a candidate can make it! As your system grows, you'll be forced to schedule more frequent and specific dates so you don't overtax your home office resources. But sooner is better. Like a cold steak, your opportunity can lose its sizzle the longer the wait for Discovery Day. Unexpected events in your prospect's world may postpone or kill the event entirely.

Discovery Day is show time, so the better prepared you and your candidate are, the more successful the results will be. Get affirmation that they are ready to join your franchise if accepted, barring any unforeseen circumstances. Coach your candidates to present themselves professionally to help ensure review committee approval. It's the time for both of you to meet, get to know each other, and confirm this is a good match.

"Be sure to put your best foot forward! It is important for our staff to know who you are, and believe that you can be successful in our business. Express yourselves. Show your personalities and interest in the franchise program. Prepare at least two questions to ask at your meetings with operations, real estate, and our senior executive staff." Prospective buyers should also be ready to answer questions for executive committee approval such as: *"Why do you feel we should award this opportunity to you?"* and *"What contributions do you believe you can bring to our system?"*

Some franchisors have the president or CEO conduct a pre–Discovery Day interview with a candidate before they are approved to attend. This interim step further qualifies the buyer's interest, expectations, and suitability before both parties invest their time and expense in the Discovery Day event.

Candidate personality profiles (see below, and check the Resources List at the end of this book) should be completed at least a week prior to Discovery Day and forwarded, along with their RFCs and other relevant information, to the executive review committee. Committee members can reference these files when considering their franchise approval before, during, or immediately after Discovery Day.

Mobile Bankers, a mobile check-cashing franchise, thoroughly qualified candidates for Discovery Day. The franchisor required each candidate to prepare a preliminary business plan (less any financial projections) for presentation to their review committee. Potential buyers were instructed to 1) express their ideas on how they would set up their business; 2) present local marketing ideas to build customers; and 3) share how they saw their role in the business initially and long term. This type of interactive assignment further engages the buyer in your business, demonstrates their skill sets, and provides a snapshot of how prepared they are for your concept.

of her franchisees. Her first 30 owners had never come to her headquarters or met her staff. I asked, *"Would you ever hire any corporate or field employee without meeting them? Yet sight unseen, you are awarding 10-year contracts to individuals who will operate and market your brand throughout the U.S!"* The founder realized the hard way this was not a good thing and changed to mandated Discovery Days.

Home office visits are anything but an option in the sales process. They are a must for franchise candidates. High-performance franchise organizations know this event is critical in successfully qualifying and recruiting franchisees. It also is an invaluable experience for candidates to gain firsthand information, meet the staff, see the culture, and validate their expectations of the system. For franchisors committed to building a quality system, the days of waiving Discovery Day are over!

A well-designed sales process should produce a minimum 70 percent closing rate of potential buyers who attend Discovery Day. A 100 percent closing rate is too high, and usually signals that cashing franchise fees is more important at the moment than the higher costs of managing or terminating "misfits" down the road. Some top-producing development pros are closing 90 percent of their qualified candidates. They credit this to their screening process and focus on developing a superior experience for their home office visitors. Here are some guidelines for cross-checking your Discovery Day program.

Get financing pre-approved

Prior to investing time and money in a home office visit, Discovery Day attendees should get their funding in order through a third party or direct financing program. Clearing this obstacle paves the way for a more productive Discovery Day. Yet some franchisors skip this preliminary procedure and instead, at the event, provide qualified attendees with sample business plans to present to lenders when they go home. This doesn't make sense for either party. Potential buyers want to know early on if they can qualify for funding. Why waste the time if they can't? Lenders are more than happy to spend 30 minutes or more to determine if a potential client is pre-qualified for financing. This step speeds up the closing process and reduces wasted energy with prospects who "don't have the dough" to make it.

Analyze individual vs. group presentations

Track your current closing rates to establish which environment may be more suitable and successful for you. A home-care franchisor discovered their greatest success with personal, one-on-one Discovery Days. Yet an advertising franchise found group presentations far more productive for their recruitment success. Their

---

Discovery Day Checklist
Complete one week before attending

✓ Personality profiles completed for the franchise owners.

✓ Preliminary or final territories established for the franchise, by towns, cities, or counties. (Use physical boundaries for confirmation rather than ZIP Codes or city lines. Physical boundaries rarely change, ZIP Codes do. This saves you from territory confusion and conflicts that could arise later.)

✓ FDD sent and acknowledgment receipt on file to satisfy the FTC's 14-day waiting period for franchisee signing.

✓ Filled-out agreements sent to candidate to satisfy the FTC's seven-day waiting period for franchisee signing.

✓ Funding for the franchise preliminarily pre-approved.

✓ Any major candidate concerns, questions, and issues discussed and satisfied.

✓ Discovery Day agenda, accommodations, directions, appropriate dress, and other details emailed or posted online in password-protected area.

---

vice president of development said, *"The presence of several people further validates our concept, and the enthusiasm of the attendees feeds off of each other, creating additional interest."* At one franchise I represented, we noticed a tendency of more multiple-unit purchases when we had larger Discovery Day groups. Some wavering participants bought more than one unit after speaking with others who had committed to several units. (I'm not saying this was a positive, just an observation about group dynamics.)

Carefully script your event

Every activity at Discovery Day must be analyzed, rehearsed, and monitored. Your goal is to make a positive impression on the candidate. Your franchise system is on stage and must exude professionalism, organization, and leadership.

According to a study conducted by Dunhill Personnel many years ago, 85 percent of what your prospects absorb at Discovery Day is visual, not informational. Minor details create major impact. What attendees observe greatly influences their decisions to join your system. *"By whom and in what car was I picked up at the airport? Were employees friendly and interested in me? Was my name posted on the company sign? Were the employees well-groomed and dressed appropriately? Did I relate to and feel comfortable in your environment? Was the home office well-maintained or were the bathrooms dirty? Did I get to meet the president or CEO?"*

To illustrate the power of what's really important to some buyers, Once Upon A Child, a children's franchise, snatched a strong candidate out of the arms of a competitor at the eleventh hour. The new franchisee changed her decision because *"the people were much nicer and I really sensed they were happy working for the system."* In another instance, a direct-marketing franchise beat out a competitor when their CEO offered his guest room to a highly qualified prospect whose evening flight was cancelled by bad weather.

Set expectations at the outset

When your candidates arrive at Discovery Day, naturally you'll start with a warm welcome. Explain the purpose, process, and activities for the day to ensure everyone is "aligned" in the right direction. This provides further clarity for your Discovery Day guests and eliminates any potential confusion that may occur during the event.

Here's one approach to setting the stage: when a group attends, ask each candidate to make a brief personal introduction including their business background, how they found out about your opportunity, and why they are so interested in your franchise. This familiarizes everyone with their peers, validates the desirability of your concept, and accelerates the bonding process among the group. It also gives you an early read into their mindsets and interest levels. Next, review the scheduled events and tell them who they will meet. Wrap up this orientation by reaffirming expectations for their visit:

"Put your best foot forward. Express yourself, ask questions, show your personality. You have all diligently conducted your research. Today it's most important for our corporate staff to get to know you, and for you to get acquainted with our professional support team. This strong relationship is the key to success for both of us. We're dependent upon each other, and we can profit together through our partnership. Our job is to build the car, start up the engine, and provide you with a road map for success. It's your job to follow the course and drive the growth of your business. This is what successful franchise relationships are all about. Today is about ensuring there can be a good fit.

"At the end of our day, I will speak with each of you privately before I present you to our executive approval committee for consideration. If a personal concern does come up during the day, please address this with me when we get together later. After the event concludes, our review committee will meet and review your skill sets, suitability

to our culture, and willingness to follow our system. Their key question is, 'Do we believe you can be successful in our franchise system?' Your development executive will contact you within the next 24 hours to inform you of the committee's decision."

Assign a tour guide

When staff are available, a personable facilitator who ushers and assists prospects throughout Discovery Day is invaluable. Their presence makes a good professional impression on your guests, showing them the attention your franchisees are given. It also elevates the stature of your development executive, who isn't always there seemingly waiting to grab their checkbook. From airport pickup to rearranging departmental presentations if needed, the facilitator keeps the schedule moving and can prevent potential mishaps and provide on-site feedback to your development team about the candidates.

Additional tips

Here are some additional practices franchisors have found increase the success of their Discovery Day presentations:

- ***Provide an advance agenda***—Furnish the schedule of events, names and bios of department executives your attendees will meet, specific travel information, and any other helpful instructions or information; ask for contact names for family emergencies. This preview heightens the importance of the event and provides useful information in assisting attendees in preparing for their trip. Savvy franchises post this on their website using a password-protected page for "Discovery Day Guests." It's more efficient and stimulates curiosity from new site visitors.

- ***Get your housekeeping in order***—Your guests are influenced by everything they see, touch, and hear at your home office. This includes bathrooms, paint, carpets, shrubbery, plants, trash, office décor, etc.

- ***Post a welcoming board***—Display your visitors' names on an attractive display stand. Recognizing their presence shows your candidates they are important to your company... and helps your staff members remember who's attending!

- ***Post department names***—Identifying different department areas with door tags or labels shows organization and professionalism, and provides your visitors with a better sense of how your company works.

- *Display your "Franchisee Wall of Fame"*—Photos of owners featuring your top franchisees and franchisee advisory council are impressive to your guests, bringing home your powerful relationship and appreciation for franchise owners. Unfortunately, not enough franchisors leverage the impact of showcasing their franchise stars at their headquarters.

- *Furnish a personalized notebook*—Provide the schedule of events, meaningful reports, presentation outlines, and other relevant material that candidates can take home with them.

- *Standardize your corporate dress*—Whether in company polo shirts or suits, establish a consistent dress code for Discovery Day. Franchising by definition means uniformity; an "anything goes" attitude toward attire does not communicate a professional image.

- *Schedule departmental presentations*—It is essential that your field support, real estate/site selection, advertising and marketing, and customer service departments participate in Discovery Day. Qualified buyers want to meet the people they will be working with. Likewise, key personnel should speak with prospective franchisees and offer their insights in qualifying them.

- *Invest in multi-media*—Quality, well-prepared presentations make the difference in motivating buyers. PowerPoint, video, TV and radio commercials, intranet, and software demonstrations enhance the impact of your messages.

- *Conduct a facilities tour*—Don't keep your guests prisoners all day in the same room. A closet remodeling franchise made this mistake until a prospect finally asked to see their warehouse and was happily surprised: *"I never realized you are producing such great product!"* He signed on the next week. Don't assume tours aren't important. Even with a no-inventory service business, prospects often don't realize the commitment of personnel and resources required to support a franchise network until they see it for themselves. Seeing is believing!

Length of meeting: *1 to 2 days*

6 The Six Steps to Selling Success: Step Six—Awarding the Franchise

Objective: Grant the franchise to qualified buyers on Discovery Day or soon after

Executive review committees are typically composed of senior franchise executives who review a candidate's qualifications before granting them a franchise. If you are a founder just starting up your franchise, employ a close business associate, franchise consultant, or other trusted advisor to be a part of your committee. They can help in your decision-making process, and provide greater credence to your professionalism.

It is the committee's decision at the conclusion of Discovery Day whether to extend a franchise offer or disqualify a candidate. Successful franchisors prominently position this venue as the final qualifier in granting new franchises to prospective buyers. It's a legitimate "country club" approach that helps safeguard the future of both the organization and prospective franchisees. Here's what your committee of advisors must answer: *"Is this individual a good fit who can be successful and a contribution to the system?"* or *"Is this a person who really doesn't match your franchise profile and will probably create problems for both of you down the road?"*

For franchisors using Discovery Day as "signing day," committee-approved candidates sign agreements and pay their franchise fees at the conclusion of the event. Celebrate this memorable occasion with your congratulations, photo shots with senior executives, and company logo gifts. Now the franchisor and franchisee join together in their journey to build a rewarding business partnership.

Turning down Discovery Day candidates

It's not a pleasant moment when you inform your prospect they are rejected by your review committee. Out of respect for the candidate, it's imperative to give the specific business reason(s) why. Just as you want to know why qualified prospects pass on your opportunity, these prospects deserve the same from you. Legitimate reasons can be: *"We are concerned you don't have the necessary social and networking skills demanded for our concept." "Our training people believe you will be overwhelmed with employee management, hiring, and training responsibilities." "Executive management has decided you aren't currently in a position with your heavy family commitments to dedicate the 12-hour days and energy to start up your business." "The consensus is our franchise procedures and policies are too restrictive for you and will frustrate your ability and motivation to grow within our organization."*

Make it clear that your particular franchise simply isn't right for them, and explain why. If you care about the welfare of the individual and your franchise system, disqualifying candidates is not a personal attack on the candidate. I've certainly had the displeasure of delivering bad news. A wonderful, physically challenged woman who qualified in all other aspects was rejected because it was evident at Discovery Day she didn't have the energy or stamina to operate our fast-paced business. Another gentleman had difficulty communicating with our operations and training executives, which would affect his learning potential as well as unfairly burden our support team.

My toughest rejection was disqualifying a proud husband without the skill sets to manage the franchise. However, we were blown away by his wife's business acumen, personality profile, and passion for our concept. We said we would award the franchise if his wife would join him full-time as co-operator of the business. Unfortunately, the husband flatly rejected the idea. He still carried the mindset of his traditional culture, which prevented him from agreeing to our requirements.

Post–Discovery Day signings

Most franchisors approve candidates and award franchises immediately after the event. The intent is not to sign up new franchisees at Discovery Day. If you're wondering, there is no right or wrong way. In successfully using this post-award process, the key is to contact the buyer the day after Discovery Day and lay out the steps to signing. I've seen time, indecision, and lack of follow-through kill post–Discovery Day deals. Executive leadership must give franchise closings top priority within their organization. Losing a five-store, multi-unit deal because it took three weeks to get the territory defined and contracts out is utterly tragic. Time kills deals. Buyers expect responsiveness, are highly impressionable, and can be easily diverted when too much time elapses. This is nothing less than we'd expect for ourselves.

<u>Length of meeting</u>: *30 minutes to 2 hours*

Here are some quick tips to accelerate your closings:

- Immediately after committee approval, call the candidate with the good news and email a confirmation letter with timelines for signing papers.

- Extend a maximum one-week offer for your franchise. If legal review needs completion, provide a few extra days. Keep the schedule tight, otherwise franchise attorneys may give this assignment a low priority and unnecessarily drag out their review.

Personality Profiles Help Decision-Making

As discussed in Chapter 2, behavioral surveys can provide effective insights into the natural characteristics and traits of potential franchisees throughout the qualification process. This behavioral information brings you closer to the real person sitting before you at Discovery Day. As providers of these profiling services advise, personality insights can be helpful with borderline decisions when you are on the fence with certain candidates. They certainly aren't to be used as the primary decision-making factor, but they can help break deadlocks in making the better choice. Knowing a candidate's inherent behavior provides a window into who they really are.

This knowledge is especially valuable within the "show time" environment of a Discovery Day. How many times have we discovered that a candidate's behavior at this corporate gathering doesn't mirror who that person really is? The performance of attendees this day will vary depending on their adeptness at selling themselves to the home office staff. There's also a challenge with candidates of diverse ethnic backgrounds, cultures, and family dynamics. In a group, the normally vivacious wife may fade into the background, or the "go-getter" son may be totally overshadowed by the presence of his investing father.

Personality surveys can help you recognize and neutralize the behavioral dynamics of Discovery Day, which is an emotional, life-changing event that will change the lives of the attendees sitting before you. These behavioral tools are highly beneficial for members of the executive review committee, who may spend as few as 15 minutes with a prospect seeking a 10-year commitment with your franchise brand.

- Set a date and time for a telephone closing, or an office closing if the candidate is local. This keeps the sale in motion. It also ensures your new franchisee signs the documents properly, avoiding delays because of pages incorrectly completed.

- Provide your overnight delivery account for returning their signed agreements.

- Countersign documents the next day, congratulate your new franchisee, and confirm their next step in starting up the business!

Confirmation Letter of Franchise Approval

Mr./Ms. Franchisee Candidate
Franchisee Operations, Inc.
One Easy Street
Las Vegas, NV 77777

Dear Mr./Ms. Franchise Candidate:

Congratulations! We are pleased to extend an offer for you to join our franchise program until November 15, 2008. You have met our qualifications for our Domidums Are Fun Factory franchise program. We certainly look forward to a mutually rewarding relationship, and the opportunity to help you in building a successful business for you and your family.

To help you prepare, these are the next steps to get you started in establishing your own Domidums Are Fun Factory:

1. Within the next few days, Glorious Gloria will be contacting you to set up a Closing Day, at which time she will guide you through the signing and return of your franchise agreements.

2. When we receive your agreements and franchise payment, your documents will be reviewed and signed by William Willy, president, and an original copy will be returned for your files.

3. Wobbly Wayne, vice president of real estate, will then call to welcome you aboard. He will have our franchise operations manual sent to you, which provides initial start-up materials, including our proprietary real estate process and forms.

4. When you complete reading the real estate section of the manual, contact Wobbly for instructions to get your location search started. He will review site selection procedures and how you will participate in the process to find a prime site for your Domidums Are Fun Factory.

Once again, congratulations and welcome aboard the Domidums Are Fun family!

Frankly Funne
Senior Vice President
Franchise Development

Overcoming buyers' cold feet

Feeling butterflies in personally uncomfortable situations is a human condition. We all know and have experienced this. It means we care and really want to do something right—whether it's our first step on stage in a community performance, preparing for the city league tennis championship, addressing an audience of 500 people, moving to a new city, taking on a new job… or getting Discovery Day approval to buy a franchise business!

Why am I bringing this up now? Because when closing time starts "closing in," reality hits some buyers like a sledgehammer. *"What am I doing? I'm leaving my job, going into debt, disrupting my family lifestyle, and starting up a new venture with no guarantees I can make this work!"* I have been gripped by this myself when starting businesses, and I'm sure many of you have as well.

The key is recognizing when this paralysis hits your prospect. Because of embarrassment, a buyer often disguises their sudden fear of final commitment with other excuses. It's your job to address and diffuse the issue swiftly, or you can lose the candidate. Your buyer probably told you earlier that they were ready to own their own business. But now it's for real, and emotion has superseded all their motivations for buying your franchise. Panic and immobilization hit. Calmly rescue your buyer from this entrepreneurial terror, reassuring them with the benefits of your franchise partnership: you're on your own but not alone; you have the best of both worlds; you have the comfort of fellow franchisees actively interested in your success as a part of the franchise family. *"We're here for you. This is what franchising is all about. I'd be especially worried if you didn't go through these feelings of uncertainty. Everyone goes through these last-minute butterflies. It's healthy and natural. This just tells me you are excited, want to be successful, and know it's going to take a lot of time and effort. It shows me that you are well prepared to own your own business."*

Engineers, bankers, and "bean counters" are often victims of "analysis paralysis." This has little to do with emotional panic. It can have everything to do with minimizing their risks of entrepreneurialism. Let them know this intellectual meltdown is common among their peers. Consequently, use "left brain" logic to turn them around. They must choose based on your investigation process, which details your business model with its policies, procedures, systems, and franchisee validations. Providing more data and guarantees isn't the answer. *"Now's the time to move up, or move on to another business. Indecision is simply no decision."* So, when the analytical type hits freeze frame, force them forward with firm deadlines and a "drop dead" date for returning signed documents. Otherwise, they won't stop asking for more facts, suck the life out of you, and drive you to the funny farm.

Timeline for selling process

Twelve weeks is the average length of time in awarding a franchise, according to 148 franchise companies surveyed in Franchise Update's latest Annual Franchise Development Report. Selling hotel franchises and other million-dollar-plus concepts certainly takes much longer. On the lower investment end, some franchises costing less than $100,000 can close within 6 to 8 weeks.

Legitimate time-robbers delaying franchise signings include life's realities of family vacations, sickness, dealing with partnerships, legal and CPA reviews of franchise agreements, or scheduling conflicts with Discovery Days.

There are no excuses for delays resulting from individuals skipping appointments or stringing out decisions over several weeks. When this happens, wave the red flag, because this means your investigation process is not properly developed or isn't being executed by your sales team!

"Our franchise buyers are more sophisticated and they would be insulted if we pushed them to make decisions. This is why our signings take seven to eight months, and really can't be shortened without losing quality candidates." This is how a sales veteran with a successful, $400,000 technology franchise greeted me when I asked about her selling experiences. Her new vice president had just hired me to review the company's total recruitment process and see if there was an inkling of truth to this saleswomen's belief. Shortening their selling cycle was a critical issue, since two more sales people had come aboard and the old-timer's influence could create problems in training the new sales reps.

After mystery shopping the sales veteran several times, we discovered she was clearly not following the process. Too bad. Her passion, enthusiasm, and relationship-building skills were quite impressive. But she always put the prospects in the driver's seat, allowing them to take control and proceed at their own pace. She was afraid to present a timeline for decision-making. Instead, she would say, *"When would you like me to get back to you?"* or *"Give me a call back when you are ready to take the next step."* Of course it took her eight months to bring new franchisees aboard! And since time kills, how many more did she lose?

Here's an example of a selling process with an eight-week template for working with franchise buyers from initial contact to signing, assuming all stars are aligned and there are no time delays:

Closing Schedule for Concepts Under $100,000 Investment

1. Prospect Inquiry	Jan. 2
2. Pre-qualification —Materials sent and received Jan. 6	Jan. 3
3. Program Review —FDD sent and received Jan. 13	Jan. 10
4. Disclosure Review —Franchisee list emailed and received, and funding preliminarily pre-approved by Jan. 21	Jan. 20
5. Franchisee Validation —Franchise agreement sent and reviewed, and personality profile(s) completed by Feb. 5	Jan. 27
6. Discover Day	Feb. 15
7. Awarding the Franchise	Feb. 16
7. Franchisee Closing —Franchise fee received and signed franchise agreements by Feb. 25	Feb. 23

Summary: Six Steps to Selling Success

1. Pre-qualification
- Present a brief description of your franchise opportunity
- Confirm basic contact and qualification information
- Screen candidate with key probing questions
- Describe candidate profile you are seeking
- Present next step in investigative process
- Instruct candidate to return RFC application within five days

2. Program Review
- Highlight topics and objectives of session
- Review prospect's RFC with qualifying and probing questions
- Ask for and address general questions, deflecting premature ones for later
- Discuss ownership benefits and advantages
- Share mission statement, culture, and values
- Summarize training, operations, marketing, and management
- Describe ideal candidate you are seeking
- Assign task(s) to involve prospect in your business

- "Start the close" by establishing expectations and your six-step process
- Review next step and prepare prospect for FDD
- Set time for next meeting

3. Disclosure Review

- Highlight topics and objectives of session
- Answer candidate's FDD questions, reviewing key areas
- Discuss prospect's assignment and give another
- Review funding options and recommend lending sources
- Probe with more open-ended questions
- Pre-sell Discovery Day
- Review next step and prepare prospect for franchisee calls
- Set time for next meeting

4. Franchisee Validation

- Review franchisee conversations
- Review preliminary approval of financing
- Review prospect's assignment
- Probe with more open-ended questions
- "Set the close" with invitation to Discovery Day
- Provide profiling survey to complete
- Prepare buyer with Discovery Day checklist
- Provide filled-out agreements to satisfy five-day FTC rule
- Set time for Discovery Day at headquarters

5. Discovery Day

- Give welcoming introduction and reaffirm expectations and approval process
- Provide agenda for the event
- Tour local franchisee operations
- Meet with training, operations, marketing and real estate executives
- Visit with president/CEO and senior executives

6. Awarding the Franchise

- Review Committee meets and awards approved franchises
- "Close the close" by approving buyers and extending one-week offer
- Set time for telephone closing, or in-office closing for local buyers
- Provide overnight delivery account for returning signed documents
- Countersign documents and welcome new franchisee into your system

---

Defining the Stages of the Buying Process

It's helpful to recognize the prospect levels in your pipeline funnel. We throw around various descriptions in qualifying who we are working with during the sales process. Identifying and separating the more serious candidates from the tire kickers provides greater perspective and direction on where to focus your efforts.

- "Leads" are inquiries submitted on your initial request for information form that appear to satisfy your preliminary requirements.
- "Prospects" are leads who have spoken with you and sent completed applications (RFCs) that meet your minimum financial, background, and experience requirements.
- "Candidates" are qualified prospects who have read your FDD, appear qualified for financing, have spoken with your franchisees, and want to attend Discovery Day.

---

3. Advanced Sales Training: Mastering the Psychology of Buying

You'll increase your closings by 30 percent or more if you understand why and how buyers buy. Years ago a sales executive complained to me, *"What an idiot! I can't believe my prospect went with our competition. Our program is better, our fees are less, and our system is proven to be stronger."* In quizzing him about the lost candidate, the troubled sales rep was clueless about the buyer's motivations, concerns, and goals in owning the business. My question is, *"Was it the buyer, or the sales rep who was the idiot?"*

In today's economy, sales pros gain the edge by moving into their prospect's world. They probe, read, adapt, and outsell their competition by fully understanding and responding to how their candidates think and behave… and by uncovering their personalities, motivations, characteristics, and hot buttons. Here are some insights on prospects' behavior that may help increase your recruiting success.

Buyers are seeking a relationship

Relationship-building is the heartbeat of recruitment. Franchising is people-driven, not product-driven! Buyers smell product-pushers 10 miles away, which is why many sales people fail at selling franchises. Buyers must feel extremely comfortable with you, trusting your ethics and your commitment to franchise owners.

Potential owners must believe you are concerned about their family, aspirations, and their future health and wealth. By gaining their credibility, confidence, and trust, you are in the driver's seat. With this bond in place, you will outperform your competition. Without it, it doesn't matter what franchise program you offer. You are vulnerable. If the prospect hasn't personally connected with you, they can disappear at any moment.

What truly is most important to the buyer? Is it the sales person, the product, or the company? As noted earlier, research conducted by Prudential Insurance found that the sales person is the greatest influencing factor in purchasing insurance. The product is second. I believe this rings true in buying franchises. Deals go south when prospects sense you are commission-hungry, or that you may not be able to deliver what you claim. They buy from professionals who will work in their best interests, and who are passionate about their franchise success.

Buyers are highly impressionable and fragile

Every word you utter to a prospect is recorded in their memory. What you say and do will greatly influence their investigation. Minor errors have major impact, e.g., when your investment costs don't match your brochure estimates; when you take two days to return their phone call; when you misspell their name on your follow-up correspondence; when you ask the same question twice; or when you are 11 minutes late picking them up at the airport.

Sales pros obsess on the accuracy of details during the sales process for good reason. Seemingly small items are a big deal to cautious buyers investing their life's savings in a franchise opportunity.

Buyers are in a specific stage of buying

Did your prospect just start looking at opportunities, or have they qualified their search to your industry? Find out quickly. Uncovering this up front will improve your effectiveness with your candidates.

Prospects in the preliminary stage who don't know exactly what they want will welcome your education and guidance. Your approach should be more consultative, providing basic franchise information this buyer should know as they evaluate your opportunity. Probing questions such as, *"How long have you been looking for a business?"* and *"What other businesses have you been considering?"* will provide direction about your prospect's current status and interests.

For buyers who have diligently researched franchise opportunities and are in the decision-making stage, your approach is certainly different. Don't bore them with the basics. Rather, direct your attention to what they have discovered in their franchise investigations. Focus on the ownership advantages your franchise offers, and continue to dig for a prospect's hot buttons to determine whether they fit your franchise profile. *"What don't you like about some of the franchises you have considered?"* and *"What are the most important factors for you in the business you choose?"*

Buyers expect responsiveness

Franchise follow-up is undergoing a service crisis. Franchise Update's Annual Franchise Development Report continues to expose poor lead follow-up by most franchisors: late or no call-backs to email requests are the norm rather than the exception; inquiring prospects often receive material two to three weeks later; and enthusiastic respondents are thrown into voicemail 60 percent of the time when they try to contact a franchise representative. Floor Coverings International, PostNet International, and Express Employment Professionals understand the strong competitive edge of establishing a quick, professional response to their franchise requests. They employ internal systems and standards that require live phone coverage and same-day follow-up to lead inquiries. PostNet has an after-hours and weekend phone service to ensure every inquiry is personally answered. When nobody else is there, you can bet these two high-performance companies are. As Tom Wood, president of Floor Coverings International, confirms, *"First to the door wins!"*

Buyers don't know how to buy a franchise

Most of your prospects haven't purchased a franchise before, so how would they know how to go about it? You're the expert, not them. It's your role to take firm control of the investigation through leadership. Define your specific investigation process for them early on, or they will create their own!

Buyers want you to guide them. High-growth companies like Great Clips know most serious franchise buyers can, and are willing, to commit to a franchise within six to eight weeks. Why is this? Because their qualified candidates have agreed to make their decisions by a specific date.

Buyers want to qualify

Many of us have experienced the value and prestige of receiving approval onto an executive board, into a country club, or into a fraternity or sorority. Qualifying to join a select group of franchisees is a lot more attractive than investing in an opportunity that opens the door to anyone waving a check. If you haven't already, create an executive committee responsible for reviewing and approving each candidate before awarding a franchise. It elevates your franchise's stature with buyers, existing franchisees, and your employees.

Buyers start the sale by personal contact

No one can be considered a potential prospect until they speak with a development executive. Without personal interaction, you simply have inquiries. This is why responsiveness to requests is critical. When one-on-one contact is made, the relationship-building and sale begin.

High-tech tools help develop inquiries and facilitate communication. Unfortunately, some companies struggle by relying too much on email campaigns. Without systematic phone follow-up they miss out on sales opportunities. There's a reason they call it "dialing for dollars!" Once you make the live connection you can begin filling your prospect funnel.

Buyers want ownership information

"How will your franchise help me achieve my business and personal goals? What are the benefits of your industry? What are the unique advantages of your franchise system? How do I qualify? What training do you provide? Can my family be involved?"

Prospects don't contact you to find out more about the custom, curved counters in your stores, special white sauce on your noodle dishes, or torque ratios of your service equipment. First and foremost, they are interested in the ownership opportunity, benefits, and lifestyle rewards your franchise offers. Focus on what your business can do for them, rather than dwelling too much on what your business does. The candidate wants to know, *"If I'm qualified, can your franchise provide the blueprint for my future success?"* Unfortunately, selling product rather than the opportunity is a big problem for many franchises. If you are guilty of this, development consultants can be quite helpful in refocusing your recruiting approach.

Buyers share what they think, if you ask

Often sales reps feel they are intruding by asking too many questions about their candidate and "where they are coming from." This is a mistake.

Prospects want you to show interest in them. Ask questions about how they feel, their family's level of support, what else they are looking at and why, what their business strengths and shortcomings are, and what they want the business to do for them. Their revealing answers provide powerful direction on how to respond to their needs and interests.

Buyers process information in stages

Avoid overdosing individuals with too much information too quickly, or you'll prompt prospects to prematurely eliminate your opportunity. Worse yet, you can overly excite a candidate at the outset with nothing left for an encore.

Our brain is most effective processing new information in modules, progressing from general content to specific details in later stages. So keep prospects engaged by wanting more and by deflecting questions for additional information you'll cover further on in the process. Script your promotional material and presentations in a step-by-step sequence, leading up to the grand finale of your Discovery Day. Don't hesitate to say, "*Joe, when we receive your qualifying application, then we can discuss financials from our disclosure documents.*"

"Spin selling" helps in successful franchise recruitment, as it recognizes buyers' emotions as they move through the process. Build their interest as they go, and avoid the danger of peaking too soon. Have you ever lost a deal you assumed was a "slam dunk"? You knew early on your prospect was all fired up, ready to sign up at that moment! The problem was you got them moving too quickly, they short-circuited, and you never heard from them again.

Buyers are guided by behavioral styles

If you haven't already, learn how to sell to the different behavioral styles of your buyers. Studying their behavioral characteristics will equip you with effective techniques for working with "driver," "analytical," "expressive," and "amiable" personalities. This powerful understanding will help you build closer relationships with your candidates and be a better closer.

Who buys on emotion and ego? Who purchases on facts and logic? Which personalities require more assistance in making the right decision? How do you adjust your language and speech patterns to the buyer type you are working with? Knowing these answers will improve your relationship skills and eliminate "personality conflicts" with your qualified buyers. This is particularly beneficial with closing candidates, who are quite vulnerable and may seize up with buyer's fright before signing the franchise agreement.

Buyers have decision-making hot buttons

Discover your prospects' buying triggers through probing questions and observation. Different buyers have different motivations. They will appreciate you asking, and will tell you what they are. Also observe what your prospects don't say. One franchise sales pro refined his Discovery Day selling strategy by closely watching how his prospects watched and responded to his 10-minute franchise video. He zeroed in on those areas that caught their attention and those that prompted yawns.

Buyers' actions reveal their intentions

It's not what prospects say, it's what they do! When a candidate breaks an appointment without an explanation, or stops returning calls, it means he isn't interested any longer. Yet some franchise reps continue to chase these individuals. Is the application sloppy and not completely filled out, or is it neatly typed with each question thoughtfully answered? Did your candidate contact three franchisees as agreed, or "just didn't have a chance to get to it yet"?

Confront and eliminate prospects who are wandering around with you. Keeping six-month-old applications on your active list is usually a waste of time. Move 'em up, or move 'em out.

A 6- to 12-month mass mailing to former prospects occasionally resuscitates a sale. But don't spend wasted time digging for the dead. Focus on those who show interest and who are responsive by following your process. They are your buyers!

Master the psychology of buying, and you'll both win

Joining your franchise system is a major decision affecting the life, security, and future of each candidate considering your opportunity. Understanding prospect behavior, apprehensions, needs, expectations, and personality styles can catapult your selling success to the next level… empowering you with extraordinary insights that can benefit you and your buyers, and beat out your competition.

4. Qualifying Prospects More Effectively

Focus on their world, not yours

Smart probing prevents delays and needless time spent working with poor prospects. However, most franchisors don't engage with their prospects to gather valuable information about their attitudes, wants, impressions, and goals. Move from your world into the world of your candidates. Find out what they see, feel, and think. Avoid being an "information pusher" and instead develop two-way conversations. Share thoughts.

Concentrate your attention on your candidates, asking open-ended questions that give you valuable direction on their direction. This shows them you are interested in them and will strengthen your personal connection. Some telling questions to consider are: *"Why are you looking now? What does franchising mean to you? What do you want your business to do for you? What do you like and not like about other opportunities you've considered? How do you initially see yourself in the business, and three years from now?"*

Knowing the answers to these questions, you can present your opportunity to target your prospects' hot buttons, build a closer relationship and understanding with them, and be viewed as a franchise organization concerned most about their interests and future as a franchise owner.

How to eliminate poor prospects

A major problem for many franchise sales people is how to say "No" to prospects early in the process (especially when an overzealous franchise broker is pushing you heavily to sign a candidate they've introduced). We all want quality franchisees. Often, systems seek aggressive growth and want to close as many deals as possible. Yet a major cause for struggling franchisees is accepting fat checks from people doomed to failure from day one. This is the dirty laundry of franchise selling that plagues some systems. *"Just say no,"* and you will win in the long run. Satisfied, successful franchisees are the catalysts that ignite major growth! Floundering, disgruntled operators can torpedo your expansion.

Six Steps To Selling Success (see above in this chapter) is a self-eliminating process that will automatically weed out 75 percent of your unqualified candidates. The other 25 percent will hang on too long and eat up your time unless you cut them loose. Learning when and how to ease these individuals out of your process frees you to focus on more desirable prospects.

Dealing with candidates who can't make decisions

Procrastination and stalling accomplishes nothing positive for you or the prospect. Keep your process in motion, with each activity moving a candidate closer to buying. There is nothing worse than: *"Let me think this over before we continue,"* or *"I still just haven't had a chance to read your material, so why don't you call me back in another week,"* or *"Oh, I'm sorry for not being available for our scheduled appointment, but I went out for ice cream with my daughter and the time got away from me."*

Cut these people loose, because chasing is wasting! Actions speak louder than words. What they are saying is your franchise opportunity is no longer important to them. Immediately confront these stall tactics with, *"It certainly appears you are no longer serious about our franchise program. Is this correct?"* If they claim they really are interested, they must agree to follow your process or they will not qualify. If they confess their interest has waned, gracefully erase them from your database. *"As you know, we work only with individuals actively considering our opportunity. Thanks for your initial interest. We wish you the best of success in your future endeavors. Good-bye."*

I much prefer working with a few motivated prospects rather than a large callback list of poor "suspects" draining my valuable time. Work the sales funnel and eradicate the time-wasters.

Ralph Ross, founder of Mobile Bankers, was quite direct with franchise candidates who challenged his program or deviated from his selection process. In initial face-to-face meetings and at Discovery Days, he would stand up from his chair and usher an individual out the front door, saying, *"I can see this is not going to work for either you or us. Our program is not for you. Thank you for taking the time to visit us."* I witnessed this on three separate occasions. He taught me that it makes no sense to tie up one's valuable time once it's evident there isn't a match. Another seasoned sales veteran, Cecil Johnson, always offered a noon exit time for Discovery Day candidates who realized they weren't a fit for his franchise. What's the use of dragging out the day when a visitor is only going through the motions?

Separate dreamers from doers

"Dreamers" love the idea of owning their own business. They envision themselves as happy proprietors of a fun ice cream store, socializing with smiling families raving about their scrumptious hot fudge sundaes in their Ben & Jerry's franchise. Gracefully disqualify these passionate individuals before they soak up your selling hours. Since they often are raving customers of yours, let them down gently. They just don't realize the difference between eating at and owning an ice cream store. Share the hard realities of working 80 hours a week, fixing broken machines with 10 people impatiently waiting to be served, and two employees on the busiest shift not showing up for work. Early on, I tried to convert these well-meaning souls and failed every time. The American Dream of franchise ownership is just too much for most people.

How about the "professional lookers," those distinguished elite who turn franchise investigation into career hobbies? Have any of you franchise veterans run into the same prospects attending franchise shows three years in a row? Or what about the "armchair entrepreneurs?" I once had a tennis buddy who bought the complete $3,500 library of *Entrepreneur* magazine's more than 80 start-up business manuals. He bragged about reading every manual cover to cover. Bill confessed he had explored owning a business for the past 15 years. Amazed, I asked him why he hadn't done anything yet. He certainly had the money to invest. He enthusiastically responded, *"The timing hasn't been quite right, but I'm still looking!"*

In short, weed out the dreamers, and work only with the "doers" motivated and driven to commit to a business they can operate within the foreseeable future. They are engaged in your franchise model and are ready to say "Yes" if the match is right. Separate the chaff from the wheat and focus your sales efforts on the real prospects.

Send them to reform school

Robert was a franchise broker who was exceptional at keeping prospects in line with the sales process. One time I was working with one of his candidates, who skipped our appointment without notice or apology. When I told Robert I was

10 Ways To Close Deals Faster

Try a few of these selling tips to sharpen your process and accelerate your inquiry-to-close cycle. These techniques are speeding deals for franchisors. See what makes sense for your development approach, and you can enjoy more closes in less time.

1. Develop an engaging, powerful website to replace your franchise recruitment package and offer electronic delivery of your FDD. This streamlines your sales process by several days.

2. Provide a response time frame for your initial prospect inquiries in your packet cover letter or email, e.g., "Please return the application within five days or we'll assume you are no longer interested in our opportunity."

3. Break your full application into two forms. This can prompt faster—and additional—responses from qualified candidates.

4. Establish a "Decision Day" time frame with your prospect after you receive and discuss their application with them.

5. Provide the steps of your franchise approval process to coordinate with the agreed-upon Decision Day. Set up all future conversations by telephone appointment.

6. Get preliminary financing pre-approval from a third-party lender by setting up a phone call between the lender and the prospect.

7. Review disclosure documents prior to the Discovery Day visit. Let your prospect know that the franchise agreement is not negotiable and is written to protect the good franchisees and the quality standards of your system. If they are using a general attorney, emphasize the benefits and cost savings of using an experienced franchise attorney. Provide the prospect with suggestions on how to speed their review, e.g., book a two-hour appointment with their attorney to go over the documents together at their office. Unfortunately, many attorneys do not give FDD reviews top priority, which can delay and drag out the sale. Keep on top so your deal doesn't hit a wall!

8. During scheduled calls, review your program with focused conversations about your core areas of training, marketing, field support, products and services, and territory and site selection assistance. This can be more expedient and productive for candidates learning about your concept than having general discussions that move aimlessly about in various directions.

9. Date your franchise agreement with a deadline for returning the documents with an accompanying check for the total franchise fee. Because you are removing their desired territory from the buyer market, let the candidate know they need to close the deal within one week after executive committee approval. You can always extend the offer beyond this, depending on the circumstances.

10. If you aren't closing a franchise in person, schedule a telephone close to guide the candidate through the document signing and overnight delivery of the contract and money. This frequently reduces the transaction time.

stood up, he contacted the perpetrator and blasted him. *"You forgot the appointment? How can Steve seriously consider you for their program after flaking out on your conference call? He certainly let me have it after I presented you as an ideal candidate for their system. This doesn't make me look good as a trusted consultant. Egg's dripping down my face and I should drop you from their selection process. What do you have to say? I'm not about to present you to other franchise opportunities if this is what's going to happen!"*

Robert put this candidate "in jail," told him to call him back in a week if he promised he would never commit such a "crime" again. It sounds a bit humorous and harsh, but it worked. Tail between his legs, the guilty candidate apologized profusely and marched perfectly through our process after that.

5. How To Work Franchise Trade Shows

Franchise shows have experienced an exciting rebirth during the past few years. The annual International Franchise Expo in Washington, D.C., as well as regional shows in the U.S. and international expos, have provided a valuable recruiting venue for generating qualified buyers. But not everybody is jumping aboard. Some franchisors confess they aren't interested in trying this successful, revitalized lead source. Actually, this no longer surprises me. Franchise shows require out-of-town travel, working weekends, and aggressively following up once you're back in the office, in addition to juggling the slew of tasks that piled up while you were gone. It's harder work than sitting at your desk and receiving email or broker leads, and some sales execs don't want to make the effort. But for those of you interested in selling more franchise buyers, shows and seminar events could be a great addition to your marketing plan.

Are you ready to exhibit yet?

Cautionary note… so much so, that I'm repeating this advice from Chapter 4! Make sure you are well prepared to exhibit at the show. If not, you can make critical mistakes that cost you sales opportunities. First, attend a show before you participate: walk the aisles, note the better booth designs and props that are attracting attention, observe how sales people approach visitors, ask questions and present their concepts, and how they get interested candidates to complete inquiry forms. Pick up any handout materials to get a sense of what may be appropriate for your business. Check out the food franchises that offer samples of their sandwiches, ice cream, cookies, smoothies, and other products. The questions you must answer in advance are: *Will it be worthwhile for you to display or distribute some of your products? Should you bring your service van, as some franchisors do?*

Every year some restless franchisors pull the trigger too soon, signing up for a trade show without proper preparation. Too often start-up franchises participate before their franchise program is ready to market. Results can be disastrous. It's "show time" for your concept, so make sure you are at your best when you hit the stage. Bad reviews will spread fast.

Pre-market to maximize your results

Focused, targeted marketing efforts in advance of a trade show can generate greater return on your investment of money, time, and resources. Here are some ideas that have proven effective:

- *Invite your database*—Send letters or email blasts to all area prospects in your contact management program promoting the show and the opportunity to meet with you. Provide free admission passes for responding, and the invitation to book a personal appointment with you. For those who want appointments, send your Request for Consideration to be returned in advance, which will qualify them to receive your disclosure documents prior to or at the event.

- *Target list mailings*—Some franchisors have enjoyed success through advance mailings to prime prospect groups within the show's metropolitan area. When I was with a direct marketing franchise, we sold master licensees at some events by purchasing magazine lists of local computer sales managers, who we knew were ideal prospects. Trade shows became a great platform for recruiting attendees through our mailings, and they produced some great franchisees for us.

- *Contact local brokers*—If you work with franchise or business brokers, visit them when you are in town. You may want to invite them and their interested candidates to the event, or meet at your hotel if more appropriate.

- *Push for publicity*—If you have a PR agency, have them pitch the local media for interviews before, after, or while you are at the event. The larger franchise shows are newsworthy events frequently covered by local television, newspapers, magazines, radio, and online news clips.

Most press have some franchisors already lined up for interviews before they enter the exhibit hall. Get your concept on their lists.

At the show

Every sales professional knows the power of face-to-face contact. Franchise shows and similar forums are the opportunity to shake hands and personally connect with business buyers. But as show veterans realize, the show venue requires a different sales process than working Internet, broker, or print leads.

- *Define expectations*—Shows are not selling events, they are prospecting events. Capturing leads is your foremost objective. This requires effective, polished "elevator conversations" that prompt their interest and request for information. Think about it: attendees are wandering about overwhelmed by several hundred franchise displays, materials are bursting from their show bags, and the babble of smooth-talking franchise execs bombards their brains. It's show time, and you'd better be prepared to produce leads that you can later convert into franchise owners. If not, you'll fail miserably and end up with nothing more than a wasted weekend, sore feet, and a pile of bills to pay.

- *Engage visitors*—Focus on stopping attendees with a friendly smile, product sample or demonstration, or a question that turns their attention to your opportunity. To get attendees talking, I often asked puzzled attendees reading our signage, *"You probably can't figure out what we do!"* Or I'd query a pleasant-looking attendee with a simple, *"What do you think of the show so far? Is it what you expected?"* You must be approachable and use whatever attracts prospects to your booth. Laser-tag and boxing franchises attract attention at shows, because their visual excitement reflects what their businesses are about. I once hired a magician who harnessed droves of spectators to our coupon advertising booth. Tragically, it was one of our worst shows. His magic performance was spectacular, but our prospecting performance bombed. There was no connection between disappearing rabbits and our franchise opportunity. The magician delivered no value, just a mesmerized audience. However, it does make sense for food franchises to give away samples of ice cream, pizza, sandwiches, and coffee to introduce buyers to their products.

- *Get their information*—Handing out brochures is helpful, but alone will not prompt many direct responses. The prime objective is to get names and contact information from potential prospects. One new exhibitor at the International Franchise Expo in Washington, D.C., was very excited because she gave out more than 300 brochures! *"Wow, that's great, but how many leads did you get?"* I asked. There was dead silence. She didn't capture names. All that money blown away, and she never exhibited again. The mistake was too traumatic for her to do it over the right way.

Don't wing it. Be prepared for your first show. Practice different approaches so you are ready when the doors open! Here are a few sample techniques to secure leads:

- Ask two or three open-ended questions that will tell you something about the attendee to see if there may be a fit, e.g., *"What are you looking for in a business? What do you think about our explosive industry growth? Which franchises do you like so far that you've seen? Why? Have you been in one of our stores? What was it like?"*

- Present a 15-second "opportunity statement" that quickly defines and promotes your franchise offer. Paint a compelling picture with three of your "wow" factors. This quickly triggers interest or disqualifies the visitor or you. No use wasting time.

- Hand engaged attendees your request form to complete, clamped to a convenient clipboard with a pen, or swipe their badges for their information if scanner machines are available. Personally, I prefer the old-fashioned fill-out forms, which force attendees to focus on your business as they complete the questions. It also allows you to discuss their information as you review it.

Quick tips for greater success

- Write down something about the attendee, their spouse, child(ren), a particular benefit that excited them, a factor important in their business selection, or any item you can address more fully when you make contact.

- Rate your leads. If you don't, you'll forget who impressed you and who needs dumping in the wastebasket. A simple "A," "B," or "C" noted on their lead forms allows you to prioritize the better prospects at the show for follow-up.

- Don't place a table in front of your booth. This creates a physical and psychological barrier for attendees. Keep the front open to provide a more inviting, less formal environment for prospects to come in and chat with you.

- Don't sit down. Who wants to meet someone sitting in a chair? Be respectful and stand up at their level when you greet them. Too tired to stand up? Leave the booth and take a break in the exhibitor's lounge.

- Don't eat in the booth. This tells a prospective buyer that diving into your ham-and-cheese sandwich is more important to you at the moment than sharing your opportunity with them. That moment may be all you have with them as they pass by.

- When your booth gets really busy, pause from individual conversations to engage others before they walk away. Acknowledge their presence and let them know you will be with them shortly. Hand out brochures as they wait, or inquiry forms to complete. Work the crowd or you'll lose prospects that lose patience.

- Gracefully excuse incessant gabbers. Sometimes a visitor latches on to you at the expense of others waiting to get their questions answered. Remember, you're gathering leads, not making sales. Set up signals with your booth mates so they can "remind you of that meeting you are late for." Another technique is to cut off your marathon discussion with a handshake and say, *"Thanks so much! Please fill out our request form and we'll get back to you after the show."* Hand them the clipboard and form, provide them a pen, smile, slowly turn away, and start conversing with your lineup of other interested attendees.

- Get troublemakers away fast. All of us encounter the nutcase who has come to hassle you, your business concept, or all the evils franchising represents. Squelch the disruption before it escalates. Immediately walk with these nutcases away from your booth area and, if necessary, signal someone to get show personnel or security to escort them out of the hall.

After the show

I recommend you call all leads within 24 hours of the show, thanking the person for visiting your opportunity. Make that individual feel special, bringing up a key observation you noted on their request form when you met. This wins big relationship points, separating your call from those of the other exhibitors. When speaking with an attendee on the phone, I started with, *"Jill, you probably didn't have time to review our opportunity yet, but I really want to thank you and Joe for visiting with us. As you shared with me, owning our service business could be a nice fit for you two, and a great opportunity for your son Bob."* I would then go silent, and if Jill jumped into a discussion, I was off and running with my prospect. If she said, *"You're right, I haven't had time to review any of the businesses yet,"* then I asked, *"Would Wednesday be an appropriate time to do this?"* and I would book a time for a conference call.

Working nearly 100 franchise shows, I learned early that speed is of the essence in capturing the fast decision-makers. Many franchisors take three, five, seven, or more days to get back to their show leads. I know, I used to be one of them! Making the first contact with prospects will distinguish you from the pack. The slowpokes miss out with those buyers anxious to move forward with their business investigation.

Post-show seminars—Some franchisors are pros at running seminars during the show, or on the Saturday, Sunday, or Monday night following the event. These sessions are designed to sell the hot candidates when emotions are high, and owning a business is consuming their minds. These forums vary from well-scripted PowerPoint presentations accommodating 30 people, local franchise store meetings, or personal appointments at the show hotel. Have a sign-up sheet posted at your booth. If you successfully promote your special event, expect 50 percent of sign-ups to show up. For after-hours seminars, call to confirm the time and place of your session. I've sold from these seminars, and I've struck out as well. It's certainly worth a test if you're in a key development market and have successful franchisees in the region available for validation.

6. Selling Deals Through Franchise Brokers

The incredible surge in outsourcing prospect generation to franchise brokers has reshaped the sales programs of many franchise systems. Once tarred by the horror stories of the 1980s, today's brokers are reborn and repackaged as the "franchise sales consultants" of the 21st century. This isn't surprising. Networks of professional consultants with years of franchising experience have swooped onto the franchise sales scene with extraordinary success. Today they deliver an estimated 3,000-plus new franchise owners annually to appreciative franchise companies. Franchise Update's Annual Franchise Development Report revealed that 50 percent of the 148 franchisors surveyed used brokers, with 85 percent of those companies closing deals.

Are you right for each other?

This is the million-dollar question you have to answer. Whatever the outcome, you could make a critical mistake if you don't explore this growth opportunity. Whether you are a start-up or veteran franchise company, a successful marriage with franchise brokers could accelerate your growth by 25 percent, 50 percent, or even more! Some franchisors pretty much hand over the development reins to broker networks that have been responsible for building their system.

Let's peel the onion to determine the pros and cons seasoned franchisors are experiencing with broker networks. This may help guide your decision-making if you are not using broker representation at this time.

Broker advantages

- *No up-front costs*—Especially for the younger, bootstrapping franchise this is a huge benefit. Brokers can reduce your sales payroll and advertising expenses, and provide you with a network of seasoned franchise consultants who can present your franchise program to pre-qualified candidates throughout the U.S. By using brokers, some attractive and well-run start-ups have enjoyed explosive franchise growth without investing any advertising dollars to promote their concept.

- *"Found" buyers*—Consultants bring you qualified owners you never would have met otherwise. Buyers you sell directly from your own marketing efforts have evaluated different concepts and selected you as the franchise they want. Buyers brokers send you often didn't know what they wanted and sought out counsel to help them weed through the opportunity jungle of thousands of franchises. From the 1980s into the 2000s, I awarded franchises to broker-referred candidates who had never thought of considering our concept... until the broker sent them our way. Broker networks are valuable in recruiting additional qualified prospects, creating a new pool of buyers for franchisors that participate in their programs.

- *Qualified prospects*—Your candidates have been pre-screened to fit your prospect profile: financial and operational requirements, skill sets, character traits, corporate culture, etc. They believe in the franchise model, are ready to start a business now, and understand they will have to follow a sales process to qualify for your franchise. Brokered franchisees I have sold became top producers, receiving system-wide honors for their outstanding achievements.

- *Free sales training*—Some broker networks offer you on-site training to help ensure your mutual selling success. This is particularly beneficial for younger franchisors without a strong sales program in place. Their assistance helps you establish an effective relationship with the broker by seamlessly connecting your recruitment approaches for maximum sales results.

- *Buyer insights*—Your broker can provide vital information about a prospect that can make the difference in closing a new franchise. Third-party consultants are sounding boards for candidates, who share with them their impressions, concerns, and interests about your franchise. This additional awareness of your candidate's status certainly helps as you guide them through your qualification process.

- *Service concepts capitalize*—Brokers are especially successful with lower investment, mobile, home, and office-based franchises. These are often easier package sales, less complicated, and pay higher commissions. Consequently, the most successful broker relationships are with service-driven concepts. If your concept falls within this category, definitely check out broker representation as part of your lead generation strategy.

Broker challenges

- *Rising costs*—$13,000 is the average commission brokers receive for franchisee placements, according to the Annual Franchise Development Report from Franchise Update. This is a generally acceptable budget expense that works for the majority of franchisors who understand and enjoy the rewards of using brokers. Unfortunately, commission payouts are soaring, with a few aggressive franchisors now "buying" broker business by paying up to $25,000 for single-unit sales.

And in isolated cases, a few pay the broker a portion of the ongoing royalty stream. The bad news here is that these financial incentives can 1) create an uneven playing field with some commissioned consultants when choosing which concepts to present to their client buyers, and 2) strain franchisor acquisition costs beyond prudent business practices. It certainly can become unaffordable for retail concepts with real estate assistance and startup costs… added expenses that service businesses don't experience. An additional cost: franchisors should attend their brokers' conferences, which do pay off in additional sales but can require travel expenses and registration fees up to $5,000 and more.

- *Co-dependency*—Some franchisors have put "all their eggs in one basket," anointing consultant/broker networks with the responsibility of building their systems. This is extremely dangerous. Accordingly, consulting systems will advise you to spread your risk by using multiple lead generation sources. I've witnessed these sobering realities time and again:

1. An influential consultant is angry because you blew a sale. This may be false, but perception is reality. He kills your lead flow at their national conference advising his colleagues to think twice before showing your concept.

2. Your franchisee validation dips and your brokers instantly cut you off since your hot concept is now not so hot.

3. The prospect pipeline for the broker network dwindles and your leads shrink significantly.

4. Brokers know they're the foundation of your recruitment success, making you vulnerable to their policies, changes, and demands. Without other sales sources you are helpless.

5. You're at a disadvantage because you never recruited a franchisee from start to finish.

A mobile service franchise once sought my counsel, confiding to me, *"We have to learn how to market and sell our own prospects, because we're headed for trouble if we don't. We've been extremely successful with brokers, but I don't like being prisoner to their prospect supply. I now must figure out how to effectively generate lead flow, follow-up with initial prospects, and produce applications."*

- *Losing control*—A few sales consultants in every broker network are what I call "sales commandos," people who try to bully, manipulate, mislead, or change your sales process to suit their battle plans. Their mercenary appetites for commissions may overpower any ethics they have for either the candidates or the franchisors they represent. Try turning down their Discovery Day candidate and you'll face a raging bull! I experienced this a few times. Fortunately, they are a minimal faction among the professional broker community, but they do need to be exposed and eliminated by their superiors for damage control. These renegades are dangerous to the franchise consultant company, the franchisor, and the prospective buyer. Broker network executives want franchisors to immediately report these wayward soldiers, who are violating their own best practices and will be punished accordingly. Unchecked, they give all of us a bad name.

- *Too many unqualified candidates*—Not all brokers are equal, and unfortunately some just don't cut it as franchise recruiters. A few will waste your valuable time by sending leads that clearly don't show the money, skill sets, or characteristics you are seeking. To prevent this, clearly define your success profile to these broker "shotgunners," and return referrals that don't meet your minimum qualifications with a corresponding note. Be sure to review with the broker the candidate's shortcomings so they won't make the same mistake again. Also, beware of becoming the "throwaway franchise" some brokers use in presenting different concepts. This is a comparison practice to clearly showcase another franchise much better suited for the candidate. Brokers selfishly use this trick to finesse a sale. It's a waste of time for you and their candidate, who should only review franchises that match their criteria. Drop the broker who habitually does this and tell them why.

- *Retail concepts struggle*—Lower investment, non-food franchises can do well using brokers. For higher-priced food concepts, often the relationship has not proven fruitful for either franchisor or broker. Prime real estate requirements, much longer opening times, and higher investments create barriers and consulting challenges most brokers don't want to address—especially when the commissions don't match what many service franchisors can pay. It simply isn't worth the effort for most. On the brighter side, a few hot, successful food-related concepts willing to invest the extra time have educated and won over the more sophisticated brokers, who have championed their causes. It's A Grind Coffee, Bear Rock Cafe, and Robeks Juice have generated new franchisees through consultants. As franchise broker systems evolve, hopefully they will realize the rewards of representing "Main Street America" to their clients. But not in today's world. Consequently, most higher-priced retail concepts don't consider franchise consultants a viable lead source, as revealed in the Annual Franchise Development Report.

How do I sign up?

Don't be shocked if you approach a broker group to represent you and they turn you down. The best consulting networks seek franchisors with hot concepts, strong validation, earning claims, and an effective selling process. They seek credible franchises that will support their buyers' efforts in building successful businesses. You must have your act together.

If you are a young franchisor, you typically need to establish a track record before the noteworthy consultants will take you on. If you are established, you may be placed on a waiting list because of a full inventory of concepts, or an abundance of franchises in your category. When you are up for consideration, a broker research analyst typically will review your FDD, promotional material, sales process, and the sales experience of your recruitment personnel. They frequently mystery shop your franchise owners to ensure good franchisee satisfaction.

10 tips to bigger broker success

I certainly enjoyed successful broker relationships over the past 20 years. Discovering qualified franchise owners through the professional efforts of franchise and business brokers contributed to the growth of several franchise companies I represented. Based on my personal experience and the insights from hundreds of franchisors who have sold broker-referred prospects, here's how to increase your popularity and closing rates with broker networks.

1. ***Present your franchise in broker's terms***—They want to know what your concept is, what's hot about it, who your buyer is, how responsive and how good you are at closing deals, and what the payoff and other

incentives are. Don't try to "build the watch" when you tell them. Just hit the hot spots that will excite and turn them on to your concept. You're competing with broker inventories of 25 to 125 franchises; information overload creates broker confusion and wastes time.

2. ***Ask what is most important to the broker***—Probe their brain just as you do with direct prospects. What are their top motivators? Is it just commissions? Your strong closing skills? Satisfied franchisees? Impressive earnings claims? Your explosive industry? Are they fans of your product? Or are they most interested in working with highly responsive franchisors who call their referrals within 15 minutes of receipt? These insights will help you better screen brokers you want… or want to ignore!

3. ***Ask how the broker likes to communicate***—Does the consultant prefer phone calls or emails, copies of your correspondence to their clients, weekly updates on candidates, or no contact at all unless you have a "hot one" who's a potential sale? Communicate the way they like to communicate. Each consultant is different. Understanding what's most effective for them will strengthen your relationships and bring more deals.

4. ***Get on their "fab five" list***—This is your mission. Some broker systems have more than 100 franchises in inventory. I believe more than half of those are buried in dust, with a handful in the morgue. Do what it takes to move up to the consultant's fab five list and you'll profit. If a broker is hot on your mobile photography franchise, you'll get scores of referrals, since many of their buyers seek low-investment service franchises.

5. ***All you need are a few good brokers***—Cast your net wide to the entire broker and consultant system with calls, emails, and franchise success stories and announcements. Then aggressively lock in on those who show interest in you. Second, contact the broker's headquarters and find out who are the top 12 consultants in the system, as well as the movers and shakers in your region. Personal phone calls and meetings, where feasible, can make a big difference. Selling without focus to the majority is a waste of time. I always targeted recruiting 8 to 10 consultants in each system who would champion my concept to their buyers, and then

use them as references when approaching other brokers. I had more than 40 quality consultants across the U.S. from 5 different networks who produced hundreds of pre-qualified candidates for our $400,000 retail concept. The other 600-plus brokers just "didn't get it," or we didn't get them. The disinterest was mutual, so why waste the time?

6. ***Establish mutual trust or you're headed for disaster***—The franchisor and consultant must always trust each other before they trust the buyer. At times a prospective buyer will play you against their consultant. *"Steve Olson still hasn't called me"* is a popular one with candidates who won't admit they didn't respond to your two phone calls and email. Or the buyer makes the consultant the fall guy, claiming to you, *"Joe told me your franchise takes an unusually long time to get open, and I don't want to experience these problems you have."* In reality, this is what consultant Joe actually stated, *"This franchise is interested only in premier locations to help ensure greater success for their franchisees. In your local California market, the real estate window for finding, approving, negotiating, building, and opening a prime 'A' street corner location typically takes from 10 to 24 months."*

Note: Always side with your consultant first, and immediately address issues before they become problems. If you allow buyers to manipulate the two of you, you both lose. If you do miss a scheduled appointment, "fess up," and immediately tell your broker. Neither of you is perfect. In this case, you admitted the mistake to the consultant, which strengthens your credibility. As always, it's all about communication.

7. ***View your active broker as part of your recruitment staff***—Treat your top consultants with the same respect and sensitivity you accord your own sales team. Praise and recognize active consultants who are contributing to your success. Send personal letters and announcements through their system praising their achievements in bringing new owners to your franchise. It amazes me when franchisors push their brokers and candidates into second-class seats. I don't understand this mentality, since I never cared where a qualified candidate came from. They're all first class and potential contributors to your franchise success.

8. ***Conduct Discovery Days for your brokers***—Inviting select brokers to your headquarters is the ultimate sell. Roll out the red carpet and bring these valued guests into your world to see, feel, touch, and taste your franchise environment. You'll see their eyes sparkle as they discover benefits of your program they never imagined. Your "wow" factors will excite them with a renewed enthusiasm for promoting your franchise. Immersed in your world, they meet with your sales staff, franchise owners, founder, CEO, and other top execs. It's show time, so wine, dine, and show your appreciation as their gracious host. Load them up with mugs, shirts, caps, and product samples so your brand impression travels back to their offices and homes. The payoffs are huge. More than 75 percent of my broker guests sold our franchises. It's well worth the investment.

9. ***Spread your risk among several systems***—A few years back, some consulting networks tried to bully their most popular franchise clients into exclusive listings. Never allow one system to hold you prisoner. Spread the wealth and sign on with more broker networks. It's your safety net. This is what may happen: five months ago your star broker system produced 35 percent of your franchise sales, but today they're blanking out and you have no backup. Recognize that continually shifting external factors will affect the ebb and flow of broker candidates. What if you have a blow-up with a consultant who then raises red flags about your concept throughout the network? Your two star brokers leave the system? A new competitive concept takes center stage? Or the broker system is now hammered by declining lead flow?

10. ***The more the pay, the more the play***—Unfortunately, greater commissions drive greater prospect submissions from the more money-motivated consultants. If you have the cash, go for it and you'll jump up on their favorite list. Personally, I refused to "buy the market" by throwing bigger bucks to further motivate brokers, and I was still quite successful generating sales with average commissions. There's no need to pay top dollar if you have a solid concept, happy franchisees, an effective selling system, and good relationships with your brokers. But the choice is yours!

7. Sales Intelligence for Superior Performance

Sales intelligence gives you the competitive edge. Growth companies know that if you're not guarding your front and backside, you'll fall behind in the race. They keep smart and savvy by gathering data, insights, and profiling information from their franchisees, sales people, and competitors. Periodic feedback sets you atop of and in tune with the highly competitive recruitment environment. You can reap the rewards and gain the inside track on building a better, more attractive franchise program for franchisees.

Those in the dark are losing buyers

During a consultation, a home service franchisor bragged to me about their established market position and quickly brushed off competitors, claiming there was no need to research or shop their development efforts. Yet shortly afterward, an industry source reported significant gains by one of their "not to worry about" competitors. This young, hard-charging franchise was rapidly closing the gap with an improved franchise program and sales team. You snooze, you lose! The cavalier franchisor eventually woke up, removed their blinders, and shifted into emergency mode to regain lost market share. Ego and denial are too expensive in today's recruitment race. Unfortunately, this franchisor's refusal to monitor their market is not that uncommon.

Shop your competition

Knowing your competition's strengths and weaknesses prepares you both offensively and defensively. By studying your leading competitor's sales presentations and techniques, you often learn how to improve your own team's performance. You may want your franchise sales people to shop the competition, as well as franchisors in other industries. This can be a fast-track training tool for your development staff. There also are some employee recruiting benefits. After shopping one franchise system some years ago, we tried to hire their sales person, who was in the process of leaving the company. We knew he was outstanding in his presentation and follow-up process because we shopped him!

When evaluating franchise sales candidates, you should also consider mystery shopping as part of your hiring procedure. This gives you the chance to see how they perform on the job before you decide if they are right for your development team.

Shop your franchisees

Learn what your franchise owners are saying to prospects, how they are presenting your opportunity, how willing and helpful they are in answering your questions, and their attitudes about the business. What your franchisees say to you may not always be what they say to prospective buyers. You need to know the real story to be a well-informed, responsive franchisor.

I was asked to mystery shop a successful retail postal franchisee who wanted to become the area developer for his region. You would immediately think he'd pass with flying colors. Not so. When I asked this motivated owner, *"If you had to do it over again, would you sign on with this franchise?"* He responded, *"Want to know the real answer? This is a great business, but it doesn't really matter which franchise in this industry you join. They're all pretty much the same. Who gives you the best deal and negotiates the best location is what counts."* Bye-bye area development opportunity for him!

Don't keep yourself in the dark. It's important to know what your franchisee partners say and how they are representing you. We know franchisees can share whatever they like with prospective buyers. I certainly did as a franchisee. As independent operators they certainly have the legal right to do so. However, it's good practice to know what they tell prospective owners so you can better prepare candidates when they make their due diligence calls. One of your recruitment priorities is educating new franchisees that system growth fuels their individual business success. Expansion is a collective effort that benefits everyone. Cost savings, greater branding, and consumer awareness are the strength of the franchise model. Don't be bashful in communicating the advantages of system growth to your franchisees through newsletters and your intranet—and remember to show your appreciation to those who actively support your ongoing development efforts.

Shop your sales staff

Aggressive growth companies measure the performance of their sales personnel just as they do their advertising. With high recruitment expenses you can't afford mediocre selling performance, which costs dearly in lost franchise deals. As I've already mentioned, a policyholder survey by Prudential Insurance revealed that the greatest influencing factor in the buying process is the sales person.

It doesn't matter how good your process is… poor follow-up, deviation from the script, or failure to build rapport can chase ready buyers to the competition. As consumers, we have all walked away from deals because of an irritating sales person, not because of the product. You must know what your quality prospects are experiencing with your sales personnel. Good or not so good, it's required intelligence for upgrading selling performance.

To make your mystery shopping most productive, inform your recruitment personnel that you are implementing a quality control program to stimulate additional franchise sales. Let them know you will periodically monitor their selling performance and provide constructive feedback to recognize their strengths and help sharpen their selling skills. This is not a witch hunt, but a best practice for producing greater sales.

Here's a quick tip (as mentioned above): wait three weeks before you begin the program, which will give you the true picture of how well your sales people perform. The first week they expect to be monitored; in fact, they often tell you they knew they were shopped, before you started! There's also the added benefit that your development team instantly raises their selling skills—just from knowing their performance will be evaluated. Keep 'em on their toes and you can both profit from better results. More sales means more corporate royalties and sales commissions.

You can be caught off guard

Franchise executives often are surprised when they first shop their recruitment personnel as they discover a need for additional sales training and support. Once problem areas are identified, remedies can be implemented quickly. Mystery shopping conducted by Franchise Update has revealed sub-par performance including: continually getting into voicemail; receiving franchise information 11 days later or not at all; receiving unauthorized earnings claims; not being asked qualifying questions; allowing the shopper to control the discussion; not establishing a time frame for making a buying decision; not scheduling follow-up calls by appointment; and ineffectively promoting the home office Discovery Day.

Coaching sales executives to strengthen areas that require attention will improve your recruitment results. For reps unable to make the needed changes, it's time to move on to a different job. Many trying to make it in our business have difficulty adjusting to some of the counter-intuitive processes of franchising selling. So cut your losses now, before you pay too big a price in lost sales and royalties. I've worked with a few CEOs who procrastinated in firing failing reps. One mall-based franchisor gave his struggling salesman a third chance to correct his faults, again with the same predictable outcome. You just can't afford nice sales people who can't sell franchises. If you really like them, stick 'em in another department! No one has ever been accused of firing a franchise sales rep too soon.

Now for the good news. Shopping your staff also showcases their sales talent in progress, identifying those recruitment pros who have strong people skills, responsiveness, and systematic approaches in representing your franchise program. This is a valuable eye-opener for executives who may take for granted the impressive accomplishments of their best sales performers. I certainly have discovered techniques, nuances, and charismatic relationship-building skills by shopping some top sales performers. Doing this also provides you with an ideal opportunity to recognize them for their accomplishments.

Shop your own website

Broken links, wrong links, stuck submissions, getting imprisoned in an area with no way back, outdated or inconsistent information on your various advertising sites... these are all common website problems that need continual attention. The real nightmare is when you realize too late that you have been losing prospects for days, even weeks. Just as with a lost phone connection, your lead flow stops abruptly.

Monitor your website and franchise ad portals at least weekly. If you don't, I guarantee you will burn dollars and prospects at some point. A major food franchise executive complained to me about how his recruitment website hadn't produced a single lead in quite some time. I asked him to give me a tour of his site. When we got to his inquiry form I stopped him, filled it out, and hit the submit button. A monstrous error message flashed in my face! He moaned in disgust, *"No wonder I haven't been getting any leads for the past several weeks!"* I wonder what that cost him in irretrievable sales. You can avoid these expensive techno-traps by auditing your site's functionality every week. If you haven't "gone shopping" yet on your own website, try it and you'll see. Your payoffs can be immediate.

My latest tale of horror involves a retail concept using multiple third-party sites that never informed several portals of their new email address for receiving leads. Five months and several thousands of dollars later, they discovered the brutal mishap. Old leads are gone leads, and there was no recouping their investment. Again, the solution is very simple: require a staff person to regularly test your online lead generation operation.

8. Do You Measure Your Advertising and Sales Performance?

Great victories in franchise development are achieved by careful measurement and refinement of lead generation and selling activities. Sadly, not enough franchisors embrace this best practice. This is astonishing! How can you grow if you don't know where to go? According to Franchise Update's Annual Franchise Development Report, 43 percent of franchisors still don't track their sales sources.

Simply stated, *"You can't manage what you can't measure."* If you're new to the franchising world, invest in marketing and sales intelligence and you'll save valuable dollars and accelerate your growth. Need assistance? Hire a proven development consultant who has successfully stepped up development for other brands. You'll recoup their fees many times over.

Tracking sales matters most

When I was growing up in the direct response business, leads that produced sales were all advertisers cared about. Whether developing inquiries for life insurance agents or for home improvement sales people, how many deals you closed was the benchmark for performance. Advertising decisions were based on marketing sources that generated sales at acceptable costs. Lead counts were never the deciding factor. Quite simple, or so I thought.

To my surprise, my ignorance was exposed when I entered franchise selling in the 1980s. It was my first experience with what I call "upside-down marketing." During the prior year, I had taken over sales development for American Advertising Distributors. This is when I discovered how some franchisors evaluate recruiting success. Company President Dick Webber scowled as he lumbered into my sales office. *"Steve, Sales & Marketing Management magazine is our most expensive lead source, so dump it."* I countered, *"But the publication's cost-per-sale is 50 percent less than our next best source, and their franchise prospects are really qualified. If you'd like, I'll show you the deals we've sold and impressive applications we receive."* Dick then pushed our quarterly leads report in my face. *"See how few prospects we get? I don't know if we can afford this publication any longer!"* Hmm… should I have made buying decisions based on driving bushels of cheap, unqualified leads? Did that work in the classic sales flick, "Glengarry Glen Ross?" I was too stubborn to give in and continued defending my advertising expenditures. I wasn't about to give up our most effective selling source because it wasn't generating lots of names.

To this day I still ask myself, *"Do I want 5 inquiries a month that produce 2 sales, or 200 junk inquiries that produce wasted time, aggravation, and expense?"* Seek the quality lead generators. Don't fall victim to the clutter of upside-down marketing… or you'll fail!

Tracking sales has become more difficult

How can you accurately measure where sales are coming from? Did an inquiry originate from a search engine, a franchisee website, or your own site? Did the buyer read your print ad, pick up your brochure at a franchise show, or see your press release—and then contact you over the Internet? Here are some of the tracking challenges franchisors must address:

- *Multiple website sources*—The average franchisor contracts with 4 to 6 external websites, and some up to 10, creating heavy lead activity that can be difficult to monitor effectively.

- *Multiple lead sources*—In addition to the Internet, other lead generators complicate tracking challenges: broker leads, trade shows, newspapers, magazines, direct mail, referrals, customers, press stories, etc.

- *Multi-source leads*—Combinations of several lead sources often contribute to the franchise sale. All need to be credited for the sale (some companies provide percentage values for each source, e.g., 33 percent customer referral, 33 percent press article, 33 percent your website).

- *Buyers confusing website names*—With more than 100 franchise websites available to buyers, it's often difficult for a candidate to remember which site it was with "franchise" in the name that prompted them to respond to you. On occasion, franchisors have incorrectly credited the wrong site for a sale because of buyer confusion!

- *Internet as facilitator, not source*—The highly interested buyer decided to contact you by going online rather than phoning. This can easily be credited improperly as an online sale... unless the sales rep digs beyond the online contact by asking the buyer what prompted them to respond.

- *Not asking buyers for the source*—Sales people by nature are focused on the sale. Some don't even bother to interview candidates about what triggered their contact. That's "busy work," which is low on their priority scale. Every sales person should ask buyers several times for the source(s) throughout the sales process.

- *Lost and tossed inquiries*—Franchisors at times lose leads. It should be a regular practice to contact ad sites to recover or compare inquiry databases as a safeguard.

- *Ad website transfers to franchise sites*—Your own franchise website should always produce your most applications and sales. Prospects who discover elsewhere online that you franchise often abandon that site and go directly to yours for the full scoop. This is great, but credit may be incorrectly given to your site, not to the advertising portal that prompted the inquiry.

- *Disconnect between marketing and sales*—This is a growing problem between marketing and sales functions that don't closely align their tracking efforts: one side is carefully measuring lead production results, while the other is intensely measuring sales results. Unless this process is seamless, you're vulnerable to bad decisions that will weaken your lead generation and sales success. I've witnessed too many misguided companies that unknowingly dropped selling sources because they didn't integrate their performance metrics.

Start with a contact and lead management program

Alert to young franchisors! If you aren't doing this already, capture your leads ASAP by installing ACT!, Salesforce, GoldMine, Outlook, or any other sales contact management program. Prospects are too valuable to lose in drawers, binders, or scribbled lists. It's never too early for a new franchisor to set up a lead management program to avoid the growing confusion they will experience with lead sources. Two thirds of franchisors now outsource this function to companies such as eMaximation, FranConnect, IFX, MyBruno, and others. Be sure to compare these services carefully before you select one, because there are differences in the capabilities and performance records of each. Contact several clients and thoroughly investigate before you sign on. Remember, your future will rely on these management tools to guide you smoothly through your expansion journey.

Tracking results that matter most

Once you master your performance metrics, you can intelligently predict and control your development growth. You'll know which newspapers produce sales and which to avoid; your least and most expensive selling sources; what percentage of qualified applications will become franchise owners; the average length of time it takes to close deals; and how many online inquiries different portals require to produce a new franchise.

You're in command when you know your performance results, what they cost you, and how efficient and effective you are in achieving them. This simplified chart highlights the key performance benchmarks that help build high-growth companies. Use this checklist to compare and evaluate the measurement criteria you are currently using to grow your system.

Key Performance Benchmarks for High Growth

	Media 1	Media 2	Media 3	Media 4
Sales Results				
# Sales				
# Discovery Day Guests				
# Applications				
# Leads				
Sales Costs				
$ per Sale				
$ per Discovery Day Guest				
$ per Application				
$ per Lead				
Sales Effectiveness				
% Sales per Discovery Day Guests				
% Sales per Applications				
% Leads to Applications				
% Sales per Leads				
Sales Efficiency	Q1	Q2	Q3	Q4
# Days for Lead Follow-Up				
# Days to Mail Franchise Materials				
# Days for Follow-Up on Mailings				
# Days to Develop Territory Descriptions				
# Days to Deliver Franchise Agreements				
# Days to Close Sales				

Sales and revenue forecasting

Master your metrics and you can project development results up to six months in advance. You can predict sales performance by measuring three key indicators in your recruitment pipeline: 1) number of active qualified prospects; 2) closing ratios at the various steps of the sales process; and 3) average number of units and revenues per transaction. With the right sales management software, you can forecast your monthly sales and revenue production in a few keystrokes. No more "winging it" in executive planning meetings! If you don't have this capability yet, ask your contact management service to build this into your current program.

Get the latest sales and lead generation statistics

How does your selling performance stack up against overall industry averages? Take a look at these results from Franchise Update's Annual Franchise Development

Report. The survey represents 148 franchise companies with a total of more than 57,000 franchise units in 42 industry categories.

You may want to order this insider's guide to sales and marketing costs, trends, and budgets. The comprehensive report is a great resource for established and emerging franchisors, development consultants, and advertising and marketing suppliers. The study is organized by industry categories, investment levels, and number of units. It also includes sales compensation surveys and other meaningful development data and is an ideal benchmark for building budgets and media plans. Contact Franchise Update Media Group at sales@franchiseupdatemedia.com, or call 800.289.4232, x202. Some sample results from the report:

Measuring Costs
57 percent track cost per sale
$7,000—median cost per sale
70 percent track cost per lead
$50—median cost per lead

Where Leads Come From	**Top Sales Producers**
65 percent Internet	35 percent Internet
16 percent referrals	28 percent referrals
3 percent print	16 percent brokers
16 percent other (trade shows, PR, etc.)	6 percent print
	15 percent other

Ready, set, grow!

If you've made it this far, congratulations! You know there's a lot to learn, remember, and execute to build a high-growth franchise organization. Here's a checklist and summary to wrap it all up. For an in-depth discussion of each point, review the preceding chapters. For ongoing information about how to continue refining your development process to increase sales and build a high-growth franchise organization, refer to the list of resources in the next, closing chapter and visit www.franchiseupdate.com/gtg.

✓ Franchise recruitment is highly specialized, employing sales principles and techniques foreign to most other business development strategies. New franchisors and sales personnel quickly realize the process is counter-intuitive, and doesn't adhere to selling fundamentals we have successfully practiced in prior lives. Avoid the shell shock and wasted time and money by doing it right: contract a proven franchise sales trainer, attend franchise sales programs produced by Franchise Update, the IFA, Franchise Times, and other reputable industry forums. You will earn back your investment tenfold.

✓ Entertain available options for selling your concept. Should you invest in top, mid-level, or up-and-coming franchise sales pros? Is it essential they are stationed at your headquarters, or can they work remotely, as is the case with 53 percent of franchise systems? Is it better to outsource your franchise development to sales specialists that can market, recruit, and close deals? What about brokers? These are real questions with no pat answers. Your growth goals, financial capability, type of concept, and need for control will determine the best path for you to take.

✓ Don't spend heavy advertising dollars until you have your act together. Once you shape up your sales process, then roll out the marketing bucks. As one bewildered service franchisor moaned at a recent franchise show in Los Angeles, *"Steve, I have no clue what I'm doing. I'm just wasting money because I don't have a system in place to sell these people!"*

✓ The Six Steps to Selling Success is a proven process that helps accelerate deals for newer franchisors and provides a refresher guide for mature systems. It's a quick-learn tutorial that breaks through the complexities of franchise selling. The principles are simple and highly effective, incorporating self-qualifying and self-closing principles. The execution is quite demanding, but followed correctly can produce rewarding results. For quality assurance, compare this six-step process with yours.

✓ Master buyer psychology and you've captured the "X factor" in selling. You can boost your sales by 30 percent or more, getting ahead by getting into your prospect's head. Join franchise sales stars who know how to probe, read, adapt, sell to, and close more deals by reading buyer personalities, motivations, characteristics, and hot buttons.

✓ Move 'em up or move 'em out! A major problem many franchise sales people face is how to say "No" to prospects early in the process (especially when an overzealous franchise broker has introduced a suspect candidate and is pushing you to sell them into your system). We all want quality franchisees. Most systems seek aggressive growth and want to close as many deals as possible. Yet a major cause for struggling franchisees is accepting fat checks from people doomed for failure since day one. *"Just say no,"* and you win in the long run. Satisfied, successful franchisees bring you new buyers; floundering, disgruntled operators torpedo your expansion.

✓ You can close more prospects and deals more quickly employing the time-tested techniques used by the pros: start closing with the opening; immediately set agreed-upon expectations; define your process with commitments to timelines; obtain preliminary pre-approval of financing; eliminate remaining objections before inviting candidates to attend Discovery Day, and design this "show time" event as a captivating experience that exceeds the buyer's expectations; and issue dated agreements that expire if not returned by an agreed time.

✓ Preparation and setting expectations are the keys to successful recruiting at trade shows. Get the most out of your trip. In advance, invite prospects in your database, send press releases, and visit the local brokers you use. Shows are not selling events, they are prospecting events. Capturing leads is your foremost objective. This requires effective, polished "elevator conversations" that pique attendees' interests and generate a response. Ask two or three open-ended questions that pre-qualify an attendee to see if there may be a fit. *"What are you looking for in a business? What do you think about our explosive industry growth? What franchises do you like so far that you've seen? Why?"* Hand engaged attendees your request form or swipe their badges if a scanner is available. Follow up with all candidates the day after the show. Stand above the rest by responding first; most companies take several days.

✓ Fifty percent of franchisors employ franchise brokers, with 85 percent of those reporting sales results, according to Franchise Update's Annual Franchise Development Report. Investments costing less than $100,000 are most successful, while companies with investments above $500,000 showing the lowest percentage of closes. Consider broker representation if you have a proven concept with good franchisee validation and earnings claims. Brokers attract a buyer market franchisors don't reach through their direct recruiting efforts or use of third party websites. Here's an opportunity to increase your growth without up-front costs. Whether you and the broker are right for each other is always the key question, so shop carefully.

✓ Sales intelligence gives you a competitive edge. High-performance franchisors know that if they're not guarding their front and backside, they'll fall behind in the race. Tune in to what's really going on by shopping your competition, franchisees, and sales staff. Let your personnel know you are mystery shopping as a training process to help them improve their sales effectiveness. It really works.

✓ Once you master your performance metrics, you can intelligently predict and control your development growth. You can't improve what you don't measure. With today's technology tools for tracking and increasing recruitment performance, there's no longer any excuse for development confusion. You'll know sales costs by lead generation sources; how to effectively develop recruitment budgets; which newspapers produce sales and which to avoid; your least and most expensive selling sources; what percentage of qualified applications will become franchise owners; the average length of time to close deals; where particular sales reps excel or need help in your sales process; and how well your Discovery Day event pays off in closing more deals.

Get Growing,
It's Closing Time!

Nearly 3,000 active franchisors continue to write the world's greatest success story in small business development. Their script is an ongoing journey developed by these champions of successful growth, leaders with the entrepreneurial passion and dedication to provide opportunities for people to live their American Dreams of independence and achievement. My hope is that "Grow to Greatness" will make a difference in your recruitment, retention, and growth of franchisees.

Keep up to date with intelligence tools

To stay in tune with the latest trends, visit www.franchiseupdate.com/gtg. This online franchise development resource provides access to the most current sales and marketing intelligence and surveys, with highlights of upcoming industry conferences and workshops.

What's more, you can opt-in to receive the Franchise Update Sales Report, delivering breaking coverage and analysis of timely issues and topics affecting franchise growth.

For more in-depth, statistical data and analysis, you can order the current Annual Franchise Development Report. The most recent report polled 148 franchise companies representing more than 57,000 franchise units in 42 industry categories. To learn more or order, go to www.franchiseupdate.com/afdr.

Online franchise resource directory

You also will find a list of industry consultants, services, and products specializing in franchise development at www.franchiseupdate.com/gtg. With the landscape of business services and technology applications changing so rapidly, this online resource list will provide you with continually updated information.

Special recognition

Thank you to all the noteworthy contributors to this book, who have helped shape the Five Success Drivers to system growth through their best practices, policies, procedures, processes, and passion. Their own exemplary achievements are a tribute to the Five Success Drivers: Total Management Commitment, Strong Franchisee Satisfaction, Compelling Franchise Program, Successful Lead Generation, and High-Performance Sales Program.

Dedication

This book has been a long journey for my family, and without their encouragement would still be an idle idea collecting cobwebs in my mind. Thanks to my confidant, best friend, and wife Jane, who graciously put up with her workaholic husband in his daytime endeavors, not to mention the many evenings and weekends locked in his office pecking out one more paragraph.

My apologies to my loyal companion Mabel, who patiently waited at my feet during her eight years of canine existence. She has been there for me, offering yawns of encouragement as long as I occasionally grabbed the leash for creative breaks. Guess what Mabel, it's time to turn the page because this project is over!

About the Author

Steve Olson is a leading authority on franchise development. He is Publisher of Franchise Update Media Group, the industry resource for franchise growth. With nearly 30 years in franchise consulting, sales, marketing, and executive management, Steve specializes in accelerating expansion for emerging and established franchise brands. He has implemented strategies and processes for more than 40 franchise clients to help them realize their growth objectives.

Steve has served on franchise boards and is a frequent columnist and speaker at conferences and workshops on franchise development. A former multi-unit franchisee, Steve was co-owner and Franchisee of the Year of a direct marketing franchise in Houston.

Made in the USA
San Bernardino, CA
04 August 2018